THE BATHROOM READERS' INSTITUTE

Uncle John's
WEIRD WEIRD WORLD EPIC

THE STRANGEST THINGS ON EARTH...UNEARTHED!

PORTABLE
PRESS

Uncle John's Weird, Weird World: Epic

Portable Press/The Bathroom Readers' Institute
An imprint of Printers Row Publishing Group
P.O. Box 1117, Ashland, OR 97520
www.bathroomreader.com
e-mail: mail@bathroomreader.com

Printers Row Publishing Group is a division of Readerlink Distribution Services, LLC.
The Portable Press, Bathroom Readers' Institute, and Uncle John's Bathroom Reader names and logos are trademarks of Readerlink Distribution Services, LLC.

All correspondence concerning the content of this book should be addressed to Portable Press/The Bathroom Readers' Institute, Editorial Department, at the above address.

Thank you!

The Bathroom Readers' Institute would like to thank the people whose advice and assistance made this book possible:

Gordon Javna	Michael Brunsfeld
Jay Newman	Peter Norton
Duncan Youel	Melinda Allman
Trina Janssen	Sean Moore
Kim T. Griswell	Rusty von Dyl
Brian Boone	Blake Mitchum
Tom Deja	JoAnn Padgett
John Dollison	Sarah Beare
Thom Little	Thomas Crapper

Outside the book: cover design by Tom Deja at Bossman Graphics, *www.bossmangraphics.com*
Inside the book: art direction and design by Duncan Youel at *www.oiloften.co.uk*
for Moseley Road Inc., *www.moseleyroad.com*
Illustrations by Sarah Beare at *www.sarahbeare.com*

ISBN-13: 978-1-62686-428-3

Library of Congress Cataloging-in-Publication Data
Uncle John's weird weird world : EPIC.
    pages cm
  ISBN 978-1-62686-428-3 (hardcover)
1. American wit and humor. 2. Curiosities and wonders. I. Bathroom Readers' Institute (Ashland, Or.)
  PN6165.U583 2015
  031.02--dc23
                        2015000226
Printed in Shenzhen, China
First Printing
19 18 17 16 15   1 2 3 4 5

Table of Contents

More contents (onto the table top)

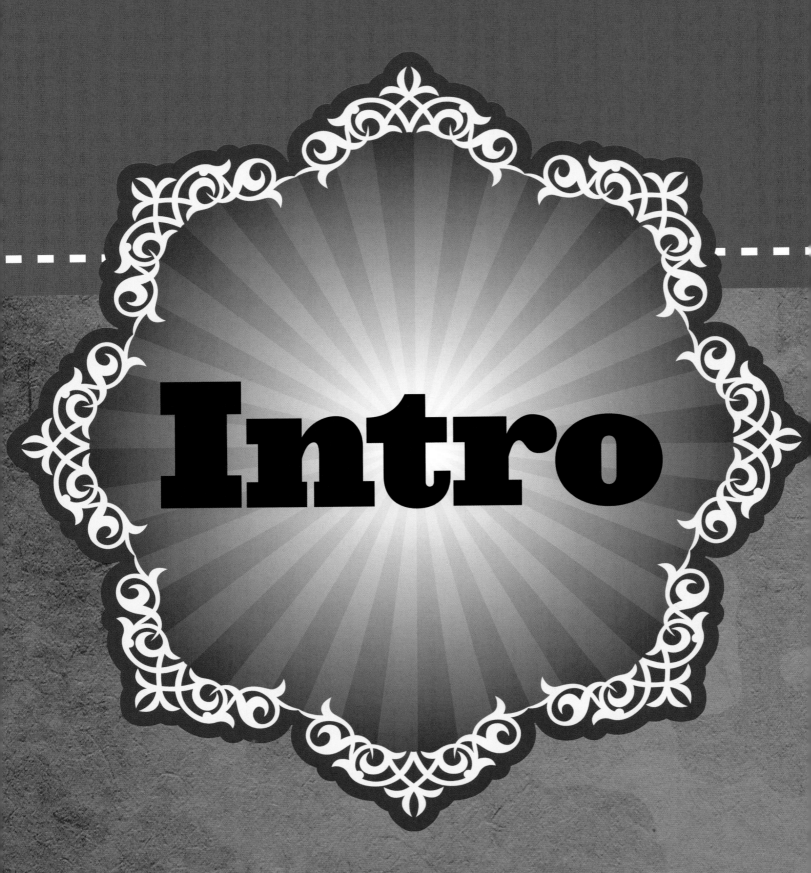

Intro

Welcome one and all to EPIC!

If you're new to the weird world of Uncle John's, here's our story: Way back in 1988, I formed a ragged band of dedicated trivia hounds. For nearly 30 years, our primary mission has been to collect the funniest, weirdest, most fascinating, most obscure, and most significant stories about the universe we live in. Whether it's pop culture, forgotten history, scientific breakthroughs, unbelievable blunders, or witty wordplay, we've probably covered it. We humbly consider ourselves chroniclers of the information age.

Now with more than 100 separate editions under our belt—with a combined total of 20 million books sold—we're at the top of our game. And one of the benefits is that we get to share our passion for information with our readers. But recently it occurred to me that we weren't reaching everyone. So as we head into our fourth decade, we started looking for new opportunities to pass along our discoveries to even more people. That's why we decided to make a hardcover book full of full-color illustrations that add a new dimension to this beloved book series.

But what to call it?

As it happens, I was pondering that dilemma while walking to work one morning when I saw an ad on the side of a bus for "EPIC TACOS!" Epic tacos? Really? That got us thinking: What exactly is "epic"? In the olden days (before 2005), that word was reserved to describe any important undertaking that took a really long time—like the Battle of Gettysburg, the movie *Ghandi,* or cleaning out your garage for the first time in ten years.

Well, if a taco can be so great that it's called "epic," then so can we. Our longevity is epic. Our quest to keep unearthing even more great material is epic. And our readership is epic.

Over the years, we've received thousands of letters from loyal readers telling us how much our books have meant to them. Parents have given Uncle John's books to their kids...who grew up and then bought them for their own kids. And so on and so forth. We are truly honored, and it makes us try even harder—to keep raising the bar on sharing great facts and trivia that's easy to digest.

That's where this book comes in. You hold in your hands 288 EPIC pages of the weirdest and wildest stuff we've ever found under the sun and over the moon—it's chock-full of incredible facts, obscure history, interesting origins, bizarre quotes, how-to tips (both silly and serious), and lots of strange pictures, too.

And as you'll soon see, we had a lot of fun putting this book together. Why? Because looking for weirdness on planet Earth is as easy as shooting a three-eyed fish in a barrel made of Tinker Toys. (Actually, that sounds quite difficult, so scratch that.) The point is, the world we live in just keeps getting weirder. You'll read about haunted trains, the physics of mirrors, the science behind Salem's witches, history's most scathing insults, amazing coincidences, famous people who barfed, and loads more.

And finally, here's an EPIC THANK YOU to our fans both old and new! Now it's time to sit back and relax with this behemoth of a book in your lap...and lose yourself in this strange odyssey we call the Weird, Weird World.

And as always... Go with the flow!

—Uncle John and the BRI

You're My Inspiration

We begin this epic journey into the Weird Zone with the inspirations behind some of the most iconic bad guys (and things) in TV and movie history.

ALIEN

In the late 1970s, screenwriter Dan O'Bannon read an article about the spider wasp, a bee that reproduces by paralyzing a spider and then laying its eggs on the spider's abdomen. When the bee larvae hatch, they eat right through the still-living spider. This macabre image haunted O'Bannon's dreams for years, but from them he was able to form the basis for the insectlike alien creature that became one of Hollywood's all-time most-feared monsters.

PATRICK BATEMAN

In the 2000 movie *American Psycho*, Christian Bale portrayed Patrick Bateman, a stockbroker by day, sociopathic serial killer by night. Bale based his characterization on another actor. According to director Mary Harron, "he had been watching Tom Cruise on David Letterman, and he just had this very intense friendliness with nothing behind the eyes."

GOLLUM

Actor Andy Serkis provided the voice and movements for the character in The Lord of the Rings films. He based the voice on the sound of his cat coughing up a hairball. Special effects artists modeled Gollum's wiry, bony frame on punk rocker Iggy Pop.

WALTER WHITE

Breaking Bad creator Vince Gilligan was inspired by a 1952 Japanese film by Akira Kurosawa called *Ikuru*, about, says Gilligan, "a midlevel corporate guy who finds out he's dying of cancer. And in the last months of his life what he chooses to do is a very good thing, it's to build a playground in Tokyo." (Walter White, however, takes a more "methy" path.)

DR. EVIL

Mike Myers's inspiration for Austin Powers's archenemy comes from the James Bond villain, Blofeld, in *You Only Live Twice*. But Dr. Evil's famous mannerism comes from this 1979 photograph of Rolling Stones guitarist Keith Richards.

"Used Cows for Sale"

Actual signs from roadsides, stores, and restaurants.

LODGING NEXT EXIT
STATE PRISON

SLOW CHILDREN
NO HUNTING

DIESEL FRIED
CHICKEN

VILLAGE OF CRESTWOOD
ENGLISH IS OUR LANGUAGE
NO EXECTIONS. LEARN IT

ACCIDENTS ARE
PROHIBITED ON
THIS ROAD

TOILET
PLEASE STAY IN CAR. WATCH
YOUR HEAD. CLEARANCE 8`6"

STOP
NO STOPPING
ANYTIME

EVACUATION
INSTRUCTIONS:
Alternate exit to the left
then right then left then
right then left to exit

ANYONE CAUGHT
COLLECTING GOLF BALLS WILL
HAVE THEIR BALLS REMOVED

SEAFOOD BROUGHT IN
BY CUSTOMERS WILL
NOT BE ENTERTAINED

Impossible!

They said it couldn't be done...

BY STEAMSHIP

"How, sir, would you make a ship sail against the wind and currents by lighting a bonfire under her deck? I pray you, excuse me, I have not the time to listen to such nonsense."
Napoleon Bonaparte, when told of Robert Fulton's steamboat (c. 1807)

BY TRAIN

"What can be more palpably absurd than the prospect held out of locomotives traveling twice as fast as stagecoaches?"
The Quarterly Review, 1825

BY AIRPLANE

"Flight by machines heavier than air is unpractical and insignificant, if not utterly impossible....No possible combination of known substances, known forms of machinery, and known forms of force, can be united in a practical machine by which man shall fly long distances through the air..."
Simon Newcomb, astronomer-director of U.S. Naval Observatory, 1902

BY SUBMARINE

"I must confess that my imagination refuses to see any sort of submarine doing anything but suffocating its crew and floundering at sea."
H. G. Wells (c. 1901)

15

Today's Menu

Funky foods from around the world.

CRACKLING ICE

Researchers from a Japanese steel company discovered that samples of Antarctic ice mixed in alcoholic drinks make distinctive, loud crackling sounds. When the ice is placed in alcohol, air bubbles trapped in the ice thousands of years ago are released with a loud popping sound. The stronger the alcohol, the louder the sound. Straight whiskey (80 proof) over the ice produces crackling sounds of around 70 decibels (equal to the noise of a loud radio) every second or so.

CRETE-DE-COQ

Cock's combs are often used by French and Italian chefs to garnish various poultry dishes. (The comb is the red, fleshy thing on top of a rooster's head.) According to experts, it's chewy but quite tasty.

CONCHA FINA

This shellfish looks like an oyster. But while oysters are often served raw (and dead), this Spanish delicacy is always served raw... and alive. Squeeze a little fresh lemon over the concha fina. When it starts fidgeting, pour it down your throat.

FRUIT BAT SOUP

A delicacy from Micronesia made with fruit bats (also called flying foxes). For the soup, the meat of the fruit bat is simmered in water, ginger, and onion and topped off with scallions, soy sauce, and coconut cream. When not in the soup, these furry bats are said to make affectionate pets.

CHIA PET SALAD

This dish features the edible sprouts of *Salvia columbariae*—related to the spice, sage. The "fur" that grows out of the ceramic cow, frog, hippo, puppy, or whatever is stripped from the pottery and tossed lightly with peppery nasturtiums and beanlike tulip flowers.

STUFFED ROAST CAMEL

It is served at traditional Bedouin wedding feasts in Middle Eastern and North African deserts. Ingredients include 1 medium-sized camel, 1 medium-sized North African goat, 1 spring lamb, 1 large chicken (some recipes substitute fish or monitor lizard), 1 boiled egg, 450 cloves of garlic, and 1 large bunch of fresh coriander. The chicken is stuffed with the boiled egg and coriander, then stuffed into the lamb, which is stuffed into the goat, which is stuffed into the camel. The camel

is then spiked with garlic, brushed with butter, and roasted over an open fire. The finished dish is placed at the center of the table. Pieces of camel, goat, lamb, and chicken are pulled off and eaten with the hands. No utensils are required. Serves 100 to 150 guests.

SCHLAGSCHOCKEN

The recipe for this dessert from Zurich, Switzerland, calls for 12 pounds of cream, sugar, eggs, honey, and chocolate, all reduced down into a single four-inch square of Schlagschocken. Warning: The Swiss are used to this rich treat, but visitors have been known to pass out from eating a single serving.

CURRIED RAT

On your next trip to Vietnam, try this local delicacy. Severe flooding in 2000 nearly wiped out the rat population in rice fields along the Mekong River, but they're back on the menu thanks to their amazingly fast reproductive rate. Rat catchers make about $4 a day selling them to restaurants. Choice rat meat goes for $1.70 per kilo ($.77 per pound). Don't like curry? Try fried rat, rat on the grill, or rat sour soup.

IGUANA EGGS

A Central American favorite. Boil the eggs for 10 minutes, then sun-dry them. The result is a slightly rubbery egg with a cheeselike flavor. How do you get iguana eggs? Catch a pregnant female iguana, slit the abdomen open with a sharp knife, and gently remove the eggs. Then rub some ashes into the wound, sew it up with needle and thread, and let the iguana go. There's a good chance you'll see her again next year for another meal.

BIRD'S NEST SOUP

Have you seen this on a menu in some fancy Chinese restaurant? Forget it. Real bird's nest soup is made from bird spit—the gooey, stringy saliva that Chinese swiftlets use to attach their nests to the walls of caves. The hardened saliva is prized for its medicinal—and aphrodisiac—properties, which makes it very expensive. The license fee to harvest one cave: $100,000. The soup is a simple chicken broth, with one good dollop of bird spit in it.

DONALD SUTHERLAND STARRED IN THE 1975 FILM *DAY OF THE LOCUST* AS…HOMER SIMPSON.

17

Rules of TV

At some point in your life, you've no doubt been watching a television show and muttered, "That would never happen in real life." And yet these things happen on the tube...a lot.

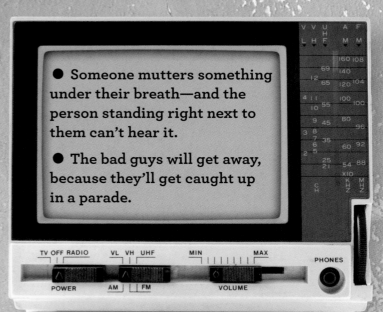

- Someone mutters something under their breath—and the person standing right next to them can't hear it.
- The bad guys will get away, because they'll get caught up in a parade.

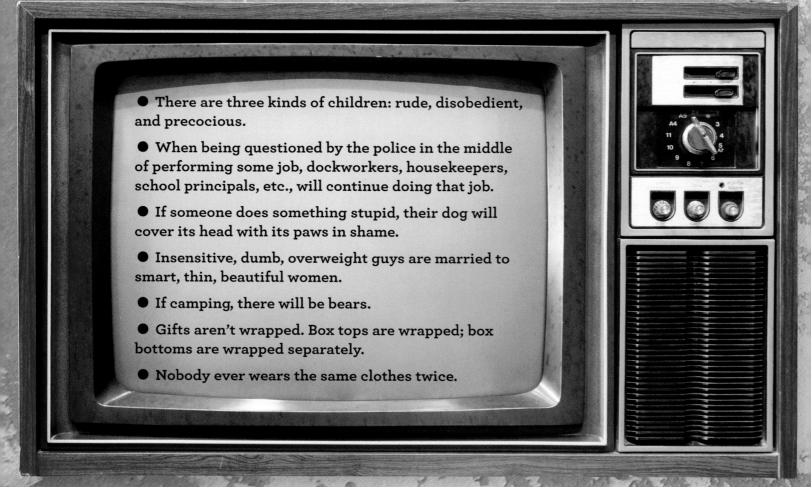

- There are three kinds of children: rude, disobedient, and precocious.
- When being questioned by the police in the middle of performing some job, dockworkers, housekeepers, school principals, etc., will continue doing that job.
- If someone does something stupid, their dog will cover its head with its paws in shame.
- Insensitive, dumb, overweight guys are married to smart, thin, beautiful women.
- If camping, there will be bears.
- Gifts aren't wrapped. Box tops are wrapped; box bottoms are wrapped separately.
- Nobody ever wears the same clothes twice.

COMMON Wii GAMING SYSTEM INJURIES: BLACK EYES, HAND INJURIES, AND TENNIS ELBOW.

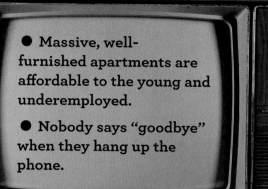

● Massive, well-furnished apartments are affordable to the young and underemployed.

● Nobody says "goodbye" when they hang up the phone.

● Best friends or duos are the complete opposite of each other.

● If a woman is pregnant and suddenly stuck in a confined space (elevator, taxi, etc.) she'll give birth immediately.

● If a woman is pregnant and makes it to a hospital, she will yell, scream, and hurl insults at the man "who did this to her."

● Kids who get caught lying or screwing something up are not punished; they are praised for telling the truth.

● Whenever someone goes grocery shopping, they will return with one sack, from which a baguette will protrude.

● Grandmas act "young"—they know the new slang, the famous people, and have dates lined up for every night of the week.

● If it's just about Christmas, that never-before-seen, kindly old man just might be the real Santa.

● A man will schedule two dates on the same night at the same restaurant. He will run back and forth between the two tables until both women catch on and storm out.

Always Spit After a Fisherman

Want people from other countries to think you're polite? Of course you do. So here are a few BRI tips about what's considered good manners around the world.

IN JAPAN: Wear a surgical mask in public if you have a cold.

IN SWITZERLAND: Buy wine for your table if you drop your bread in the fondue.

IN ITALY: Don't allow a woman to pour wine.

IN SAMOA: Spill a few drops of kava, the national beverage, before drinking.

IN BELGIUM AND LUXEMBOURG: Avoid sending a gift of chrysanthemums. They are a reminder of death.

IN SWEDEN: Wait until you're outside your guest's house before putting your coat on.

IN JORDAN: Leave small portions of food on your plate. Also, refuse seconds at least twice before accepting.

IN GREECE: Cheerfully participate in folk dancing if invited.

IN PORTUGAL: Signal you enjoyed a meal by kissing your index finger and then pinching your earlobe.

IN CHINA: Decline a gift a few times before accepting. Use both hands to give or receive one.

IN KOREA: Allow others to pass between you and the person you are conversing with. Don't make anyone walk behind you.

IN IRAN: Shake hands with children. (It shows respect for their parents.)

IN SPAIN: Say "buen provecho" to anyone beginning a meal.

IN FINLAND: If you pass the salt at the dinner table, don't put it in anyone's hand—put the salt shaker down and let them pick it up.

IN FIJI: Fold your arms behind you when conversing.

IN NORWAY: When a fisherman walks by, spit after him. It's a way of wishing him good luck.

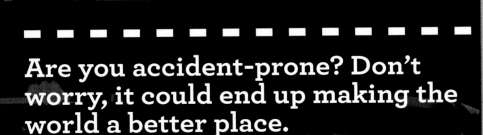

Are you accident-prone? Don't worry, it could end up making the world a better place.

Accidentally Excellent

Although Benedictus thought this was interesting, he went back to his regular work. A few days later, he read a newspaper story about a woman who had been killed by a broken windshield in a car accident. Benedictus rushed to his lab. By the next night he had invented the world's first safety glass, which can be found in virtually every car in the world today.

SUPERPRINTS

In 1977 Fuseo Matsumur, an examiner in a Japanese crime laboratory, was placing hairs on microscope slides during a murder investigation. Suddenly he noticed his own fingerprints developing on the glass slides. He mentioned it to his partner, Masato Soba, who asked what he had used to affix the hairs to the slides. Fuseo said he was using *cyanoacrylate ester*, better known as super glue. Soba began experimenting and soon discovered that super glue vapors are absorbed by the perspiration and oils left by fingerprints, turning them white. The use of cyanoacrylate fumes to reveal latent (hard-to-find) fingerprints became one of the biggest breakthroughs in the history of fingerprint forensics.

THAT'S JUST SILLY

In 1943 General Electric engineer James Wright was attempting to create artificial rubber, desperately needed for the war effort because the Japanese had invaded rubber-producing areas in Southeast Asia. In one

FIRST GLASS

One day in 1903, French chemist Edouard Benedictus was working in his lab when he accidentally knocked an empty glass flask off his workbench. When he picked it up, he noticed something strange: The glass had shattered into many pieces, but they remained stuck together in the shape of the bottle. Upon further investigation, he found that the flask had been filled with collodion, a syrupy chemical solution that, when evaporated, leaves a clear film. The film had coated the inside of the glass and held the pieces together. (Collodion, though quite toxic, was used in those days to seal cuts after surgery.)

SOME GENIUS: ALBERT EINSTEIN NEVER LEARNED TO DRIVE.

nothing else is
Silly Putty!
I take up comics—*in full color!*

I stretch!

I Bounce!

I make things!

BUY ME WHEREVER TOYS ARE SOLD—

BUY ME WHERE YOU BOUGHT THIS COMIC!

LEFT: Silly Putty advertisement from 1950
CENTER: Alexander Fleming, busy making history in his lab
BOTTOM: Culture flasks growing penicillin, 1943

experiment, Wright tried mixing boric acid with silicon oil. The substance that resulted was amazingly bouncy and could be stretched great distances. Those weren't very useful qualities, but the substance sure was fun. Wright's family members and friends—and even friends of friends—played with the "nutty putty" for years, until someone finally thought to market it. By the mid-1950s, Silly Putty was one of the most popular toys in the country.

THE NOBEL PRIZE FOR ACCIDENTS GOES TO...

...Alexander Fleming. In 1928 the Scottish scientist was experimenting with staphylococcus bacteria, the germs that cause staph infections, when he absentmindedly left some petri dishes exposed. Mold grew on the bacteria...and killed them. It was later determined to be penicillium mold, and Fleming named the active ingredient in the mold penicillin.

He wasn't able to create a medicine from it, but 12 years later two other scientists at Oxford University, Howard Florey and Ernst Chain, succeeded. The accident-inspired invention came just in time: Penicillin was mass-produced during World War II and has saved millions of lives since then. In 1945 Fleming, Florey, and Chain were awarded the Nobel Prize in medicine.

THE "COMMON COLD" CAN BE CAUSED BY MORE THAN 100 DIFFERENT VIRUSES.

Little Things Mean a Lot

"The devil's in the details," says an old proverb. It's true—the littlest things can cause the biggest problems.

A LINE OF CODE

In 2011 a Microsoft programmer working on the first major update of Windows 7 for the European market accidentally left out a line of code that would have given Europe's 15 million Windows users a choice of Web browsers—such as Safari or Firefox—with which to run the update. Without that line of code, users could only run Internet Explorer (owned by Microsoft). Result: The goof broke a 2009 commitment Microsoft had made to the European Commission to offer a choice of browsers. The software giant had to pay fines and restitution totaling $731 million.

A MISTRANSLATED WORD

When 18-year-old Willie Ramirez was rushed to a Florida hospital in 1980, he was in a coma. His family spoke only Spanish, and kept repeating the word *intoxicado*. Believing Ramirez to be intoxicated, doctors treated him for a drug overdose. However, *intoxicado* also means "poisoned," which is what the family was trying to say—that he was suffering from severe food poisoning. By the time the doctors caught the mistake, Ramirez had nearly died. He survived...but was left a quadriplegic. His family sued for malpractice and was awarded $71 million from the hospital... which now has a professional interpreter on call.

A FEW FEET OF CABLE

In 2011, 75-year-old Hayastan Shakarian from the nation of Georgia was searching through a field, looking for old copper wire scraps to sell, when she dug down with her shovel and cut through a fiberoptic cable. Not knowing what it was, she removed a few feet of it. And just like that, millions of people in neighboring Armenia lost their Internet connections. (Georgia supplies 90 percent of Armenia's Web access.) The blackout lasted twelve hours—halting Armenia's e-commerce, news service, airports, and several other systems. Normally, the cable would have been farther below ground, but recent rains and mudslides had left the area exposed. Shakarian—dubbed the "spade-hacker" by the press— was charged with damaging property, but at last report, hadn't been sent to jail.

A DECIMAL POINT

While designing the *Isaac Peral*, part of the Spanish Navy's "next generation of submarines," an engineer mistakenly put a

ABOVE: Fiberoptic cabling
LEFT: A 3D-render of what the *Ariane 5* looked like before it blew up
BELOW: The iconic de Havilland Comet was the strongest passenger plane in the world...except for one "minor" design flaw that caused two major tragedies.

decimal point in the wrong place that resulted in the completed sub being 77 tons heavier than the specifications had called for. In 2013 the Spanish Navy reported that it will cost millions of dollars to "slim it down" so the sub won't sink when it's launched.

A SOFTWARE GLITCH

The European Space Agency's *Ariane 5* rocket took 10 years to develop at a cost of $7 billion and blew up 39 seconds into its maiden flight in 1996. The rocket—designed to put the Europeans ahead in the commercial space race—was carrying a payload of four satellites costing a total of around $500 million. According to the investigation, the guidance system shut down 36.7 seconds after launch due to a software bug that was "unable

to convert a piece of data from a 64-bit format to a 16-bit format." That caused the system to "think" it was going off course— which it wasn't—so it initiated a self-destruct sequence that destroyed the rocket in midair.

SQUARE WINDOWS

In separate incidents in 1953 and 1954, three de Havilland Comet jetliners crashed mid-flight. Investigators were baffled as to what went wrong with two-year-old state-of-the-art aircraft. The culprit turned out to be... square windows. Because the steel surrounding each window had four right angles, the hull steadily became weaker in those areas. And unlike earlier, slower planes without pressurized cabins, the Comets were flying faster, higher, and for more flight hours than any passenger plane had before. Before long,

the stress became too much to hold the plane together. The Comet fleet was grounded for five years, and the problem was fixed. That's why, today, all jetliner windows have rounded "corners."

Smell Ya Later

Looking for love? Throw away those personal ads. Cancel your online dating service. You've already got what it takes to find a mate. Just take a deep breath...through your nose.

THE POWER OF PHEROMONES

The word comes from the Greek words *phero*, "I carry," and *hormone*, "to excite." So pheromone literally means "I carry excitement." And they do. Pheromones are chemicals that send signals between members of the same species. In animals and insects, pheromones can command sexual arousal or sexual receptivity. Humans have more of a choice—or at least they think they do. Pheromones are supposedly odorless, but mammals detect them with an organ inside the nose—called the *vomeronasal organ* (VNO)—a pair of microscopic pits on the skin inside the nostrils. When the VNO picks up a chemical order

from pheromones, get out of the way!

THE BIRDS AND THE BEES (AND COCKROACHES)

Scientists first stumbled onto nose power when they studied pheromones in animals and insects.

● Male mice emit pheromones so potent they actually promote the sexual development of nearby female mice.

● A male moth can detect the pheromones of a female moth from more than a mile away—it has no choice but to fly toward her.

● Male cockroaches may be the most pheromone-crazy creatures of all. When a glass rod is doused with female cockroach pheromones, the males try to mate with the rod.

GUYS IN SWEATY T-SHIRTS

But how does all this apply to us? Human love is deep and spiritual—right? Skeptics claim that the VNO isn't functional in adult humans; it can't possibly react to pheromones. Here's what the research has revealed:

● Underarm sweat has a pheromone component produced by the chemical *androstenol*. An experiment showed that exposure to androstenol made females more inclined to have social interactions with males (easy, boys, that's *social* interactions).

● When women were asked to smell unwashed T-shirts worn by different men, they liked the smell of men whose immune systems were different from

Lavender + Pumpkin Pie = Men

Cucumbers + Licorice = Women

their own. Since different genes emit different smells, the women may have been sniffing for an evolutionary advantage—a combination of immune-system genes that would be better at fighting off infections.

● Extracts of skin cells with pheromones contained in open flasks made people (male and female) warmer and friendlier. When the flasks were closed, the camaraderie faded.

● Pheromone-laced perfume increased women's sexual attractiveness. Women got more requests for dates and sexual intimacy.

● A set of female twins—one doused with pheromones, the other with witch hazel—secretly traded places at a singles' bar. The one wearing the pheromones was approached nearly three times as often as her witch hazel–wearing sister.

● Men "under the influence" of pheromones found plain women more attractive—and beautiful women less so.

STOP PAYING THROUGH THE NOSE

There are lots of pheromone products on the market, but are they really the love potions they purport to be? Scientists aren't sure. One thing they agree on is that the nose plays an important part in mating. People who are born blind or deaf engage in normal sexual behavior, but people born with no sense of smell tend to have diminished

sexual behavior.

Further research revealed that men were most aroused when they caught a whiff of lavender combined with pumpkin pie. Women went wild over licorice and cucumber. Women were definitely turned off by the scent of cherries and barbecue smoke. What smells turned men off? Well, none, actually. It seems it's pretty tough to discourage a guy who's got love on his...nose.

ABOUT 4,000 STARS ARE VISIBLE FROM EARTH WITHOUT A TELESCOPE.

27

There are Elvis impersonators, and then there's this guy. He seems so convinced that he actually is the King...that we're not going to rule out that possibility.

The Tagish Elvis

ALL SHOOK UP

"The UFO came over my head," said Elvis Aaron Presley. "And it zapped me with its light. I had this vision that I was wearing a maroon-coloured outfit, and the rhinestones on it were glowing. And I said, 'Holy sh*t, what's going on here? That's Elvis! But it's me, too!'" He said he could actually feel Elvis' DNA supplanting his own. Memories of the real Presley flooded his mind, as did the reason for his bizarre transformation: The U.S. government had hypnotized Elvis Presley in 1977 and sent him to the Yukon to live in obscurity as "Gilbert Nelles." Thirteen years later, he was "reactivated." The aliens told him so.

After the encounter, Nelles dyed his reddish-blond hair black and legally changed his name to Elvis Aaron Presley. Now he wears a sequined jumpsuit, oversized sunglasses, has jet-black sideburns, and speaks in the same Southern cadence as the King.

SUSPICIOUS MINDS

But it's not like Nelles was "normal" up until his alien encounter. He'd been known in the small Yukon town of Tagish to be a bit...eccentric. He'd tell people to watch what they say, because the CIA was monitoring him. He spent his evenings at bingo and karaoke, and made a modest living painting landscapes onto gold pans and selling them to tourists.

Locals say their Elvis really started losing it in the cold winter of 1990. That's when he built himself a cabin in the woods out of old, discarded telephone poles. The chemicals used to preserve the poles emitted noxious fumes—which may be to blame for his visions and belief that he's Elvis. But to hear the man tell his odd tale, he doesn't come off like a loony. He sounds more like...Elvis (the latter, drug-addled Vegas version). And he's got lots of faithful fans: "People actually kiss my feet and say, 'Elvis, the Lord has brought you back to us!'"

VIVA LAS VEGAS

In the three decades since his transformation, the Tagish Elvis has become something of a celebrity. One of his proudest moments was when he performed with (the real) Chubby Checker in Las Vegas. One of his lowest points also happened in Sin City: He was assaulted at a party by a group of men, who left him with two black eyes.

Back in the Yukon, you might see Elvis tooling around in his old pink Cadillac (decorated with plaster cherubs). And if you head up there to do some gold panning, you might be lucky enough to be serenaded by the King himself—he has a kiosk set up at a mining site. Bonus: He really does sound a lot like Elvis Presley!

And he doesn't just sing covers. He's written and recorded three albums of Elvis-style music: *Still Living* (1996), *Armageddon Angel* (2003), and *A King's Ransom* (2007). He was even the subject of a 2008 independent documentary film called *The Elvis Project*.

Kung Fu Elvis

JAILHOUSE ROCK

Aside from singing, one of Elvis' favorite things to do is sue people. His legal adventures began in 1996 when his wife, fed up with her husband's paranoid visions, told him she was moving out of the cabin. Enraged, Elvis accused her of being yet another pawn in the U.S. government's attempts to control him and then shot his gun toward her, but missed. When Mounties showed up and arrested him, one of them mentioned that he should seek "professional help." Elvis filed a $1-million lawsuit against the RCMP for defamation. The judge dismissed the case and charged him $10 for "wasting everybody's time."

But that was just the beginning. According to CBC News, "Elvis has sued just about every legal authority in the country, including police officers, lawyers, judges, the RCMP Complaints Commissioner, and even the Solicitor General of Canada." He even once sued adult magazine magnate Larry Flynt for featuring the Tagish Elvis as the "*ssh*le of the Month" in *Hustler*. Elvis wanted millions, but said he would be satisfied with a simple apology. So Flynt, not wanting to go to court, printed a short "sorry for calling you a crazy *ssh*le" note in the next issue.

Elvis would always represent himself in court. Dressed in full Elvis regalia, he was known to break out in song during his depositions. His rambling affidavits consisted of hundreds of pages of alien abduction and mind control stories. Finally, in 2003 a judge in Whitehorse called Elvis a "vexatious litigant" whose suits were all "gibberish." He was fined $10,000 and banned from filing lawsuits. Elvis left the building... but not before threatening to sue the judge for $120 million.

DON'T BE CRUEL

Where do troubled individuals eventually wind up? Politics, of course. In 2005 Elvis ran for the leadership position of the Yukon Liberal Party, but garnered only five votes. He fared somewhat better the following year, when he got 40 votes while running as an Independent for the Yukon legislature, promising to fix the corrupt court system. He lost, but tried again in 2011, using the slogan, "Be A Hound Dog, Vote Elvis Presley, Make Yukon Graceland." He lost again.

FAMILY GUY CREATOR SETH MACFARLANE MISSED HIS FLIGHT ON ONE OF THE DOOMED 9/11 PLANES.

"Elvis" in the *Dragons' Den*.

HEARTBREAK HOTEL

Those defeats, however, were nothing compared to the drubbing he took on national television. The Tagish Elvis performed before his largest audience ever in 2010 when, at age 54, he appeared on the game show *Dragon's Den*, in which contestants pitch their business proposals to a panel of grumpy rich people. Wearing a white jumpsuit, Elvis burst on stage singing an "Elvis original" (that he wrote) called "Country Child." Then he told the Dragons about the aliens. Not surprisingly, the Dragons mocked him, but Elvis stood his ground and pitched his pitch: For only $58,000, he'd sell them a 15-percent stake in his next two albums. He also offered up his memorabilia for sale. The answer: No. And not just no, but Dragon Kevin O'Leary called him a "nutbar." Elvis responded, "I'm making a chocolate bar called the Nutbar. We should go into business together." The answer: still no. Inspired by the insult, Elvis has since released the "Elvis Presley Nut Bar Experience Chocolate Bar" (which contains no nuts).

"Elvis" gets the runs.

"Elvis" takes a question.

RETURN TO SENDER

Currently residing in Ross River, Yukon, he's still doing what he does best: being Elvis Presley. As he says on his website, "I have an affinity for writing smooth lyrics set to upbeat dancing music containing a country, pop, rock, easy-listening style flavored with a First Nation cultural musical styling, creating a new unique musical genre with a spiritual depth easily absorbed by all."

"Elvis" being Elvis

THE EIFFEL TOWER, NOW A BELOVED SYMBOL, WAS ONCE LAMBASTED BY CRITICS AS UGLY AND UNSAFE.

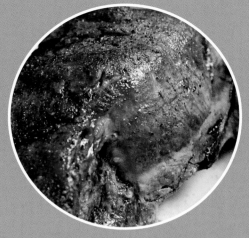

A mouth-watering butt roast

Butt Roast: A particular cut of pork taken from the pig's...shoulder.

Boston Butt: This variation on the butt roast originated in Boston.

Butt Rubbing: The practice of rubbing spices and other dry seasonings into a butt roast. (For Boston butts, the practice would be known as Boston butt rubbing.)

Butt Log: A log cut from the lowest, widest part of a tree trunk, just above the stump, or "butt."

Buttle: A verb that describes what butlers do: They "buttle."

Butts, Alfred Mosher: The unemployed American architect who invented the board game Scrabble in 1938.

David Bensusan-Butt: A wartime British civil servant and author of the Butt Report.

Water Butt: The British name for a rain barrel.

Know Your Butts

The inventor of Scrabble, Alfred Butts

Lots of things that have nothing to do with rear ends are known as butts. Here's a whole load of non-butt butts for you to ponder.

(Special thanks to BRI reader Seymour Butts for sending them in.)

Major Archibald Butt, the biggest butt that went down with the *Titanic*

Major Butt: A military aide to presidents Teddy Roosevelt and William Howard Taft, Archibald Butt was present when Taft threw out the first presidential baseball in 1910. He was also onboard the *Titanic* when it struck an iceberg on April 14, 1912, and he went down with the ship.

The Butt Memorial Bridge: A bridge in Augusta, Georgia, built in 1914 and dedicated to the memory of Major Butt.

Sackbut: A style of trombone popular during the Renaissance and Baroque eras.

Butt Rot: When the butt of a living tree suffers from a fungal infection, it's said to have "butt rot."

The Butt Report: A secret World War II report critical of British bombers for an inability to hit their targets. The Butt Report spurred changes in tactics and technology that vastly improved bomber accuracy.

Japanese popular culture has made two major contributions to the rest of the world: video games and really weird stuff. Here's where the two meet—weird video games from Japan.

Land of the Rising Fun

I'M SORRY (1985)

Former Japanese Prime Minister Kakuei Tanaka serves as the main character in this bizarre game, which satirizes the politician and his involvement in various bribery scandals in the early 1980s. Players control Tanaka as he makes his way through a series of maze-like levels while gobbling up gold bars, kind of like in *Pac-Man*. But unlike *Pac-Man*, whose enemies are a group of multicolored ghosts, *I'm Sorry*'s protagonist faces an onslaught from a group of celebrity enemies, including Michael Jackson, Carl Lewis, Madonna, and Japanese sumo wrestler Shohei Baba. If one of Tanaka's pursuers manages to capture him, they strip him down to a diaper and whip him as he begs for mercy.
Bonus: The title, *I'm Sorry*, is a play on the Japanese word *sori*, which means "prime minister."

TOYLETS (2010)

This one consists of an LCD screen placed above a urinal that contains pressure sensors capable of turning the player's "stream" into a game controller. The four *Toylets* games, from simple to bizarre:
● *"Mannekin Pis"* measures how hard the player can pee.
● *"Graffiti Eraser"* washes graffiti off walls.
● *"The Northern Wind, The Sun and Me"*: The player must provide enough "force" to make a video gust of wind blow up a woman's skirt. (The harder you pee, the harder the wind blows.)
● *"Battle! Milk From Nose"*: A test of "strength" against the previous player, in which the player's stream is translated into milk spraying out of his nose. If your stream is stronger, your milk stream knocks your opponent out of the ring.

THE TABLECLOTH HOUR (2010)

This game gives players the opportunity to do what usually only magicians can pull off— yanking a tablecloth out from underneath an elaborate place setting, leaving the dishes and silverware intact and in place. The screen shows a red sheet loaded with cute, anthropomorphized dishes and silverware. The player must then press a button at just the right moment to pull the tablecloth in order for the dishes to remain perfectly still (You win!) or fly off the table (Game Over). Believe it or not, *The Tablecloth Hour* is actually the second in a series of games about table settings. *Ultra Low Dining Table* has a completely opposite objective: The more objects that fall off the table, the more points the player scores.

SUB MARINE CATCHER (1994)

For decades, American arcades and pizza parlors have had "claw games," where the player controls a claw in order to grab and win a stuffed animal or a toy. Japanese arcades have a variant called *Sub Marine Catcher*. Instead of snatching a Hello Kitty doll or a miniature teddy bear, players can fish a live lobster out of a tank. Should they manage to snag one of the crustaceans, lucky winners are presented with a bag of water by an arcade clerk so they can take their prize catch home.

BOONG-GA, BOONG-GA (2001)

In the U.S., bullies employ the "wedgie" to terrorize their victims. In Japan, they have kancho, a less cruel, slightly less intrusive bit of mischief in which the prankster pokes someone in the butt (crack) with two fingers. *Boong-Ga, Boong-Ga* is a video-game version of kancho. Players select from a list of eight characters to "punish." Among them: "Ex-girlfriend," "Ex-boyfriend," "Mother-in-Law," "Gold Digger," and "Gangster."

Bonus: Game play is interactive—players poke a denim-covered fake butt, which is attached to the front of the game's cabinet.

ZAGAZIG IS A CITY IN EGYPT; WAGGA WAGGA IS A CITY IN AUSTRALIA.

33

The national parks in the western United States boast some of the most beautiful scenery in the world. They can also be deathtraps if you're not careful. Here are some things to watch out for.

NATIONAL PARK NIGHTMARES!

FLASH FLOODS!

Flash floods are the number-one weather-related killer in the United States, claiming about 200 lives every year. And during the summer months, the Grand Canyon, like much of the desert in the American Southwest, is prone to them. In August 1963, a downpour dropped 1.5 inches of rain on the canyon rim. After sitting out the rain about halfway down the canyon, a man and his son resumed their trek on Bright Angel Trail. All of a sudden, a 10-foot wall of muddy water carrying rock, sand, gravel, and desert vegetation burst out of a side canyon onto the trail, washing the two hikers away.

Since that tragedy, at least four other hikers have been killed by flash floods in the Grand Canyon, and many more in the various narrow slot canyons of northern Arizona. The gorges of Utah's Zion National Park have been the scene of flash flood tragedies, too.

Even under blue skies, hikers have been killed by flash floods generated by thunderstorms as far as 25 miles away. That's because desert soil isn't able to absorb large amounts of rainfall. Result: The canyons in the Southwest can funnel huge walls of water downhill in minutes. The only warning is a deep roaring sound. Once you hear that, you better start scrambling to high ground as fast as you can.

LIGHTNING!

Lightning is the number-two weather-related killer in the United States; an average of 67 people are killed and 300 injured every year. Outdoorsy types are at the greatest risk, of course, especially along high mountain trails on exposed rocks in areas of frequent thunderstorms. (The safest place to be during a thunderstorm is in an enclosed building or in a hard-topped vehicle.)

One of the least safe places to be: on top of Half Dome at Yosemite National Park in California. On July 27, 1985, five hikers climbed the cables (which the park service installs for the summer months) up the sheer rock slope of Half Dome. In their excitement to get to the top, the hikers ignored the thunderstorm brewing overhead, as well as a big warning sign at the base of Half Dome that read:

Danger: If a thunderstorm is anywhere on the horizon DO NOT PASS BEYOND THIS SIGN. Lightning has struck Half Dome during every month of the year.

The hikers proceeded anyway. Two bolts of lightning struck the granite rock that day; two young men were killed and three were injured—one of the worst accidents in Yosemite's history. Lightning also killed a hiker 50 miles to the south in Sequoia National Park.

Travel on Sub-dome and Half Dome
DANGEROUS
During and after lightning and rain storms
SERIOUS INJURY AND DEATH
Have resulted from:
- Falls on wet, slick rock
- Lightning strikes to hikers on exposed terrain

EVALUATE THE WEATHER BEFORE
PROCEEDING PAST THIS POINT

BOILING GEYSERS!

Yellowstone has more geysers, hot pools, mud pots, and boiling springs than any other place on Earth. Not surprising, then, that it's had more than 19 deaths and 100 burn injuries due to visitors stepping, falling, or diving into hot water. In fact, hot springs deaths in Yellowstone are more common than grizzly bear kills. One young man died when he dove into a hot pool to try and save a dog that had jumped in. Both man and dog died. Now pets are forbidden in the thermal areas.

Yellowstone has dozens of signs warning you to stay on the boardwalks, to keep a close watch on your children (who account for a high percentage of the injuries and deaths), and not to step on the thin crust around the thermal pools. Most of the springs are hotter than 150°F, and some get as hot as 205°F (higher than water's boiling point at that altitude).

Another hot spot is Lassen Volcanic National Park in northern California. The colorfully named Bumpass Hell is a geothermal area of boiling mud pots, steam vents, and hot springs. The story goes that in 1865 a local cowboy named Kendall Bumpass stepped through the thin crust surrounding one of the mud pots, badly scalding his leg. When he showed a newspaperman the site of the accident, he did it again, this time burning his leg so badly that it had to be amputated. So "Bumpass Hell" is an apt warning. **Read the signs the park service has put up for you, watch the skies for storms, don't go where you're not supposed to, keep a close eye on the kids, and don't say we didn't warn you.**

Uncle John's STALL OF FAME

Uncle John is amazed—and pleased—by the creative ways people get involved with bathrooms, toilets, toilet paper, and so on. That's why he created the "Stall of Fame."

health-care organization. Petey's goal: to "humanize" the company and promote same-day results for urine tests. The campaign is targeted toward "a younger demographic that understands irony, YouTube, and social networking." (Petey has a Facebook page.) In 2008 HealthPartners gave Petey a sidekick—Pokey the Syringe.

Honoree: Petey P. Cup
Notable Achievement: Becoming the first and only (so far) mascot shaped like a urine sample container
True Story: He's nearly seven feet tall, he walks on two legs, and his body is a giant jar of pee. The yellow spokescup (with blue lid) was created by HealthPartners, a Minnesota-based nonprofit

Honoree: Adam Baker, an amateur painter from Reno, Nevada
Notable Achievement: Taking life's lemons and making lemonade...in the bathrooms of every state in the union
True Story: When the 42-year-old Baker learned about a contest to paint the official portrait of Governor Kenny Guinn, Baker poured his heart and soul into a loving depiction of Guinn and sent it off to the state capitol...

only to learn that the winner was a painter from out of state. Rather than get mad, Baker decided to get even: He took his gubernatorial portrait on an extended road trip to every state capitol building in the country, taking care once he arrived to position Governor Guinn in front of the urinals in the men's room and take a few snapshots. So is his portrait a winner? See for yourself.

As for the Guinn Administration, a spokesperson says that Baker's tour of restrooms "says a lot of what he thinks about his own work."

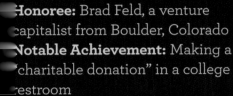

Honoree: Brad Feld, a venture capitalist from Boulder, Colorado

Notable Achievement: Making a "charitable donation" in a college restroom

True Story: Feld gave $25,000 to the University of Colorado. Now the second floor men's room in the technology building displays a plaque bearing his name. Underneath is printed this piece of advice: "The best ideas often come at inconvenient times. Don't ever close your mind to them." Feld's first choice was a restroom at Massachusetts Institute of Technology, his alma mater, but the school declined. The University of Colorado jumped at the chance and would like to remind people that the women's room adjacent to Feld's is still up for grabs.

Honoree: Sim Jae-duck, a.k.a. "Mr. Toilet," a South Korean lawmaker and president of the World Toilet Association

Notable Achievement: Making the best seat in the house into the entire house

True Story: In the town of Suwon, South Korea, Sim tore down his house and in its place built a 24-foot-tall, toilet-shaped building. It's made of steel, and it's painted white to resemble porcelain. Even bigger than the toilet house is the reason it was built: to serve as the "headquarters" for the World Toilet Association (not to be confused with the much larger World Toilet Organization), which is dedicated to improving sanitary conditions for the 2.5 billion people who lack access to clean water and bathrooms. Formed in 2007, the WTA held its inaugural meeting at Sim's toilet house—whose official name is *Haewoojae*, Korean for "a place of sanctuary where one can solve one's worries."

Honoree: Thelma Brittingham, a resident at the Holiday Retirement Village in Evansville, Indiana

Notable Achievement: Having a birthday party for toilet paper

True Story: Trying to bring some fun to the home's senior citizens, Brittingham decided to research the history of toilet paper in the hopes of tracing it back to its date of birth. Her findings: TP was first used in Europe on August 26, 580 A.D. (No word on how she determined that.) So now, each year the retirees put on a birthday party on the special day. Brittingham says, "When some people heard we were celebrating toilet paper's birthday, they asked me, 'Have you lost your mind?'"

Honoree: Gerardine Botte, director of Ohio University's Electrochemical Engineering Research Laboratory

Notable Achievement: Turning pee into power

True Story: Urine contains ammonia, and ammonia can be broken down into hydrogen and nitrogen, which can provide energy. So why do the millions of tons of ammonia made by humans and farm animals each year just evaporate in waste treatment plants and in ponds on farms? That's the question asked—and answered—by Botte and the science whizzes at OU. After a long process of trial and error, the team is perfecting a device called an electrolyzer that uses electric current to break down the ammonia into its component parts, which can then be turned into fuel. Within a few years, many waste treatment plants and farm waste ponds may be converted into power plants with an endless supply of raw fuel. The technology may even lead to pee-powered automobiles. One of the most beneficial aspects of ammonia energy: it creates no greenhouse gases, effectively turning one of our dirtiest byproducts into one of our cleanest forms of energy.

These people made it into the *Guinness World Records* and probably wish they hadn't.

Unplanned World Records

FARTHEST-FLYING HUMAN PROJECTILE (involuntary)

On December 6, 1917, a ship loaded with munitions exploded in the harbor at Halifax, Nova Scotia, killing more than 1,900 people and destroying the entire Richmond district of the town. It was the largest man-made explosion of the pre-nuclear age, estimated at 2.9 megatons. One man, William Becker, was lucky: He was in a rowboat about 300 feet away from the ship when it exploded, propelling him 1,600 yards—the length of 16 football fields—across the harbor. He swam to safety and lived until 1969.

SHORTEST MARRIAGE

On September 11, 1976, 39-year-old Robert Neiderhiser dropped dead at the altar just after he and his fiancée, Naomi Nicely, were pronounced man and wife at a Presbyterian church in Greensburg, Pennsylvania.

WORST STUDENT DRIVER

On August 3, 1970, Miriam Hargrave, 62, of Yorkshire, England, finally passed her driving test...on her 40th attempt. After so much effort, she still couldn't drive. After spending so much money on her driving lessons—$720 was a lot of money in 1970—she couldn't afford to buy a car.

OLDEST SURGERY PATIENT

James Henry Brett Jr. was 111 years and 105 days old when he had hip surgery in Houston in November 1960. He died four months later (from old age, not from the surgery).

SLOWEST-SELLING PUBLISHED BOOK

In 1716 the Oxford University Press printed 500 copies of a book titled *Translation of the New Testament* from Coptic into Latin, by David Wilkins. It took 191 years to sell them all.

TOP: View of the harbour district of Richmond, Halifax, showing the complete destruction caused by the munitions explosion on December 6, 1917

Inventor Dean Kamen holds over 150 patents for medical technology and social welfare devices. But it's for his one major failure he'll be remembered: the Segway.

LEFT: Dean Kamen
RIGHT: The oft-maligned Segway proved successful as a humorous vehicle on TV's *Arrested Development*.

Segue into Segway

EDISON REBORN?

Dean Kamen has been obsessed with the power of technology since he was a teenager. He never cared much for school, skipping homework to read complicated physics texts and create laser light shows. While still in high school, Kamen designed the audiovisual system at New York's Hayden Planetarium and the New Year's Eve Times Square ball drop. By 18, he was earning $60,000 a year, more than his father, an editor at *Mad* magazine.

He began inventing when his brother, a medical student, complained about how hard it was to administer intravenous drugs without having to keep patients constantly hospitalized. Solving his brother's dilemma consumed his life—he was even kicked out of college for spending too much time on it. But by 1976, at age 25, Kamen had patented the Auto-Syringe: a pocket-size infusion pump that delivers a steady stream of medication, freeing patients from hospital beds.

(Today it's mostly used in insulin pumps for diabetics.) Kamen manufactured and marketed the device himself, and eventually sold his company for $5 million.

THE NEXT BIG THING

Barely 30 and a multimillionaire, Kamen took his money and created DEKA Research and Development. It was his dream job: Companies would pay him to invent stuff. Under this arrangement, Kamen developed 150 devices, including a portable

Dean Kamen shows off the IBOT

Meet Ginger

A Segway on patrol

dialysis machine that freed patients with kidney diseases from constant visits to dialysis centers, and the IBOT, a robotic wheelchair that could climb stairs and raise its user to standing level. Following these successes, Kamen knew his next project would have to be nothing short of earth-shattering to meet expectations, especially his own.

For the better part of the decade, Kamen spoke very little about his next invention. The less he said, the more interest he generated in "It" (that was the codename). All Kamen would say was that It would revolutionize the world— and would "be to the car what the car was to the horse and buggy."

Science and technology magazines speculated wildly on what It might be: Was It a personal hovercraft? A solar-powered engine? By 2000 no pictures or details had been released, although Kamen had been working on It (now being

called "Ginger") for almost ten years and had raised $90 million from investors. Kamen opened up a little in early 2001: He talked about the potential impact of Ginger, but not the invention itself. He promised it would end urban congestion, air pollution, and oil dependency. Kamen leased a giant factory in New Hampshire set to produce 10,000 units a week to meet what was sure to be an insatiable demand.

What could possibly live up to such hype? Unfortunately, not Ginger.

WOW, IT'S A...SCOOTER

Kamen finally unveiled his top-secret invention to end all inventions on *Good Morning, America* in December 2001. The device's real name was the Segway Human Transporter. According to Segway Inc., the device was the "first self-balancing, electric-powered transportation device. With the

ability to emulate human balance, the Segway HT uses the same space as a pedestrian, and can go wherever a person can walk." Resembling a podium on wheels, the Segway ran on synchronized gyroscopes that constantly balanced the rider at speeds of up to 13 mph.

By and large, the public didn't think a scooter had the capacity to alter world transport, nor was it worth the years of buildup or the $90 million investment. And there were all sorts of problems Kamen and his engineers didn't foresee. Segways were banned from the narrow sidewalks of older cities like New York and Boston. They were far too expensive ($5,000) to make people give up their cars. But perhaps most importantly of all—they looked silly.

HOW MANY DO YOU WANT?

In an attempt to build consumer confidence, Kamen went to

Out and about with a Segway club

It even goes off-road!

trendsetting corporate clients first. Disney bought a few Segways for its theme parks, and Amazon.com and the U.S. Postal Service let workers test them out. Segways became available to the general public just before Christmas 2002. The general public didn't notice.

I'M A STAR

One segment of the country embraced the Segway: the media, but only as an oddity. A high-profile flop and a novelty, it was ripe for lampooning. The scooter showed up on the sitcoms *Frasier*, *Arrested Development*, *Father of the Pride*, and in the Ben Stiller movie *Envy*. All this coverage didn't help sell the Segway or improve its goofy image; it was still considered an extravagant toy for kooky millionaires. The Segway was recalled in 2003 after three riders were mildly injured falling off. At that point, only 6,000 had been sold. The Segway has yet to catch on in the way Kamen predicted or anticipated, but he rides his virtually all day long through his office and around Manchester, New Hampshire. He hasn't lost hope, though. One day, Kamen insists, everyone will be riding Segways.

Q: WHAT IS PUNCTATE PRURITUS? A: THE MEDICAL TERM FOR AN ITCHY SPOT.

41

Page 42 created with a great deal of "forti-tude"

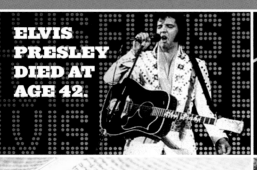

ELVIS PRESLEY DIED AT AGE 42.

The angle at which light reflects off water to create a rainbow is 42 degrees.

THE CITY OF JERUSALEM COVERS AN AREA OF 42 SQUARE MILES.

The Torah (the holy book of Judaism) is broken into columns, each of which always has exactly 42 lines.

FOX MULDER (*The X-Files*) lives in apartment number 42.

There are 42 decks on the *Enterprise NCC-1701-D* (the *Next Generation* ship).

The only number retired by every major-league baseball team is Jackie Robinson's 42.

A WONDERBRA CONSISTS OF 42 INDIVIDUAL PARTS.

THERE ARE 42 OREO COOKIES IN A 1-POUND PACKAGE.

THE RIGHT ARM OF THE STATUE OF LIBERTY IS 42 FEET LONG.

The number of dots on a pair of dice: 42

Dogs have a total of 42 teeth over their lifetimes.

In *The Catcher in the Rye*, Holden Caulfield lies and says that he is 42.

THE WORLD-RECORD JUMP BY A KANGAROO IS 42 FEET.

THE NATURAL VIBRATION FREQUENCY OF WHITE MOUSE DNA: 42

THE NATURAL VIBRATION FREQUENCY OF HUMAN DNA: 42

There were 42 generations from Abraham to Jesus Christ.

According to Douglas Adams's *The Hitchhiker's Guide to the Galaxy*, "The meaning of life, the universe, and everything" is the number 42.

Believe it or not, there is a support group called Abduct Anon for people who believe they've been kidnapped by extraterrestrials. Are you about to be abducted by aliens and subjected to medical experiments? Or has it happened already? Here are some signs that Abduct Anon and other UFO groups say you should be on the watch for.

How to tell if you've been
Abducted by Aliens

Think this scene from *Close Encounters of the Third Kind* (1977) looks far-fetched? Director Steven Spielberg consulted with actual ufologists while making the film, who told him that this odd behavior has been documented by people who claim they were abducted.

AT BEDTIME

● You have chronic insomnia, and you hear a tapping or humming noise just as you're dropping off to sleep.

● You dream of aliens and UFOs directly, or you dream of vaguely mysterious beings but remember none of the details except one: The beings had very large eyes.

● You have the feeling you're being watched, especially as you're dropping off to sleep. Or you wake up in the middle of the night because you think someone—or something—is watching you. You may even see one or more shadowy figures standing around the bed, staring at you.

SADDAM HUSSEIN'S FAVORITE AMERICAN FOODS: RAISIN BRAN AND DORITOS.

43

- You sleepwalk. You've gone to sleep in one place and woken up in another with no explanation for how it happened. (And alcohol is not involved.)

- For the first few seconds or minutes after awakening, you are paralyzed and cannot move your body.

- When you wake up you find small drops of blood on your pillow, but there's no explanation for how they got there.

ON THE ROAD

- Your car breaks down unexpectedly with no explanation, often soon after you've spotted a UFO.

- You pull over to the side of the road...and the next thing you remember is standing next to or driving your car. Hours or even days may have passed, but you have no memory of what has happened in the meantime.

- Your "broken-down" car is running again, and you have no explanation for that, either.

- You have the sense that you have levitated or passed through solid objects such as the doors or roof of your car, perhaps as the aliens lifted you into their spacecraft.

DURING THE DAY

- You see smoke, fog, or haze at a time and in a place for which there is no logical explanation.

- You have an unexplained, irresistible desire to walk or drive to a particular location, where you believe something "familiar, yet unknown" will soon happen. You may experience a heightened level of anxiety in the days leading up to this strange happening.

- You find yourself building a mountain in your living room, just like Richard Dreyfuss did in *Close Encounters of the Third Kind* before setting off to meet the aliens in person.

PHYSICAL CHANGES

- You get frequent nosebleeds and you don't know why.

- You have unexplained soreness or stiffness, or a mysterious rash on one or more parts of your body. There may also be evidence that your skin has been scraped (and a sample taken).

- You find new scars on your body and you have no idea how they got there. (And alcohol is not involved.)

- When you go in for your annual physical, your doctor finds strange, tiny probes implanted in your body.

WHAT'S UP, DOC?

- You may have a dim memory of a very probing (hint, hint) medical exam conducted against your will.

- You may also have memories of having your head placed in some kind of restraining device as long needles are inserted into your nostrils or ears, or something drills into your skull. These sensations may be accompanied by a burning smell. Human medical examiners who look you over after the fact find no signs that such procedures have taken place.

AFTER THE FACT

- There may be evidence that the scene of your abduction has have been "staged" to look as if nothing has happened, but a few incorrect details might be noticeable. For example, if you went to bed wearing pajamas, you may wake up nude or dressed only in underwear, with the pajamas folded neatly and placed at the foot of the bed.

- You may even wake up in the wrong room of the house. If you were abducted from your car, you may find that items in the car or in the trunk have been moved around.

- Your ability to remember

things suddenly becomes stronger, and you may even develop psychic powers that enable you to see events in the future.

● You suddenly get a sense of mission or the feeling that you have been chosen (by the aliens) for an important purpose, but you don't know what it is. This often replaces feelings of low self-esteem that you had before the alien encounter.

● Electronic appliances behave strangely when you pass by. Computers crash, clocks lose time, radio and TV reception is distorted, and streetlights go dark as you walk under them.

● You develop a new phobia of some kind. Did you suddenly become afraid of spiders? Heights? Enclosed spaces? Crowds? The aliens may be to blame.

● You become obsessive-compulsive or develop addictions that you didn't have before.

● You become less trusting of other people, especially doctors, police, and other authority figures, than you were before.

● You have an uncontrollable urge to take vitamins.

● You develop an interest in UFOs, astronomy, or physics. Or, conversely, an aversion

to being around other people when they are discussing these subjects.

DON'T LEAVE EARTH WITHOUT IT

If this topic has unsettled you, fear not! The St. Lawrence Agency of Altamonte Springs, Florida, sells a UFO abduction insurance policy that pays out $10 million, with a double-indemnity payment of $20 million "if the aliens insist on conjugal visits." Cost: $19.95 plus $3.00 for same-day shipping. The policy pays out $1 per year for 10 million years or until the death of the policy holder, whichever comes first.

IN THE BLUE CORNER

IN THE RED CORNER

WAR PLAN RED

When this bizarre story surfaced a few years ago, it reminded us of this quote, attributed to Warren G. Harding: "I can take care of my enemies all right. But my damn friends—they're the ones that keep me walking the floors nights."

NORTHERN EXPOSURE

If you had to invade another country, how would you do it? Believe it or not, the United States military spent a lot of time pondering that question in the late 1920s, when it came up with a plan to invade its closest neighbor, Canada.

There was certainly a precedent for the two nations battling it out. The Continental Army invaded Canada during the American Revolution, and the U.S. Army made repeated incursions during the War of 1812. In 1839 the state of Maine only narrowly avoided a shooting war with the province of New Brunswick over a border dispute. Then, in 1866, about 800 Irish-American members of a group called the Fenian Brotherhood tried to occupy part of Canada for the purpose of using it as a bargaining chip to force Great Britain to grant independence to Ireland. (They were quickly driven back across the U.S. border.)

That last invasion had an upside for Canadians: It convinced the last holdouts in the independent provinces of New Brunswick, Nova Scotia, Ontario, and Quebec that they'd be better able to defend themselves against the next invasion if they banded together to form the Dominion of Canada, which they did on July 1, 1867.

THE GREAT WAR

Of course, these skirmishes paled in comparison to World War I, which raged from 1914 to 1918. That war, which was precipitated by the assassination of Archduke Ferdinand of Austria, caught most of the belligerents by surprise. It also lasted longer and was far more costly in blood and treasure than anyone ever dreamed a war could be. None of the nations that fought in it wanted to be caught off guard again; many began planning for whatever war might be lurking around the corner.

The American military drafted a whole series of color-coded war plans to cover just about every conceivable scenario: War Plan Black was a plan for war with Germany; War Plan Orange dealt with Japan, a rapidly growing power in the Pacific. Other colors included Green (Mexico), Gold (France), Brown (The Philippines), and Yellow (China). There was even a War Plan Indigo, in case the United States had to invade Iceland, and a War Plan White that dealt with civil unrest within America's own borders.

SEEING RED

War Plan Red was America's plan for going to war with the British Empire, in the unlikely event that Britain (code name: Red) decided to "eliminate [the United States] as an economic and commercial rival." Since Canada (code name: Crimson) was part of the Empire and shared a 5,527-mile border with the U.S., much of the plan dealt with invading Canada and knocking it out of action before the British could use it as a staging ground for attacks on the U.S. Here's how an invasion of Canada would have gone:

The United States (code name: Blue) would attack and occupy Halifax, Nova Scotia, Canada's largest Atlantic port. The attack would deny Britain access to the rail and road links it would need to land troops in Canada and disperse them across the country. Next, the U.S. Army would attack across the border along three fronts: Troops would attack from either Vermont or New York to occupy Montreal and Quebec City; from Michigan into Ontario; and from North Dakota into Manitoba. Meanwhile, the U.S. Navy would take control of the Great Lakes. The effects of these attacks would be to seize Canada's industrial heartland while preventing similar attacks on America, and to further disrupt the movement of Canadian troops from one part of the country to another.

Troops would cross from Washington into British Columbia and seize Vancouver, Canada's largest Pacific port. The U.S. Navy would blockade the port of Prince Rupert, 460 miles to the north. Once the crisis passed and relations between America, Canada, and Great Britain returned to normal, the U.S. troops would be withdrawn from Canadian territory, right? No. "Blue intentions are to hold in perpetuity all Crimson and Red territory gained," the military planners wrote. "The policy will be to prepare the provinces and territories of Crimson and Red to become states and territories of the Blue union upon the declaration of peace."

THE FOG OF WAR(S)

So how seriously was the United States considering invading Canada? In all probability, not very. War Plan Red doesn't go into nearly as much detail as War Plan Black (Germany) or War Plan Orange (Japan), which military planners correctly assumed were much more significant threats. The intent of the other color-coded plans may have been to make war plans involving Germany and Japan seem less controversial. Why the subterfuge? After the horrors of World War I, in which nearly 10 million soldiers died, many people concluded that planning for wars only made them more likely. The U.S. military didn't feel this way, of course, and one way they may have gotten around public opinion was to come up with all kinds of improbable war plans to make the real plans more palatable. A public that would not have tolerated the idea of preparing for war with Germany and Japan would be less alarmed by the idea of the United States preparing for war with Germany, Japan, Canada, Iceland, Jamaica, Monaco, and Andorra.

WHAT'S GOOD FOR THE GOOSE...

Any sting Canadians may have felt when War Plan Red was declassified in 1974 was offset by the knowledge that Canada had drafted its own plans for invading the United States, and had done so several years before War Plan Red was approved in 1930. "Defense Scheme No. 1," as it was called, was created in 1921 by James Sutherland "Buster" Brown, Canada's director of military operations and intelligence. In many respects it was the opposite of War Plan Red: In the event that an American attack was imminent, Canadian forces would strike first, attacking and occupying key cities such as Albany, Minneapolis, and Seattle.

Unlike with War Plan Red, these cities wouldn't be annexed or even occupied for any longer than was absolutely necessary. The idea was to knock the U.S. off balance, then retreat back into Canada, blowing up bridges and destroying roads and railroads along the way in the hope of delaying the inevitable American counterattack until British reinforcements arrived. The plan received mixed reviews from the Canadian military: One general called it a "fantastic desperate plan that just might have worked"; other officers thought Brown was nuts. It remained on the books until 1928, when it was scrapped as impractical.

Nudes and Prudes

Nudity can be shocking...and so can prudery.

NUDE... On Christmas Day 2003, Minneapolis firefighters with sledgehammers knocked down the chimney of Uncle Hugo's Bookstore and rescued a naked 34-year-old man who was trapped inside. The man claimed he had stripped naked in order to fit down the 12-by-12-inch chimney, and that he was looking for some keys he had accidently dropped down the shaft. Police didn't buy it—and charged him with attempted burglary. "He doesn't appear to be a hard-core criminal," said Lieutenant Mike Sauro, "just stupid."

PRUDE... Acting on a neighbor's complaint, in May 2004, police in Barnsley, England, ordered a local man named Tony Watson to do something about the naked lawn gnomes in his front yard or face arrest for "causing public offense." Watson, an ex-army sergeant, complied by painting bathing suits on the gnomes. "We have to take complaints from members of the public seriously," a police spokesperson told reporters.

NUDE... Indianapolis police arrested Erica Meredith, 25, as she was picking up her eight-year-old daughter at school in January 2004. The charge: "Disseminating matter harmful to minors," a felony punishable by up to three years in prison and a $10,000 fine. The crime: She was driving her boyfriend's car, which had a three-by-five-foot painting of a naked woman airbrushed on the hood. The prosecutor dropped the charges after the boyfriend agreed to airbrush a bikini onto the painting.

PRUDE... In 1998 the U.S. Navy charged a career officer with indecent exposure and conduct unbecoming an officer following an incident at the Pensacola Naval Air Station in Florida. The incident: Lieutenant Patrick Callaghan, 28, had mooned a friend while jogging on the base. "There are people who are real offended when you take your pants down in a public street," Callaghan's commanding officer, Captain Terrence Riley, explained. At first, Callaghan faced dismissal from the Navy for the prank, but officials let him off with only a letter of reprimand in the end.

NUDE... In 2004 a businessman named Bill Martin bought a run-down nudist colony outside of Tampa, Florida, for $1.6 million and made plans to open a new business on the site. What kind of business? A Christian nudist

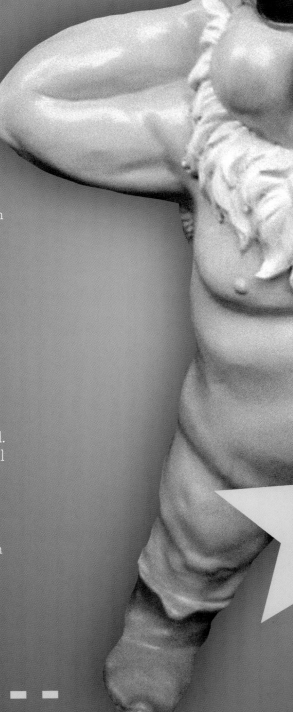

RIGHT: The "Naked Rambler" rambles into the record books.

colony. "The Bible very clearly states that when Adam and Eve were with God, they were naked," says executive director David Blood. "When people are right with God, they do not have to fear nudity."

PRUDE... Mel Culver, a teacher in Waukesha, Wisconsin, asked the school district to remove the 2001 *Guinness World Records* from all 17 elementary schools in the district. The book contains photos of models wearing "the world's most valuable bikini" and "the world's most expensive bra and panties." "Boys are asking to go to the library for the sole purpose of looking at these pictures," Culver wrote in her complaint. "The news of the pictures is spreading like wildfire." (The review committee voted 9–0 to reject her request.)

NUDE... In January 2004, Stephen Gough, 44, known as the "Naked Rambler," accomplished his goal of walking the length of the United Kingdom wearing only socks, walking boots, and a hat. His purpose: To encourage greater acceptance of the naked body. The 900-mile trip took seven months. Gough was arrested 16 times along the way and served two stints in jail for indecent exposure.

PRUDE... In 1999 school officials in two Georgia school districts spent two entire weeks applying touch-up paint to a picture of the famous painting "Washington Crossing the Delaware" in more than 2,300 fifth-grade social studies textbooks. Why? They feared that kids would mistake the ornamental orbs of Washington's pocket watch, which lay across his right thigh in the painting, for his family jewels. "I know what it is and I know what it is supposed to be," said Muscogee County Schools Superintendent Guy Sims. "But I also know fifth-grade students and how they might react to it."

Par for the Curse

As if golf pros don't already have enough obstacles hindering them from playing well, some tournaments may harbor an additional, unseen hazard...

A beautiful day for golf.

THE MASTERS PAR-3 JINX

On the Wednesday before the start of the Masters, golfers can take part in a nine-hole, par-3 competition. Yet many of golf's fiercest competitors don't even bother to compete in the par-3 contest. Why? They say it's cursed. Since the friendly competition was first held in 1960, not a single winner has ever gone on to win the Masters in the same year.

THE RYDER CUP CAPTAIN'S DOWNFALL

Most American pros would be honored to lead the Ryder Cup team against Europe's best, but golfers in the know keep their distance. Since 1993, every team captain followed up the event with one of his worst seasons ever. A few examples: Tom Watson (1993) sank to 43rd place in 1994. Tom Kite (1997) finished 159th the next year. Ben Crenshaw (1999) was 240th in 2000. Hal Sutton (2003) played in only a handful of tournaments in 2004, and barely made the cut in most of them.

CHIEF LEATHERLIPS'S REVENGE

The Wyandot tribe once thrived in what is now Dublin, Ohio. White settlers called the chief "Leatherlips" because he always told the truth. But although they respected him, they settled on land stolen from the Wyandots. In 1810 Leatherlips's own tribe executed him for allowing the settlers to move in without a fight. A century and a half later, Jack Nicklaus built Muirfield Village on the Wyandots' sacred burial grounds, and according to local legend, this angered Chief Leatherlips. The proof: over its 25-year run, the Memorial Tournament held each May has been dumped on by torrential rains more than half of the times it has been held. Normally, May is a dry month in central Ohio with only a 3 percent chance of heavy rain on any given day. Inexplicably, that increases to more than 50 percent when the pros are there. Could the spirit of Chief Leatherlips be drowning out the Muirfield Memorial Tournament?

Anarchy in the E.R.

Having to go to the emergency room (ouch!) is bad enough. Having to admit that your condition is the result of doing something stupid only adds insult to the injury, as these excerpts from actual E.R. reports attest.

* "42-year-old female states, 'I was playing a computer bowling game and passed out; struck chin on unknown object. I've been drinking.'"

* "18-year-old male accidentally shot himself while putting BB gun in his pants at home. Gunshot wound to penis."

* "61-year-old female was smoking on the porch while wearing oxygen. House caught fire. Smoke inhalation."

* "37-year-old female went to sit in recliner at home, missed chair, fell on arm. Elbow pain."

* "21-year-old male used a surfboard to slide down a flight of stairs; fell off surfboard. Sprained left ankle."

* "Male, 41, was accidentally hit in the head with bowling ball while playing catch with it at a bachelor party. Neck strain, head injury, bruising."

* "53-year-old female was sitting on a rocking chair when she fell backwards off of porch. Back pain."

* "Female, 41, was having sexual intercourse in a recliner with partner when the recliner fell, throwing patient into glass door on bookshelf. Lacerated lip."

* "18-year-old male, drumming, bent over and got a drumstick up his nose. Bloody nose."

* "32-year-old male had a glow stick in his mouth and ran into a pole while at a haunted house. Dental fracture."

* "18-year-old male dropped his lighter, went to pick it up, was sprayed in the face by a skunk. Eye irritation."

* "52-year-old male was sleeping when son put tail of toy dinosaur in his ear. Ruptured eardrum."

* "53-year-old male fell off toilet as he had explosive diarrhea; struck head on counter. Ate moldy tortilla, bad milk, and moldy cheese."

THERE ARE 40,000 TOILET-RELATED INJURIES ANNUALLY IN THE U.S.

1947

The year Everglades National Park was established.

The 'Glades by the Numbers

Florida's Everglades National Park is North America's only subtropical preserve, a collection of islands, waterways, mangrove forests, and ponds that are known for being a home to an abundant array of wildlife (especially mosquitoes).

2

Major Native American tribes (the Seminoles and the Miccosukees) that once called the Everglades home.

5

Wingspan, in feet, of the endangered wood stork. In the 1930s, 4,000 mating pairs of wood storks lived in the Everglades; today, only 250 pairs remain.

4

The number of venomous snakes in the Everglades: eastern diamondback rattlesnake, dusky pygmy rattlesnake, cottonmouth, and coral snakes.

8

In feet, the highest elevation in the park.

1/3

The area of Everglades National Park covered with water.

350

Number of bird species that live in or migrate through the Everglades. Two—the smooth-billed ani and the short-tailed hawk—live nowhere else in the United States except Florida.

15

In feet, the minimum "safe distance" the NPS recommends for alligator viewing. If the animal hisses or opens its mouth, back off!

90

° F...Average summer temperature in the Everglades; the average humidity hovers around 90 percent.

800,000

Number of football fields that would fit in Lake Okeechobee.

120

In miles, the length of the Everglades' "River of Grass," water that flows out of Lake Okeechobee and travels over fields of saw grass. The river is 50 miles wide and, in most places, less than a foot deep.

10,000

The number of islands that make up the Everglades National Park.

43

The number of different mosquito species found in the Everglades; 13 of these bite humans, so be sure to keep your can of Off handy.

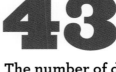

It's a Weird, Weird Crime

In the history of the BRI, we've written about smart crooks, dumb crooks, and even nice crooks. But these crimes were committed by crooks of an entirely different breed.

BED RIDDEN

Police in Ferrol, Spain, charged Antonio Navarro with driving while intoxicated on a highway. He was only going 12 mph, and he wasn't driving a car. Navarro is a quadriplegic, and police busted him driving his motorized bed on the freeway. Where did he need to go in such a hurry? Navarro was on his way to a local brothel.

STOOL SAMPLE

Police in Newark, Ohio, arrested 28-year-old Kile Wygle for drunk driving in March 2009. But Wygle wasn't driving a car—he was

driving a motorized bar stool, which he had built himself. (It's powered by a lawn mower engine.) Adding insult to injury was the fact that Wygle was the one who called police. He was riding his stool—drunk—at 20 mph. He lost control, fell off, and called 911 for medical assistance. Instead of paramedics, police arrived.

IF CONVICTED, HE WILL A-PEEL

In 2007 a man walked into a 7-Eleven in Monrovia, Maryland, just past midnight and attempted a holdup. The unidentified man

didn't have a gun or any kind of weapon at all—he merely demanded that the clerk give him money. The clerk refused, so the man started picking up items off the counter to use as weapons. After repeatedly hitting the clerk with a banana, the attacker fled (empty-handed) before police arrived.

SMALL CRIMES DIVISION

Swedish police are trying to bust a ring of thieves who steal valuables from bus travelers' luggage. Criminal teams work in

SEWELL VC

07 FD 90

twos: The first person rides inside the bus; the second, who by the crime's nature must be a "little person," hides inside a suitcase. The suitcase is placed in the bus's baggage compartment... and the weird (but clever) robbery begins. As soon as the baggage compartment door is closed, the little person comes out of his suitcase and begins to rifle through other people's bags and suitcases, looking for valuables. He pockets whatever he finds, and then returns to his own suitcase before arrival at the destination. Police are looking at crime records to identify "criminals of limited stature."

GETTING TANKED

Grand theft auto is a common crime; grand theft tank is not. At about 4:00 one morning in February 2009, an 18-year-old British army soldier stationed in northern Germany decided to steal one of his squadron's tanks. The unnamed serviceman, who had never driven one before, broke into the eight-ton Scimitar tank and made it about a third of a mile outside of his camp before the vehicle ran off the road and got stuck. So he returned to base and stole another tank. This time, British military police followed him. They blocked the soldier's path, forcing him to swerve and crash into a tree.

KIDNEY REMOVAL

In 2007 the Seattle Museum hosted "Bodies...The Exhibition," an educational display of preserved corpses and internal organs. One of the display kidneys was stolen. Police are still searching for the culprit, but do not fear the kidney will turn up on the black market, because even though the kidney is real, it's not "usable," as it's been filled and covered with plastic resin.

Dozens of American towns have special claims to fame: They have the "world's largest" something. Here are some examples.

THE WORLD'S LARGEST...

...GOLD NUGGET is in Las Vegas, Nevada. (Where else?) It was discovered in Australia in 1980 and purchased by the Golden Nugget casino for $1 million. Known as the Hand of Faith, it weighs 62 pounds and it's the size of a cat.

...BASEBALL BAT is in Louisville, Kentucky. This 120-foot, 34-ton, hollow steel bat rests against the Louisville Slugger Museum.

FOR 3,000 YEARS, HEMP WAS THE WORLD'S LARGEST AGRICULTURAL CROP.

SAKS FIFTH AVENUE

...COWBOY BOOTS are in San Antonio, Texas). They're white and brown, and 40 feet tall. They sit outside Saks Fifth Avenue.

...LOON is in Virginia, Minnesota. Sitting on Silver Lake is this steel and fiberglass bird, which measures 20 feet across. It's been tethered to the bottom of the lake since 1982. (The original loon was stolen in 1979.)

...BALL OF STRING is in Weston, Missouri. This 19-foot-wide, 3,712-pound ball of string was made by a farmer in the 1950s. It now it sits on a red, white, and blue platform in a local bar.

...TIME CAPSULE is in Seward, Nebraska. It's not just a box in the ground—it's a 45-ton vault, buried in 1975. There are more than 5,000 items from the 1970s inside, including a leisure suit and a Chevy Vega. (It's scheduled to be opened in 2025.)

...THERMOMETER is in Baker, California. At the gateway to Death Valley, one of the hottest places on Earth, stands this working thermometer, which is 134 feet tall, and built to commemorate the highest temperature ever recorded at Death Valley: 134°F, in 1913.

...FISHING BOBBER is in Pequot Lakes, Minnesota). It's called "Paul Bunyan's Fishing Bobber" (but it's really just the town water tower painted red and white to resemble a piece of tackle).

Uji! Hanabata!

When people from different cultures meet, they often develop a unique "bridge" language, or "pidgin," to communicate. Drawing from European, Asian, and native languages, Hawaiian pidgin is a tasty stew of words and expressions that you'll seldom hear on the mainland. Some examples:

HOWZIT? Aloha!

WHAS DA HAPS? What's up? What's happening?

WHADASCOOPS? Another word for Whas da haps?

LEDDAHS (Pronounced "LEH duhs"): See you later.

BAKATARE ("Bah kah TAH ray"): Crazy

WEED: With

COCKROACH: To sneak or steal.

GO HOLOHOLO: Go out

MOEMOE ("Moe ay MOE ay"): Go to sleep.

UJI! ("OOH gee!"): Eew! Yucky!

SKEBEI ("Skeh BAY"): Dirty old man

COOL HEAD MAIN TING: It's not a big deal.

HANABATA: Boogers

MAKE ASS: Make a mess

OKOLE: Butt; rear end

GRIND: To eat

GRINDS: Food

ETE: A nerd

I OWE YOU MONEY O' WOT? Stop staring at me!

USEDTATO ("USED tah toe"): Used to

LEPO: A loser. It can also mean "filthy."

STINK EYE: The evil eye—a dirty look

JUNK: Crummy, bad

JUNKS: Junk, stuff

STUFFS: Stuff, junk

MINES: Mine

CHICKEN SKIN: Goosebumps

PRESSURE OUT: Freak out

YOU'RE FIVE TIMES MORE LIKELY TO WRITE A *NY TIMES* BESTSELLER THAN DATE A SUPERMODEL.

TTFN Sweater Girl!

Supremo Uncle John thinks this whizzo page of expressions from the 1940s is unputdownable.

Veronica Lake personified the classic Peek-a-boo.

Beefburger: Another name for hamburger, which was considered misleading.

Steakburger: A high-class, high-priced beefburger.

Slimline: Sleek styling of consumer products such as radios and televisions, inspired by streamlined trains and planes.

TTFN: Good-bye (short for "Ta-ta for now!").

Mug: A violent robbery. From the boxing expression, "hit in the mug (face)."

Sweater girl: A movie starlet who wears tight sweaters to call attention to her bust.

Robomb: Short for *robot bomb*, the name given to German V-1 rockets before such weapons became known as guided missiles.

Oceanarium: An aquarium big enough to hold dolphins, whales, or other large creatures.

Peek-a-boo: A woman's hairstyle in which the hair falls over one eye, but not the other.

Unputdownable: Just what it sounds like: a book or magazine article that's so good you can't put it down.

Vacky: An evacuee. During World War II, British women and children moved from the cities to the safer countryside.

Shortie: A prefix for extrashort garments—shortie skirts, shortie pajamas, etc. It was eventually replaced by *mini*.

Tail-end Charlie: The person who mans the gun in the tail end of a World War II bomber.

Step out: To parachute from an airplane.

Toecover: A cheap, useless item given as a gift.

Whizzo: Wonderful.

Delhi belly: Intestinal disorder experienced by western visitors to India.

Atomize: Destroy something with a nuclear weapon.

Squillion: An unspecified, very large number, like zillion.

Supremo: The highest military officer in the land, kind of like generalissimo.

Nurembergs: Hemorrhoids.

These little London "vackies" are setting off for the countryside in advance of Britain declaring war on Germany.

A sweater girl in the classic pose

To Tell the Truth

Can we ever really know for sure if someone is telling a lie? Most experts agree that the answer is no—but that hasn't stopped society from cooking up ways to sort out the liars from the honest people.

ANCIENT LIE DETECTORS

● The Bedouins of the Arabian peninsula forced suspected liars to lick red-hot pokers with their tongues, on the assumption that liars would burn their tongues and truth tellers wouldn't. The method was cruel, but it may have also been accurate, since the procedure measured the moisture content of the suspect's mouth—and dry mouths are often associated with nervousness caused by lying.

● The ancient Chinese forced suspected liars to chew a mouthful of rice powder and spit it out; if the rice was still dry, the suspect was deemed guilty.

● The ancient British used a similar trick: They fed suspects a large "trial slice" of bread and cheese, and watched to see if they could swallow it. If a suspect's mouth was too dry to swallow, he was declared a liar and punished.

● The preferred method in India was to send the suspects into a dark room and have them pull on the tail of a sacred donkey, which was supposed to bray if the person was dishonest...at least that's what the suspects thought. The way the system really worked was that the investigators dusted the donkey's tail with black powder (which was impossible to see in the unlit room). Innocent people, the investigators reasoned, would pull the tail without hesitation...but the guilty person, figuring that no one could see them in the darkness, would only pretend to pull the tail but would not touch it at all.

LET'S GET PHYSIOLOGICAL

The first modern lie detector was invented by Cesare Lombroso, an Italian criminologist, in 1895. His device measured changes in pulse and blood pressure. Then, in 1914,

another researcher named Vittorio Benussi invented a machine that measured changes in breathing rate. But it wasn't until 1921 that John A. Larson, a medical student at the University of California, invented a machine that measured pulse, blood pressure, and breathing rate simultaneously. His machine became known as a *polygraph*, because it measured three types of physiological changes. Today's polygraphs use these methods, as well as more sophisticated measurements.

Q & A

The most common questioning method is called the Control Question Test (CQT), in which the polygraph operator asks three types of questions: neutral questions, key questions, and control questions.

● Neutral questions like "What kind of car do you drive?" are designed to measure the suspect's general level of nervousness, because nearly anyone who takes a polygraph test is going to be nervous.

● Key, or "guilty," questions quiz the suspect on information that only the guilty person would know. (For example: If the person taking the test were suspected of murdering someone, and the murder weapon was a knife, questions about knives would be considered key questions.)

● Control, or "innocent," questions would be indistinguishable from key questions by someone who did not have knowledge of the crime—but the guilty person would know. Questions about weapons not used in a murder would be considered control questions. An innocent person with no knowledge of the murder weapon would show the same level of nervousness during all the weapon questions—but

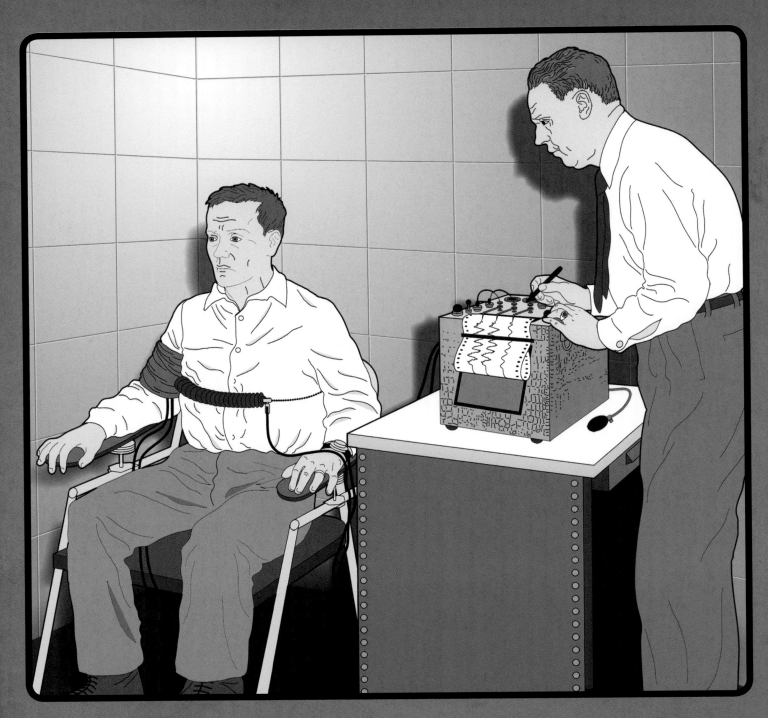

the guilty person would be more nervous during questions about knives—and would be easy to identify using a polygraph...at least in theory.

BEATING THE SYSTEM
Modern-day lie detectors are pretty sophisticated, but they have the same flaw that the ancient methods did—they all assume

that liars, out of guilt or fear of discovery, will have some kind of involuntary physical response every time they lie. But that isn't necessarily the case, according to most experts. "I don't think there's any medical or scientific evidence which tends to establish that your blood pressure elevates, that you perspire more freely, or that your pulse quickens when you tell a

lie," prominent defense lawyer William G. Hundley once said.

Still, many people believe that the polygraph is a useful tool when used in concert with other investigative methods, especially when used on ordinary people who don't know how to cheat. "It's a great psychological tool," says Plato Cacheris, another defense lawyer. "You take the average guy

John A. Larson, who invented the modern Lie Detector in 1921

and tell him you're going to give him a poly, and he's concerned enough to believe it will disclose any deception on his part." (Cacheris is famous for having represented Aldrich Ames, a CIA spy who passed a lie detector test in 1991 and then went on to sell more than $2.5 million worth of secrets to the Russians before he was finally caught in 1994.)

Aldrich Ames after his arrest in 1994

FAKIN' IT

Two tricks to help you beat a lie detector:

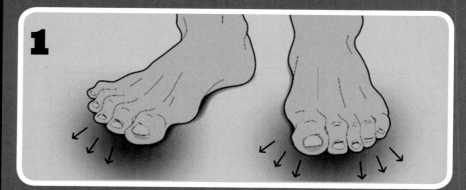

Curl your toes or press your feet down against the floor while answering the "innocent" questions. It can raise the polygraph readings to the same range as the "guilty" questions, which can either make you appear innocent or invalidate the results.

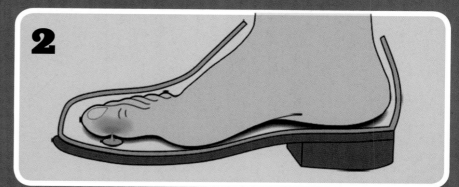

Stick a tack in your shoe and press your big toe against the sharp point during the "innocent" questions. Both toe-curling and stepping on a tack during the innocent questions have the same effect: They raise the stress level of your body.

"Police in Radnor, Pennsylvania, interrogated a suspect by placing a metal colander on his head and connecting it with a metal wire to a photocopy machine. The message, 'He's lying,' was placed in the copier and police pressed the copy button each time they believed the suspect wasn't telling the truth. Believing the 'lie detector' was working, the suspect confessed."

From NEWS OF THE WEIRD

WHO'S JOE SHLABOTNIK? CHARLIE BROWN'S FAVORITE BASEBALL PLAYER.

63

Before this page became a part of EPIC, it was a tree. While we can't bring back the poor tree that sacrificed its life for your reading pleasure, we can honor these other special trees.

Upstanding Citizens

THE BUDDHA BODHI TREE

The Bodhi, or peepul, is a species of fig tree that is native to India. The most famous one grows in the town of Bodh Gaya. It is there, Buddhists believe, that while the monk Siddhartha Gautama sat beneath a Bodhi tree in 528 B.C., he gained enlightenment and became the Buddha. A descendant of that same tree still stands at the site. Another famous Bodhi: In the third century B.C., a cutting from the "Buddha" tree was planted in Sri Lanka, where it has been protected ever since and still flourishes today—2,300 years later.

THE TREATY OAK

Once the largest in a circle of 14 oaks that Tonkawa Indians called the Council Oaks. Treaty Oak was the spot where, according to legend, Stephen Austin signed a

FREDERICK DOUGLASS' WHITE OAK

In 1877 Frederick Douglass, former slave, author, public speaker, presidential advisor, minister, and antislavery activist, purchased one of the most beautiful and desirable homes in the Washington D.C. area. He called it Cedar Hill. In front of the house stood a towering white oak tree. On February 20, 1895, Douglass left a women's rights conference and walked home, feeling ill. Once home, Douglass sat beneath his white oak, suffered a heart attack, and passed away. Cedar Hill is now a National Historic Site and on a clear day, the immense oak can still be seen from downtown Washington.

treaty with the Tonkawas for the land that is now Austin, Texas. With a 127-foot canopy spread, the 500-year-old tree was one of the finest examples of oaks in the world. But in 1989 someone tried to poison Treaty Oak. Arborists were able to save the tree, but it lost more than half of its canopy, making it a shadow of its former self. Good news, though: In 1997 Treaty Oak, the last of the Council Oaks still standing, produced its first acorns since the attack, and will hopefully make a full recovery.

THE "SMOKEY" ROOSA SYCAMORE

In 1969 NASA announced its third trip to the moon for January 1971. One of the Apollo 14 astronauts, Stuart Roosa, had been a smoke jumper for the U.S. Forest Service before joining the space program (he was nicknamed "Smokey"). When Ed Cliff, Management Research Director for the Forest Service, heard about the lunar mission he asked his friend Smokey Roosa to take a variety of seeds (pine, sweet gum, fir, sycamore, and redwood) to the moon so that they could be planted on Earth as "moon trees." Roosa liked the idea and took the seeds into space. But they were subjected to a post-return decontamination process that appeared to have killed them. Undaunted, Cliff planted them anyway...and a few actually grew. One of them, a sycamore, still stands in front of the Forestry Science Building at Mississippi State University.

"Except during the nine months before he draws his first breath, no man manages his affairs as well as a tree does."
George Bernard Shaw

WASHINGTON'S TULIP POPLARS

George Washington: President, general, landscaper. Landscaper? At Mount Vernon, his estate in northern Virginia, Washington found solace in creating gardens. One of his favorite American trees was the tulip poplar. A pair of 100-foot specimens, planted by Washington himself, still thrive on the grounds of Mount Vernon. The Marquis de Lafayette, a close friend of Washington's, was also fond of the tulip poplar and brought a few saplings back to France. He presented them to Marie Antoinette, who had them planted at Versailles. The last of the Lafayette poplars died during the winter of 1999, but, as a reminder of the two men's friendship, the trees were replaced with offspring from Washington's original tulip poplars at Mt. Vernon.

LEMONS CONTAIN MORE SUGAR THAN STRAWBERRIES DO.

Incident at Havering

A sheepish tale of political intrigue from the United Kingdom.

BAAACKGROUND

In September 2005, a zoning meeting took place in the town hall of the East London borough of Havering. The meeting concerned a proposal to convert an exotic horse and sheep farm into a mobile home park. To do so would require a zoning change and the council would have to approve it. Such zoning changes are commonplace throughout the world, but this one was different. Councilman Jeff Tucker, who represented the area where the proposed mobile home park would be built, got up to speak in favor of the idea. And that's when the trouble started. Somebody in the room apparently did not agree with Tucker. The anonymous adversary began making loud, sheeplike "baa" noises whenever Tucker tried to talk, drowning him out. Despite the fact that there were only a handful of people in the room—including just five city council members—nobody could figure out who made the noises...and nobody would own up to it.

BAAAD FORM

Councilman Tucker was enraged (and the proposal failed). He lodged a complaint with the Standards Board for England, an oversight agency for governmental disputes. The board didn't think it worthy of their time to determine who made the sheep noises and why, so they referred it back to the Havering council. The Havering Standards Hearings Sub-Committee began an investigation. They narrowed down the source of the "baa"-ing to four culprits, all of them city councilors. One of the suspects, councilor Denis O'Flynn, called the process "an extremely expensive example of the worst kind of bureaucracy" and "the height of stupidity."

Fourteen months later, Havering Borough Council issued a 300-page report, the result of an investigation that cost £10,000 (about $20,000). What did they find? The source of the sheep noises was Denis O'Flynn. The punishment: nothing. By the time the investigation was completed, O'Flynn was no longer a city council member...and no longer subject to any disciplinary action.

The Garden of Ghastly Delights

Hollywood has created its share of gore fests— from *Friday the 13th* (1980), to *A Nightmare on Elm Street* (1984), to *Scream* (1996). But all bloody, creepy slasher movies owe a large debt to the shock-theater pioneers in France, courtesy of turn-of-the-century Parisians who got their horror up close and personal at the Grand Guignol.

ON SACRED GROUND

The Théâtre du Grand Guignol (pronounced with a hard G, like *gross*) was a small 280-seat theater founded in 1897 on the slopes of Montmartre in Paris. Over a century later, the Grand Guignol still means one thing: blood. And lots of it. Movie critics today still use the term "Grand Guignol" to describe a sort of over-the-top kind of blood and gore—with good reason. Eye gougings, stabbings, flayings, impalements—all were "performed" in front of a live audience.

The theater was located in a small building that was originally a convent, a setting that lent itself surprisingly well to the sinister. The seats looked like pews, and two leering wooden angels hung over the stage. The stage, only 20 by 20 feet, was so close to the front row, one critic joked that the audience could shake hands with the actors without leaving their seats. With the addition of dim red lighting and the abundance of shadows, the theater oozed the macabre even before the curtains opened.

THE PUPPET MASTER

Oscar Méténier, a former police secretary, founded the Grand Guignol in April 1897. Named after a popular children's puppet, the Grand Guignol was meant to be a big puppet show for the adult set. It would use live actors instead of puppets and specialize in one-act plays that showed slices of life from the Parisian underworld. Eventually, Méténier left the Grand Guignol and handed it over to Max Maurey, who continued the one-act plays. But he turned slice-of-life drama into what one critic called "slice of death." In 1901 Maurey discovered the Grand Guignol's signature playwright, André de Lorde, the man who would earn the title "Prince of Terror" because of his gruesome plays. The son of a physician, Lorde spent his childhood listening to

WHAT? BEES DON'T HAVE EARS.

the screams of patients in his father's office. Result: a lifelong fascination with pain and death. He turned that fascination into more than 100 terrifying plays that were performed at the Grand Guignol.

NOT FOR THE FAINT OF HEART

Maurey, Lorde, and the cast judged the success of each production by the number of audience members who fainted—an average of two per evening. One popular play featured a young girl imprisoned in a madhouse with three old women who gouged her eyes out with a knitting needle. Horrified at what they had done, the crones turned on one of their own and seared off her face with a hot plate. Another play set a record with 15 faintings. Interestingly, it was mostly men that fainted, probably because they didn't look away at the worst parts.

As a publicity stunt, Maurey hired a physician to be present at all performances, although some accounts say that one doctor was not enough. A Guignoler, attempting to revive his fainting wife, called for the doctor. From the lobby Maurey replied that the doctor had just fainted as well!

A THOUSAND DEATHS TO DIE FOR

An actress at the Grand Guignol named Paula Maxa went by the nickname the "High Priestess of the Temple of Horror." She

IN HOW MANY AGATHA CHRISTIE MYSTERIES DID "THE BUTLER DO IT?" NONE.

69

kept a diary of her career that catalogued her 10,000 stage deaths in 60 different macabre fashions—including getting scalped, strangled, disemboweled, guillotined, hung, burned alive, devoured by a puma, and cut up into 93 pieces and glued back together (pictured, opposite page).

RECIPE FOR DISASTER

The stage tricks that made the Grand Guignol the most realistic horror in town were closely guarded secrets—some were even patented. This was probably more to disguise the simplicity of the tricks than to keep other theaters from stealing them. The cornerstone was 10 different recipes for fake blood, each congealing at a different rate for different types of spurting and oozing wounds. The stage managers even used local butchers and taxidermists as sources of animal eyeballs. Why? They bounced best when they hit the stage.

The theater hit its peak in popularity after 1915, which some historians attribute to the Guignol's filling a gap left when public executions were discontinued. Society women in particular flocked to the Grand Guignol in the 1920s and 1930s to scream and swoon into the arms of their male companions—or just the stranger in the next seat over. Audiences often included royalty, among them the king of Greece, Princess Wilhemina of Holland, and the sultan of Morocco's children.

A SLOW DEATH

But after the real-life horrors of World War II, the Grand Guignol fell out of favor and never regained its former popularity. By the 1950s, audiences went to new horror movies (that stole some of their tricks straight from the Grand Guignol), and only curious tourists and college students frequented the theater. The Guignol tried in vain to generate new interest through publicity stunts (like staging the kidnapping of their own scantily clad leading ladies), but it was no use; the crowds didn't come. But the Guignol did go out with a scream. Performed by Maxa, it was so long and loud, that it permanently damaged her vocal chords. The little theater of horrors finally closed its doors forever in November 1962.

THE SILVER SCREEN RUNS RED

Though the little theater on the slopes of Montmartre is long gone, its aesthetic lives on. A number of cheap horror films have been set in a Grand Guignol–style theater like *Mad Love* (1935) and *Theatre of Death* (1966). Vincent Price's classic *Theatre of Blood* (1973) uses the Grand Guignol as its template. The blockbuster *Interview with the Vampire* (1994) even set a scene of frenzied vampire feeding on the Grand Guignol's stage.

Even more numerous are the films that owe their gore to the Grand Guignol. Though it's unlikely that directors Tobe Hooper (*The Texas Chain Saw Massacre*), John Carpenter (*Halloween*), Quentin Tarantino (*Kill Bill*), or Sam Raimi (*The Evil Dead*) ever saw the Grand Guignol in its waning days, film critics and historians alike have compared the over-the-top bloodbaths in their movies to the bloodbaths that took place at the Parisian theater.

Paula Maxa dies for the 6,736th time.

Hotter'n a Burnin' Stump
(It's a Texas thang...)

Whether five-alarm or just smoke-alarm, there's nothing like a bowl of Texas chili to fill a belly up!

NO BEANS ABOUT IT

If you know beans about chili, allow us to tell you something really important: Texas chili has no beans. Not a one. Maybe in other states you'll find a bean or two. But in Texas, chili is just a fiery molten stew made of beef, onions, tomatoes, spices, and lots and lots of chili peppers. Everybody has a special recipe, but no true Texan would add a legume to the mix.

CONSIDER THE SAUCE

Chili's past is a little bit shady since nobody quite knows who invented it or when. Some say it was invented by cattle drivers and trail hands during long cattle drives. Others speculate that chili's origins go much farther back in time to the Mayans, Aztecs, and Incas. Still others give credit to Canary Islanders who started immigrating to the San Antonio region as early as 1723. They were known for concocting tasty dishes using local peppers, meat, onions, and most important of all, cumin.

And let's not forget the Chili Queens of San Antonio, a group of women who, legend has it, earned the moniker when they stirred up and sold vats of the meaty goo on street corners and in front of the famed Alamo in the mid-nineteenth century. No matter who you thank for it, there's no denying the melting-pot influence of a variety of cultures on this hot and spicy dish.

HOT STUFF

Even the field of chili technology is a heated battleground. The invention of chili powder enabled cooks to streamline their recipes a bit, but just who invented chili powder also remains a mystery. We do know that chili powder is indeed a Texan invention, but was it German immigrant Willie Gebhardt, who moved to San Antonio near the turn of the century and registered his Eagle Brand Chili Powder? Or was it Fort Worth grocer DeWitt Clinton Pendery's own blend of spices that was the first true chili powder?

Either way, chili's popularity grew and grew during the late nineteenth century. It first hit the global stage at the 1893 World's Fair in Chicago, where a booth offered San Antonio Chili for all to taste.

TOP CHILI DOG

One of the most famous chili contests is the Chilympiad, a festival that began in 1969 in San Marcos, Texas. Every year during the second week of September, competitors bring their chili recipes out for battle. All chili has to be made from scratch and all contestants have to be male. Luckily, the gals have their own contest in Luckenbach called Hell Hath No Fury Like A Woman Scorned. Winners of both festivals automatically qualify for the World's Championship Chili Cookoff, held every year in Terlingua, Texas. The world championship is held during the first weekend in October. Men and women compete for a $25,000 grand prize and the title of world champion. A number of colorful characters have won this contest, but their recipes have even more colorful names:

- Capitol Punishment (1980)
- Bottom of the Barrel Gang Ram Tough Chili (1984)
- Shotgun Willie Chili (1985), named after Willie Nelson
- Tarantula Jack's Thundering Herd Buffalo Tail Chili (1989)
- Road Meat Chili (1991)
- Warning Shot Chili—Runs for Your Life (2002)

IN FRENCH FOLKLORE, DREAMING ABOUT POOP IS AN OMEN THAT GOOD FORTUNE IS ON THE WAY.

73

It's Feral Cat Day!

Here are the stories behind some fun animal-themed holidays.

SQUIRREL APPRECIATION DAY, January 21

Origin: This holiday was created in 2001 by Christy Hargrove, a wildlife rehabilitator from Asheville, North Carolina. At first, the holiday was just a fun way to get local kids interested in the region's many squirrel species, some of which are endangered.

But over the last few years, Squirrel Appreciation Day has grown more and more popular at schools throughout the United States. Why is it in January? That's when food for squirrels is the most scarce, so celebrants are encouraged to put out some seeds, nuts, or suet for the furry little creatures. The holiday is also a great way to pass on some cool squirrel facts, like this one: The word goes back to the Greek *skiouros*, a combination of "shade" and "tail," which meant "creature who sits in the shadow of his tail."

NATIONAL PIG DAY, March 1

Origin: Ellen Stanley didn't think that people gave pigs enough credit as intelligent animals that make great pets. So in 1972 the art teacher from Lubbock, Texas, cofounded National Pig Day with her sister Mary. Today it's celebrated by pig owners (and plain old pig lovers) all over the country. A recommended present for your favorite pig: apples—pigs just love apples!

INTERNATIONAL MIGRATORY BIRD DAY, Second Saturday of May

Origin: This holiday was started in 1993 by ornithologists at the Smithsonian Migratory Bird Center and the Cornell Laboratory of Ornithology. Their goal: to increase awareness of the many migratory bird species in the Western Hemisphere. Government-sponsored events take place on the big day from Canada down to Latin America. Want to take part? Go to *www.birdday.org* and download a bird-count form. Then print it out, go for a birdwatching walk, and submit your data back to the website.

THE FRISBEE WAS ORIGINALLY CALLED THE PLUTO PLATTER.

NATIONAL COBRA DAY
On the fifth day of the moonlit fortnight in the Hindu month of Shravan (translation: sometime in July or August)

Origin: This Hindu holy day, known locally as Nag Panchami, has been celebrated all over India for centuries. In the state of Punjab, huge "dough snakes" are made from flour and butter and carried in noisy, colorful processions through the streets, after which the "snake" is blessed and buried. In the state of Maharashtra, snake charmers carry baskets with live cobras inside them through crowds of celebrants. The charmers play their flutes and cry out, "Nagoba-la dudh, de Mayi!" ("Give milk to the Cobra, oh mother!") Women come running out from their houses dressed in their finest saris. The serpents are released and the women sprinkle spices and flowers on their heads and feed them sweetened milk.

NATIONAL FERAL CAT DAY,
October 16

Origin: This holiday is celebrated all over the world by feral cats who get together for mice-and-beer parties. Okay, not really. It was actually started in 2001 by humans at Alley Cat Allies, a national cat-protection organization in Bethesda, Maryland. Their goal is a serious one: ending the mistreatment and killing of feral cats in the United States. (An estimated 70 percent of the cats that go to U.S. shelters are killed.)

LEARN ABOUT BUTTERFLIES DAY,
March 14

Origin: This holiday is so unofficial that we couldn't even find out who created it. But we're guessing it was a teacher, because every March 14, schoolkids all over North America learn about butterflies. They watch butterfly videos, read butterfly books, and draw pictures of not just butterflies but caterpillars and cocoons, too! (We're not sure why a holiday about a summertime insect takes place in the winter, but it does give the kids something to look forward to.)

DUTCH NATIONAL OWL DAY,
November 3

Origin: Created in 1986 by one of the world's premier owl experts, Johan de Jong, founder of the Dutch Barn Owl Working Group, the holiday helps raise money and awareness for the endangered European barn owl. The group's efforts have paid off, and the barn owl's numbers are steadily rising. This success has prompted de Jong to get the day recognized around the world, as there are many more endangered owl species. You can do your own part by holding a National Owl Day celebration in your community this November. They're a real hoot!

PENGUIN AWARENESS DAY,
January 20

Origin: This began in the 1980s as a lark by biologists studying penguins in the Antarctic. Few people (in the Northern Hemisphere, anyway) gave the holiday much thought until 2006, after two penguin-themed movies had taken the world by storm—the French documentary *March of the Penguins* and the animated musical *Happy Feet*. Thrilled with the sudden interest, penguin advocates publicized the holiday as a means to educate people about the world's endangered penguin species. Suggested activities for Penguin Awareness Day:

● Organize a field trip to the nearest zoo that has penguins.
● Rent a tux (or just wear black and white) and waddle around handing out literature about penguins.
● Rent one or all of these lesser-known penguin films: *The Adventures of Scamper the Penguin* (a 1988 cartoon about a young Adélie penguin), Little Kings (a 1999 documentary about penguin expert Mike Bingham), or our all-time favorite, a 1950 animated short called *8 Ball Bunny* in which Bugs Bunny must help a lost "peng-u-in" find his way home to the South Pole. (Every time the little guy cries an ice cube, it just breaks Uncle John's heart.)

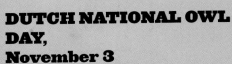

In case you don't know, an oxymoron is a phrase made of two words that appear to be contradictory. Here are some of our newest favorites.

Instant Classic

- Cautiously optimistic
- Bigger half
- Rock opera
- Boneless ribs
- Resident alien
- White chocolate
- Global village
- Minor crisis
- Act naturally
- Defensive strike
- Slumber party
- Oven-fried
- Deafening silence
- Graduate student
- Educated guess
- Free trade
- Instant classic
- Calculated risk
- Wilderness management
- Vegetarian meatball
- Wireless cable
- Detailed summary
- Fresh from concentrate
- Extended deadline

- Negative growth
- Paid volunteer
- Small fortune
- Controlled chaos
- Doing nothing
- Going nowhere
- Athletic scholarship
- Open-book test
- Primitive technology
- Audio book
- Civil disobedience

- Forgotten memories
- Virtual reality
- Accurate stereotype
- Down escalator
- Bittersweet
- Sharp curve
- Unbiased opinion
- Alone together
- Short distance
- Outer core
- "The rumors are true"

IDENTICAL TWINS HAVE THE SAME DNA BUT DIFFERENT FINGERPRINTS.

In 1979 a man who thought humanity was being overrun by idiots sought to even the score by breeding super-babies. Here's the amazing story of Robert Graham.

The Nobel Prize Sperm Bank

FAR LEFT: Hermann J. Muller
CENTER: Robert K. Graham
RIGHT: William Shockley
OPPOSITE, TOP: A young Doron Blake, the first child conceived via the Sperm Bank
OPPOSITE, BOTTOM: Robert K. Graham at his Repository for Germinal Choice

WHO'S YOUR DADDY?

Hermann J. Muller, an American scientist who worked in the Soviet Union during the 1930s, was a pioneer in the science of *eugenics*: selective breeding designed to create a pure, superior race of people. (Another supporter of eugenics: Adolf Hitler.) Muller wanted to create his master race by impregnating Russian women from a sperm bank stocked with samples from the Soviet Union's top scientists. The hoped-for result: ultra-smart babies. Unfortunately for Muller, the technology required for storing specimens had not yet been invented.

GRAHAM: QUACKERS?

American scientist and businessman Robert K. Graham was an admirer of Muller. In the mid-1960s, Graham became convinced that dumb people were corrupting the gene pool and taking over the world. Graham, the father of eight, believed that intelligent people had an obligation to breed in order to offset all the stupidity. The answer, he thought, was sperm banks, which were brand new at the time (the first two opened in 1965—one in Tokyo, Japan, and the other in Iowa City, Iowa). But Graham didn't have the money to start one, so instead he started a charity to finance the rearing expenses of children born to cash-strapped college professors and scientists.

In 1978 Graham sold his company, Armorlite (through which he'd invented plastic eyeglass lenses), to the 3M Company for $70 million. That was more than enough to start a sperm bank. So in 1979 Graham, now 74 years old, placed a half dozen liquid nitrogen freezer tanks in a storage shed on his San Diego, California, estate and named it "The Hermann J. Muller Repository for Germinal Choice." Later that year, he dropped Muller's name and moved his sperm freezers to an office in nearby Escondido.

It was time for Graham to start recruiting world-class "daddies." And the only sperm he'd accept would be from Nobel Prize-winning scientists. Graham solicited the 30 Nobel laureates who lived in California. Most were appalled by the idea, but three actually agreed to participate...on the condition of anonymity.

LIQUID ASSETS

Graham didn't publicly announce the existence of the Repository until a 1980 interview with the *Los Angeles Times*. There was instant backlash—Graham was compared to Hitler, and the media nicknamed the Repository "the Nobel Prize Sperm Bank." Graham was forced to hire armed guards to protect the bank. It didn't get any better when physicist William Shockley revealed himself to be one of the three donors. Shockley was a brilliant physicist, but was better known for his racist sociological theories—he once told a reporter that because African Americans were reproducing faster than whites, America's collective IQ was dropping.

The media furor died down by late 1980, but Graham suddenly found himself with no donors. Not wanting to be associated with Shockley, the other two of Graham's three donors pulled out of the project. Then Shockley did, too, considering himself too old (70) to produce viable sperm. Graham was forced to abandon the Nobel-only concept and opened the bank up to athletes, businessmen, and lesser scientists, provided they had a genius-level IQ.

Graham and his assistant, Paul Smith, approached candidates at scientific conventions, contacted professors and doctoral students at UC Berkeley, and wrote to men they found in *Who's Who of Science*. They had some success— about 19 donors had signed up by 1983. But they had to be even more selective when female applicants— answering an ad in a *Mensa* magazine—told Graham and Smith that they wanted their genius- donors to be, if at all possible, tall, athletic, and handsome.

SOMETHING FOR THE LADIES

Graham required female applicants to be married (to infertile men), well educated, and financially stable. (One other requirement: Graham's wife asked him to exclude lesbians.) Soon he had a waiting list. Several hundred women applied; only two were rejected: a woman with depression and a diabetic.

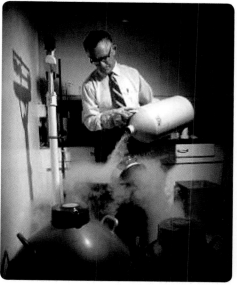

Potential mothers chose donors from a typed, mimeographed catalog that listed donors' personal details, including general health facts, eye color, ancestry, height, and weight. Each donor was assigned a color and a number and given a summary:

"Mr. Fuchsia No. 1 is an Olympic gold medalist. Tall, dark, handsome, bright, a successful businessman and author."

"Mr. White No. 6 is ruggedly handsome and outgoing, a university professor and expert marksman who enjoys the classics."

Once a woman was accepted, vials of frozen sperm were mailed to her doctor, who would then thaw out the sperm and implant it during ovulation. Fertilization would often take several tries; 75% of applicants never got pregnant at all. At least it was free—Graham personally paid all Repository expenses at a cost of more than $500,000 per year. He considered it charity work. (Sperm donors weren't paid.)

FROZEN IN TIME

In total, the Repository for Germinal Choice resulted in 218 children. Did they all turn out to be geniuses? It's impossible to say. Only one child conceived via the Repository has identified himself. Doron Blake, born in August 1982, was a child math and music prodigy and attended prestigious Reed University. No other mothers or children have ever come forward. And other than Shockley, no donor has come forward, either.

Robert K. Graham died in 1997 at the age of 92. He considered leaving a trust to continue to fund the sperm bank, but left the choice to his wife and children. Having never liked the project, they closed down the Repository for Germinal Choice for good in 1999. All the sperm left behind in freezer tanks— along with all of the bank's records about the identities of its donors, the mothers, and the offspring—was destroyed.

Today's sperm banks are open to the general population (no IQ test required). Potential parents still choose from boastful anonymous donor "catalogs." But modern sperm banks exist to help people who would otherwise be unable to have children—a far cry from Graham's goal of intellectually dominant super kids.

Take the Plunge

Next time you're out hiking with friends and you come across a waterfall, impress them by telling them what kind of waterfall it is.

Most of us just think of waterfalls as, well, waterfalls, but geologists, hydrologists, and just plain old waterfall lovers know that they actually come in many different types. Some are broad categories, while others are more specialized, and some waterfalls can be a mixture of more than one variety. Here are the different classifications, followed by a few examples of waterfalls you might have heard of—or even saw for yourself.

Cataract: A general term used to describe large waterfalls that involve the flow of very large amounts of water, a cataract is usually accompanied by rapids both above and below the falls itself.

Plunge: If you see water rushing over the top of a steep cliff and free-falling—not touching the cliff face—for all or a part of its height, you've got a plunge waterfall.

Cascade: Unlike a plunge waterfall, a cascade's water flows down a slope, cascading over rocks or ledges on its way down.

Block: A block waterfall is formed when a river or large stream flows over a wide and relatively even ledge, giving the falling water a wide "block" shape. It's also called a sheet waterfall, because the falling water resembles a sheet. Both terms are normally used for waterfalls wider than they are tall. If they're taller than they are wide, they're called curtain falls.

Fan: A type of cascade waterfall, a fan starts out narrow and gets wider as the water flows downward, spreading out and giving the falls the look of an open fan.

Horsetail: Unlike a fan, a horsetail is a cascade that remains narrow as it flows downward, resembling a long horse's tail.

Punchbowl: This is a plunge waterfall that forms when a strongly flowing stream or river surges through a small opening and straight down into a round pool—the pool itself is the

creation of the falling water over a very long period of time.

Segmented: When a stream or river is separated at or near the top of its height and falls as two or more falls, they're known as segmented waterfalls.

Tiered: A tiered waterfall is a single waterfall made up of several smaller steep falls that drop down a series of rock steps.

Slide: This waterfall flows down a smooth, even surface.

Chute: A chute is a cascade waterfall that flows—usually very fast and with lots of white water—between the walls of a narrow canyon.

TOP: Upper Yosemite Falls, in Yosemite National Park, California, is the tallest waterfall in North America.
OPPOSITE LEFT: Watson Falls plunges over a cliff in Oregon's Umpqua National Forest.

Yosemite Falls in California is 2,425 feet high, making it the tallest waterfall in North America. It has three sections: The Upper Falls is a 1,430-foot plunge, making it alone one of the tallest falls in the world; the Middle Cascades drops a further 675 feet; and the Lower Falls plunges another 320 feet.

Angel Falls in Venezuela is the highest waterfall in the world, at a staggering 3,212 feet. More staggering: 2,648 feet of that is the initial plunge, before the water even hits the cliff face.

Victoria Falls, on the Zambezi River in Zambia and Zimbabwe, is a classic block waterfall, and stands about 360 feet high. It's about 5,604 feet—that's well over a mile—wide.

Niagara Falls is actually three waterfalls: Horseshoe Falls, American Falls, and Bridal Veil Falls. The first two are block waterfalls; Bridal Veil is a curtain waterfall.

In 1935 architect Frank Lloyd Wright designed what remains one of his most famous works, Fallingwater, a home in southwestern Pennsylvania that incorporates a waterfall into its design. The cascade waterfall, which is part of a five-mile-long creek called Bear Run, is probably the smallest world-famous waterfall. The house itself was declared a National Historic Landmark in 1966.

The Mustache Report

Uncle John found these stories right under his nose.

'V' FOR VICTORY

Who hates amazing mustaches? The Taliban. In 2009 the terrorist organization threatened to kill Malik Amir Mohammad Khan Afridi of Pakistan unless he shaved off his V-shaped facial fur (which he grew to honor a local politician). Afridi refused, so the extremist group held him in a cave for days until he caved and shaved off his 30-inch-long 'stache. Undeterred, he and his family fled to another town in Pakistan, where he grew it back. But when extremists in Afridi's new town told him he could only keep the mustache if he paid them $500 a month—or he would be killed—he fled again in 2013. At last report, Afridi was still in hiding. It's the only way to keep his wife and ten kids—and his 30-inch-long 'stache—safe.

ABOVE: Malik Amir Mohammad Khan Afridi and his 30-inch face furniture

THE STRONG, SILENT TYPE

In 2005 Suzy Walker of Kirkland, Georgia, started going everywhere—even to restaurants and movies—with a life-size mannequin...that sported a fake black mustache. She told reporters that she did it because the mannequin, so altered, looked exactly like her husband, a Navy sailor deployed on a submarine. "When I put the mustache on him, I couldn't believe the resemblance," she said. Her husband said he'd become the butt of jokes around the sub, but that he didn't mind—he thought it was funny.

THE 'STACHE MAKES THE MAN

In 2004 police in northern India were offered an extra 65 cents a month if they grew mustaches after a researcher found that officers with mustaches are taken more seriously. But superintendent Mayank Jain said that mustaches would be monitored...to make sure that they didn't give any officers a "mean look."

Fuzzy Facts

SPEED-0

In the 1972 Olympics, mustachioed Mark Spitz put on one of the greatest swimming performances in history, winning a record seven gold medals and breaking world records in all seven events. Years later, he told *Time* magazine that a Russian coach at the Games had asked him about the mustache. Spitz jokingly replied that it "deflects water away from my mouth, allows my rear end to rise and makes me bullet shaped in the water, and that's what had allowed me to swim so great." The next year, Spitz said, "Every Russian male swimmer had a mustache."

HER WAY

In 1991 Barbara Mossner of Mount Clemens, Michigan, was ordered to pay her ex-husband $2,800 for damaging his record collection... and for drawing a mustache on his Frank Sinatra poster.

● In the 19th century, it was illegal for British Army officers to shave their mustaches. The rule was repealed on October 6, 1916.

● During the Victorian era, wax was often used to keep large mustaches in shape. That created a problem for men drinking hot beverages—the heat would melt the wax into the drinks. In 1830 Englishman Harvey Adams invented the "mustache cup." The cups had a "mustache guard" across the rim, with a small hole that allowed mustached men to safely sip their tea. Mustache cups became popular all over Europe and the United States, and are still made today.

● There are 27 words for "mustache" in Albanian. *Madh* describes a bushy one, *posht* is one that hangs down at the ends, and *fshes* is a long mustache with bristly hairs. (They also have 27 different words for "eyebrows.")

● In 2006 author Dax Herrera sold his mustache, called "the Captain," on eBay for $105.

● A snood is a type of hair net used to protect and shape mustaches.

● Mustache quiz: How many of the Beatles have mustaches on the cover of *Sgt. Pepper's Lonely Hearts Club Band*?

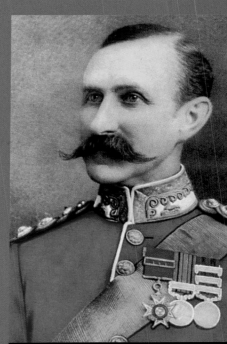

Quiz answer: All four Beatles have mustaches.

Swan Songs

One minute you're a rock star, the next minute...you're gone. Here are some musicians whose lives ended on a somber note.

JEFF BUCKLEY (1966–97)

The up-and-coming rock star was in Memphis, Tennessee, to record some new music with his band. On the night before recording was to begin, Buckley decided to take a swim in one of his favorite spots in the North River Harbor along the Mississippi River. A roadie, Keith Foti, was there with him, but opted to stay dry. Buckley was in a good mood, though, and jumped in the water fully clothed— heavy boots and all. He was doing the backstroke while singing Led Zeppelin's "Whole Lotta Love" when the wake from a passing tugboat approached. Foti turned away to shield a guitar from the wave. When he turned back around, Buckley was gone. His body was found five days later.

CHET BAKER (1929–88)

Baker was an influential jazz trumpeter and singer whose life was marred by heroin addiction and prison time. After his career had stalled, he was making a comeback in 1988, and he was having a pretty good year—musically, anyway. Baker was still struggling with drug addiction. He was staying in an Amsterdam hotel room by himself...and a lot of heroin and cocaine. In the middle of the night, Baker opened the window of the second-story room. Somehow, he fell out and hit his head on a metal post and died. The death was ruled an accident, not a suicide—there was no note. And who tries to kill himself by jumping out of a second-story window?

TOP: Jeff Buckley shortly before his untimely death in 1997
RIGHT: Jazz legend Chet Baker in his youthful prime, photographed in the 1950s before his career nosedived into heroin and jail

ANNE BOLEYN, SECOND WIFE OF HENRY VIII, HAD SIX FINGERS ON HER LEFT HAND.

RANDY RHOADS (1956–82)

A guitarist for Quiet Riot, Rhoads was also Ozzy Osbourne's lead guitarist. During a tour stopover at the Leesburg, Florida, estate where Ozzy's bus driver, Andrew Aycock, lived, Rhoads reluctantly agreed to take a short flight in a 1955 Beechcraft Bonanza. Rhoads was afraid of flying, but he was persuaded to go up because the other passenger, hairdresser Rachel Youngblood, had a heart condition, so Aycock promised not to do anything too scary. But Aycock did do something scary: He buzzed the tour bus where several band members were sleeping. After two successful buzzes, Aycock looped back around for a third one. But he got way too close, and the Beechcraft's wing clipped the back of the bus. The plane spun out of control, took out the top of a tree, and then crashed into the mansion's garage. It exploded into a ball of fire, and all three passengers were burned alive.

TERRY KATH (1946–78)

In 1978 Kath, the original front man for the band Chicago, and his wife were partying at a roadie's house in Woodland Hills, California. Kath loved guns, and he had two of his favorite pistols with him. At one point, he placed the barrel of a .38 revolver on his temple and pulled the trigger several times. Click, click, click. Nothing happened. Then Kath picked up his semiautomatic 9 mm pistol. "Don't worry," he assured them. "It's not loaded." He even showed them the empty magazine to prove it. But Kath didn't check the chamber. There was bullet in it. He put the pistol up to his temple, pulled the trigger, and died.

JOHNNY ACE (1929–54)

Ace, a well-known blues singer in the 1950s, was touring with Big Mama Thornton's band. Between sets of a Christmas Day gig in Houston, Texas, Ace, Thornton, and the rest of the band were sitting around a table. As he often did, Ace pulled out his .22 caliber revolver. He was drinking, which he also often did. According to bass player Curtis Tillman, "He had this little pistol he was waving around the table and someone said, 'Be careful with that thing.' And Johnny Ace said, 'It's okay! Gun's not loaded, see?' And he pointed it at himself with a smile on his face, and 'Bang!' Sad, sad thing.'"

THE DAY THE MUSIC DIED

Once upon a time, there was a rock star who really liked having clean underwear when he was on tour. One night, in order to get to a gig early so he'd have enough time to wash his clothes, he skipped the tour bus and chartered a plane. He also footed the tickets for two of his tour mates, one who had the flu and another who won the last seat in a coin toss. It was February 1959. Ritchie Valens won the coin toss (over Waylon Jennings), the Big Bopper had the flu, and Buddy Holly needed fresh skivvies. The plane crashed; all on board were killed.

TOP: Buddy Holly and the Crickets
ABOVE: Ritchie Valens
TOP LEFT: Randy Rhoads in the 1970s

IF YOU'RE AVERAGE, YOU'LL SPEND ABOUT 10 MINUTES TODAY DOING NOTHING.

85

Mama Mia!

ANNA WHISTLER

Known as: Whistler's Mother

Background: In October 1871, James Whistler decided to paint a portrait of his mother. "I want you to stand for a picture," he said. Mrs. Whistler agreed. "I stood bravely two or three days—I stood still as a statue!" she told a friend. But in the end she was too frail to stand for the long hours the portrait required. So Whistler painted her sitting down instead. Today, the painting, officially called *Arrangement in Grey and Black: Portrait of the Painter's Mother*, is the 2nd most recognizable portrait in the world...after the *Mona Lisa*.

Here's a look at three famous American mothers. (And you'll never guess who gave Uncle John the idea for this article.)

ELIZABETH FOSTER GOOSE

Known as: Mother Goose

Background: In the 1750s, Boston printer Thomas Fleet heard his mother-in-law, Elizabeth Goose, singing nursery rhymes to her grandson—including "Hickory Dickory Dock," "Humpty Dumpty," and "Little Bo-peep." Fleet began writing them down, and in 1765 published them in a book called *Mother Goose's Melodies for Children.*

MARY HARRIS JONES

Known as: Mother Jones

Background: Mary Harris was a schoolteacher in Monroe, Michigan, in the 1850s. She married George Jones in 1861, moved to Chicago, and started a dressmaking business. But the great Chicago fire of 1871 wiped her out. Soon afterward she became active in the U.S. labor movement, and for the next 50 years traveled all over the country organizing workers in steel mills, railroads, coal mines, and the garment industry. She remained an active organizer until shortly before her death in 1930 at the age of 100.

All About Corduroy

A few lines about fabric with lines

Wes Anderson, the king of corduroy

● Corduroy is a type of fabric characterized by its ribbed, or "corded," texture. It was first made in the textile manufacturing center of Manchester, England, in the late 1700s.

● The word *corduroy* dates to the 1780s. Its exact origin is unknown, but most etymologists believe it's a combination of the words *cord*, as in a ropelike cord, and *duroy*, an obsolete type of fabric once made in England. Some sources say the word derives from the French *corde du roi*, meaning "king's cord." This is false.

● Corduroy is a type of woven textile known as a cut-pile fabric. The weaving process results in one of the fabric's surfaces being loose loops of thread, or pile. After weaving, the fabric is passed through a machine that cuts the loops relatively close to the surface. The process also "brushes"

the fabric, causing the threads to tuft. All of this results in the fuzzy texture that cut-pile fabrics are known for. Other cut-pile fabrics include velvet and velour. A pile fabric in which the loops of thread are not cut: terry cloth. In corduroy manufacture, the pile is cut into orderly vertical ribs and valleys—giving corduroy its "corded" texture.

● The ribs (or cords) are known as "wales." Corduroy comes in different types, based on the width of the wales: Broadwale has wide wales—4 to 6 per inch of fabric; Midwale has medium-sized wales—8 to 10 per inch; and Pinwale, also called pincord—has 12 to 16 wales per inch.

● Filmmaker Wes Anderson is a corduroy freak. He had his personal tailor, Vahram Mateosian, design a corduroy wardrobe for the cast of his 2001 film *The Royal Tenenbaums*.

● Eddie Vedder was inspired

to write Pearl Jam's 1994 hit "Corduroy" when he saw an "Eddie Vedder" corduroy jacket being sold for $650. It was modeled on one Vedder wore, which he said he bought in a thrift store for $12.

Eddie Vedder of Pearl Jam sporting his cord jacket onstage

CITY DWELLERS HAVE LONGER, THICKER, DENSER NOSE HAIRS THAN COUNTRY FOLKS DO.

Man With a Camera

Bringing a war to the folks back home isn't without its risks.

HAVE CAMERA, WILL TRAVEL

English photographer Tim Page spent his 21st birthday dodging bullets and mortar fire to chronicle the war in Vietnam. By that time, Page had been bumming around Europe, the Middle East, and southern Asia for four years.

Although a novice with a camera, Page arrived in Vietnam as an accredited UPI freelance photographer. More vagabond hippie adventurer, occasional smuggler, and black marketeer than photographer, he'd been offered the job based on photos he'd shot for UPI of an attempted Laotian coup. At the time, the Vietnam conflict was ramping up and UPI was short-staffed in Saigon. It was 1965, and by year's end, 200,000 American troops would be fighting there. During that year, working primarily out of Saigon, Da Nang, and Hue, Page built a reputation for getting the best shots of the worst events.

SUCCESS OUTSIDE THE BOX

Daily situation briefings (known as the "five o'clock follies") and the structured photo opportunities laid on by military information officers were not for him. Instead, he went where the action was—flying in-country on Hueys, patrolling on swift boats and cutters, and hunkering with Special Forces in remote jungle base camps.

By the time he was repatriated from Vietnam, Page's photos had appeared in hundreds of newspapers and magazines, including *Time*, *Life*, *Paris Match*, the *Daily Telegraph*, and *Der Spiegel*. But fame came with a cost. Drugs, death, and rock 'n' roll were the meat of his diet, and none were particularly nutritious. Each would continue to affect his life long after he returned to peace.

In addition, in pursuit of that ultimate "shot" during his first 18 months in Vietnam, Page was wounded three times and more than once had to put aside his camera and pick up a rifle.

TOP: Tim Page and his tools of the trade
ABOVE: Page's 1965 photo of the 1st Air Cavalry marching in the Ia Drang Valley

LEFT: Page's uncanny ability to capture candid images of soldiers' raw emotions showed war in a whole new light.

BATTLE SCARS

During 1969's Operation Starlite—the first major battle between U.S. and veteran North Vietnamese regulars—Page suffered minor shrapnel wounds. Despite the wounds, some of which were in his right hip and buttock, he persevered. His Starlite photos earned him a six-page spread in *Life* magazine. Later that year, in Da Nang, he was wounded again, this time by shrapnel when a grenade exploded a few feet from him.

The third incident was the result of friendly fire from the USAF. Operating from Da Nang in the predawn hours of August 11, 1966, the Coast Guard cutter *Point Welcome*, on patrol near the mouth of the Ben Hai River, drew friendly fire from a B-57 returning from a bombing run. The plane made two runs, wiping

out the cutter's bridge, killing two guardsmen—the first deaths of U.S. Coast Guard personnel in Vietnam—and wounding several others. Two F-4s then made several strafing runs. Abandoning the ship and trying for shore in life rafts, the survivors came under small-arms and mortar fire from enemy junks and shore positions. They were later picked up by the cutter *Point Caution*, and the wounded, including Page, who'd received multiple shrapnel wounds, were transferred to a hospital.

BACK FOR MORE

After his recovery, Page was assigned by *Time-Life* to cover the Six-Day War from Beirut, but in early 1968, he was back in Vietnam. By then, the war had changed. The battle for Khe Sanh was raging, and in March of that year, the Vietcong brought the

conflict to Saigon in a prolonged battle that came to be known as Mini-Tet. Page roamed the streets with his cameras throughout.

In 1969, in the Parrot's Beak area, a land mine blew shrapnel into Page's head moments after he jumped from a Huey into a firefight. He was briefly pronounced dead during his evacuation, but medics revived him. Later, while on the operating table, he flatlined three more times. He lived, but his war was over. The injury not only left Page with a permanent plate in his head, but also partially paralyzed. He moved to the United States for long-term rehabilitation.

ONE MORE JOB

The war would eventually end for other Vietnam photojournalists, though differently than for Page. Between 1962 and 1975, more

than 300 photojournalists from both sides were killed. Page's best friend from the earliest Saigon days, Sean Flynn (son of film star Errol Flynn), was among them. In 1970 Flynn was captured in Cambodia, then held prisoner for more than a year. Page helped spearhead a 20-year search for Flynn to determine the circumstances of his death, but his eventual fate remains a mystery.

BACK TO THE REAL WORLD

As the war entered its final stages, Page became active in the antiwar movement in the United States. After the war, he continued to work as a photojournalist, still traveling extensively throughout Southeast Asia. He authored several books, many as platforms for the 250,000 photographs in his portfolio. He is currently an adjunct professor of photojournalism at Griffith University in Brisbane, Australia. Along with several other Vietnam photojournalists, Page became part of the amalgam that shaped Dennis Hopper's memorable character in the movie *Apocalypse Now*. He has also become a prominent anti–land mine activist.

Years later, Page said, "Vietnam was the first war in color, the first war for freelancers, the first war for photo agencies, the first war for television." He called it "an incredible small period of time when we could capture anything we wanted to." By comparison, he said, "Today, the inhumanity and horror of conflict are never more than a station break away—Iraq is almost conducted like an American football game. Never drawn. Only won."

TOP LEFT: One of Tim Page's most famous photos shows a Huey helicopter evacuating wounded soldiers after their convoy was ambushed.
TOP: Tim Page shot this picture of his close friend and fellow photojournalist Sean Flynn, who became a PoW and was never heard from again. He was the son of actor Errol Flynn.
ABOVE: One of Page's pop-culture legacies: Dennis Hopper's drug-addled photojournalist character in *Apocalypse Now*

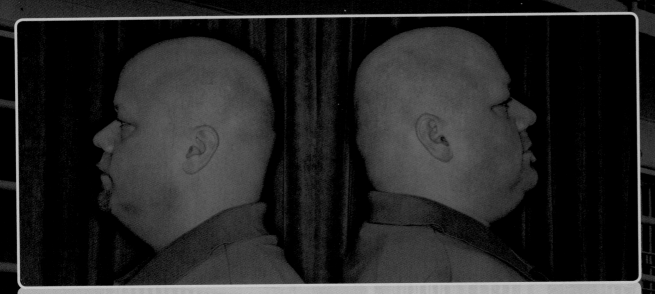

Two Timing

We recently read a newspaper story about an identical twin who switched places with his brother so that the brother could escape from prison. That got us wondering—how often does this happen? Answer: More often than you might think.

TWINS: Bernic Lee and Breon Alston-Currie, 19, of Durham, North Carolina.

BACKGROUND: In May 2002, both brothers were being held at the Durham County jail. Bernic Lee was awaiting trial for murder, and Breon was being held on an unrelated robbery charge.

TWO-TIMING: On the day that Breon was scheduled for release, the jail's computer crashed. The guards, working from a handwritten list of inmates to be released, went to Bernic Lee's cell and asked him if he was Breon. Bernic Lee said yes. His face matched the photo on the release form (they're twins, remember) and he gave the right home address, but he didn't know Breon's Social Security number. No problem. It's not uncommon for inmates to not know their own Social Security numbers, so the jailers released him anyway.

WHAT HAPPENED: Bernic Lee spent about seven hours on the outside, then turned himself back in. He later pled guilty to second-degree murder and was sentenced to 9 to 12 years in prison. County officials never figured out whether Breon played any part in the snafu. "I have no information to believe that," says the jail's director, Lt. Col. George Naylor. "I have no information *not* to believe it, either."

IN INDIA, A "HIMALAYAN BLUNDER" MEANS A VERY SERIOUS MISTAKE.

92

TWINS: Two 18-year-old twins living in Sweden in December 2004 (Their names were not released to the public.)

BACKGROUND: One of the brothers was serving a 10-month sentence in the Kronoberg jail for assault and robbery. Then one day the other brother came to visit. The two were indistinguishable, except for a birthmark on the incarcerated twin's body.

TWO-TIMING: The brothers were allowed a 45-minute, unsupervised visit. Guess what happened! They switched clothes and the one without a birthmark used an ink pen to make a fake one. When the visit ended, the brother who was serving time walked out of the jail and disappeared.

WHAT HAPPENED: For all we know, the innocent twin might have served the entire 10-month sentence for his brother, were it not for one thing: that night, he panicked at the thought of having to spend a night in jail, called for a guard, and confessed the deception. As of late December, the guilty brother was still loose, and the "innocent" one, temporarily out on bail, was facing the prospect of doing some time of his own. "He thinks he's going to walk," Warden Lars Aake Pettersson told reporters. "But that's probably not going to happen."

TWINS: Carey and David Moore, 27
BACKGROUND: Both brothers were serving time in the Nebraska State Penitentiary in October 1984.

TWO-TIMING: One afternoon they met up in a conference room in the prison and switched clothes when nobody was looking. Afterward Carey, posing as David, was released into the prison yard. David, posing as Carey, was escorted back to Carey's cell. The ruse was exposed when Carey reported for David's kitchen duty. The kitchen supervisor realized that "David" wasn't really David and reported the incident to the guards.

WHAT HAPPENED: When confronted, the twins admitted the switch. It's doubtful that it was anything more than a prank, though, and even less likely that the brothers would have kept it up much longer—David was serving 4 to 6 years for burglary; Carey was awaiting execution on death row.

TWINS: Tony and Terry Litton, 19, of Cardiff, Wales
BACKGROUND: Tony was about a year into a two-year sentence for burglary when Terry came to visit him at the Cardiff prison in March 1990.

TWO-TIMING: Somehow, the brothers managed to strip down to their underwear and switch clothes in the middle of a bustling visitors room without attracting the notice of the guards. When the visit was up, Terry went back to Tony's cell, and Tony walked out of the prison with the rest of the visitors. A word of advice to identical twins: If you and your sibling plan to trade places, don't have your names tattooed to the backs of your necks. Tony and Terry did; when an inmate noticed that Tony's now read "Terry," he alerted a guard. The twins' dad, Ken Litton, couldn't figure out why they pulled the stunt, especially since Tony was about to come up for parole anyway. "This time they've gone too far," he told reporters. "The police won't see the funny side of it."

WHAT HAPPENED: Tony was caught three days later and returned to jail to serve out his full sentence (no parole this time), plus extra time for the escape. Terry served some time of his own for helping him. (No word on whether they were allowed to visit each other in prison.)

IT WAS ALL A DREAM!?!?

When *Roseanne* viewers learned the final season was a dream, they were fuming mad. Why even tell a story if it never happened? More often than not, there's a real-world explanation for why shows pull this stunt.

SHOW: *Dallas* (CBS, 1978–91)

DREAM: In the final episode of the seventh season in May 1985, Bobby (Patrick Duffy) is run down by a car and killed. A year later in the eighth season finale, Bobby's wife Pam (Victoria Principal) wakes to the sound of running water. She goes into the bathroom...and there's Bobby, alive, taking a shower. His death—along with the entire eighth season—had been one long dream of Pam's.

REALITY: Bobby was originally killed off because Duffy was bored with the role and wanted to leave the show. But he was also a big ratings draw, and *Dallas* dipped from #2 to #6 the following year, so producers begged Duffy to come back. Because he couldn't find any better work, he did.

(Never mind that Bobby's return demolished logic—for example, several characters who left the show during the dream season, and who therefore didn't really leave, remained gone.)

SHOW: *Married...With Children* (Fox, 1987–97)

DREAM: At the start of season 6, Peg (Katey Sagal) announces she's pregnant. A few episodes later, Al (Ed O'Neill) becomes a private detective, solves a murder, earns $50,000, romances a beautiful heiress...and then wakes up to his old humdrum life. The season thus far, pregnancy included, had merely been Al Bundy's crazy dream.

REALITY: Sagal's character became pregnant only because

Sagal did in real life. Sadly, she miscarried, so Peg's pregnancy was hastily written out of the series and never talked about again.

SHOW: *Life on Mars* (ABC, 2008–09)

DREAM: This American remake of a British show ended much differently than the original. (Spoiler alert: In the British version, the main character was revealed to have been in a coma.) In the updated version, a New York City cop named Sam (Jason O'Mara) is hit by a car in 2008 and wakes up in 1973. He joins the NYPD and tries to find a way home, but keeps seeing flashes of his 2008 life. Sam can also see tiny robotic vehicles scurrying about. In the series finale, Sam

in the head by a golf ball. The screen goes black, then a light turns on. Newhart is in bed. He says, "Honey, you won't believe the dream I just had." His wife wakes up and rolls over, and it's not Joanna (Mary Frann), it's Suzanne Pleshette, in character as Emily from Newhart's previous series, *The Bob Newhart Show*. He tells her that he dreamed he was as an innkeeper in a small Vermont town, making all 184 episodes of the surreal *Newhart*—and all its characters, including Larry, his brother Darryl, and his other brother Darryl—nothing but a dream in the mind of Dr. Robert Hartley from *The Bob Newhart Show*.

REALITY: The dream idea came from Newhart's wife, Ginnie. He liked it, saying it "really fit the show," but was apprehensive because the hospital drama *St. Elsewhere*'s twist ending (it was all in the mind of an autistic boy) had received harsh criticism from viewers. But Newhart decided to film the ending just to see how it would play out. As the cameras began rolling, a facade was removed to reveal the bedroom set from Newhart's former show...and the studio audience broke out into loud applause even before Pleshette's surprise appearance. Right then, Newhart later said, he knew he'd made the right choice. *TV Guide* later named it "the most unexpected moment in the history of television."

learns that his 1973 world is a dream...and so was his 2008 world. Sam isn't even a cop—he and the other characters are astronauts in the year 2035 on the first manned mission to Mars. The events of the show took place in a collective dream shared while they were all in an induced hibernative state to make the months-long flight go by faster.

REALITY: Why such a bizarre twist? The writers

wanted a different ending than the U.K. version (to keep a surprise at the end for viewers who'd watched both series), and they wanted a finale that would truly surprise, but would still make sense to viewers. It also explained the cryptic title.

SHOW: *Newhart*
(CBS, 1982–90)

DREAM: In the final episode of the series, Dick Loudon (Bob Newhart) gets whacked

The Lyin' King

Over the years. we've reported how Disney animators massaged, rewrote, censored, and sanitized classic fables and fairy tales for mass audiences. But this is the first time we've ever heard of them "borrowing" so much of another artist's work. Did they? Or was it just a coincidence?

INSPIRATION

In 1950 a Japanese artist named Osamu Tezuka created *Jungle Taitei* (*Jungle Emperor*), a story about an orphaned lion cub who is destined to rule the animals in Africa. From 1950 to 1954, it was a Japanese comic book series, and in 1965 Tezuka turned it into Japan's first color animated television series. The following year, all 52 episodes were released in the United States under the name *Kimba the White Lion*. Over the next few years, Kimba enjoyed some success in syndication, mostly on local or regional TV stations, and Tezuka freely acknowledged that the work of Walt Disney—*Bambi* in particular—was an inspiration for the story of his lion hero. In 1994, nearly 30 years after the creation of *Kimba* and five years after Tezuka's death in 1989, Disney released its feature-length animated film *The Lion King*—about an orphaned lion cub destined to rule the animals in Africa.

FALSE PRIDE

Officially, the executives and animators at Disney denied they had ever even heard of *Kimba*. But fans of the original *Kimba the White Lion* were incensed with the many similarities they found between the two projects. A group of more than 1,000 animators in Japan sent a petition to Disney asking the studio to acknowledge its debt to the original series. Disney refused, citing only *Bambi* and Shakespeare's play *Hamlet* as influences. Walt Disney reportedly met Tezuka at the 1964 New York World's Fair and mentioned that he someday hoped to make something similar to Tezuka's earlier creation, *Astro Boy*. But Disney died in 1966, 28 years before *The Lion King* was made. If he really was a fan of Tezuka's work, would he have approved of the project?

COPYCAT

Some of the most striking similarities between *The Lion King* and *Kimba the White Lion*:
● The main characters' names are remarkably similar: Simba and Kimba.
● Both are orphaned as cubs and destined to become rulers.
● Each lost their father in treacherous circumstances.
● In *The Lion King*, Simba turns to a wise but eccentric baboon (named Rafiki) for guidance. In *Kimba the White Lion*, Kimba turns to a wise but eccentric baboon (named Dan'l Baboon) for guidance.
● One of Simba's friends is a hysterical yet comical bird (named Zazu). One of Kimba's friends is a hysterical yet comical bird (named Polly).
● Simba has a cute girlfriend cub named Nala. Kimba has a cute girlfriend cub named Kitty.
● Simba's chief nemesis is Scar, an evil lion with a scar over his left eye. Kimba's primary nemesis is Claw, an evil, one-eyed lion with a scar over his blind left eye.
● In *The Lion King*, Scar enlists the aid of three hyenas (Shenzi, Banzai, and Ed). In *Kimba the White Lion*, Claw enlists the aid of two hyenas (Tib and Tab).

ABOVE, LEFT TO RIGHT: These four stills from Kimba should look very familiar to Disney fans. RIGHT, BELOW: Kimba is white, and Simba is brown—which proves that the two movies are totally different, and any other similarities between them are purely a coincidence (according to Disney, anyway).

● Kimba and Simba each speak to the spirit of their father, who appears in the clouds.

● The image of Simba standing on Pride Rock in *The Lion King* is almost identical to an image of Kimba as a grown lion, standing on a jutting rock surveying his kingdom in *Kimba the White Lion*.

CAT FIGHT

Disney may have "borrowed" the idea, but they were legally protected. Mushi Productions, the company that made *Kimba the White Lion*, went bankrupt in 1973 and U.S. rights to the show ran out in 1978. That means *Kimba* was in the public domain. Someone tried to release it to home video in the U.S. in 1993, but was delayed by a lawsuit from an undisclosed company. At the same time, details of Disney's new movie began to surface. In an online chat in 1993, Roy Disney mentioned Kimba, the lead character in Disney's next animated film, *The Jungle King*. (Kimba's original English title was *The Jungle Emperor*.)

IN 1968 STEVEN SPIELBERG AND GEORGE LUCAS TOOK A DIRECTING CLASS TAUGHT BY JERRY LEWIS.

97

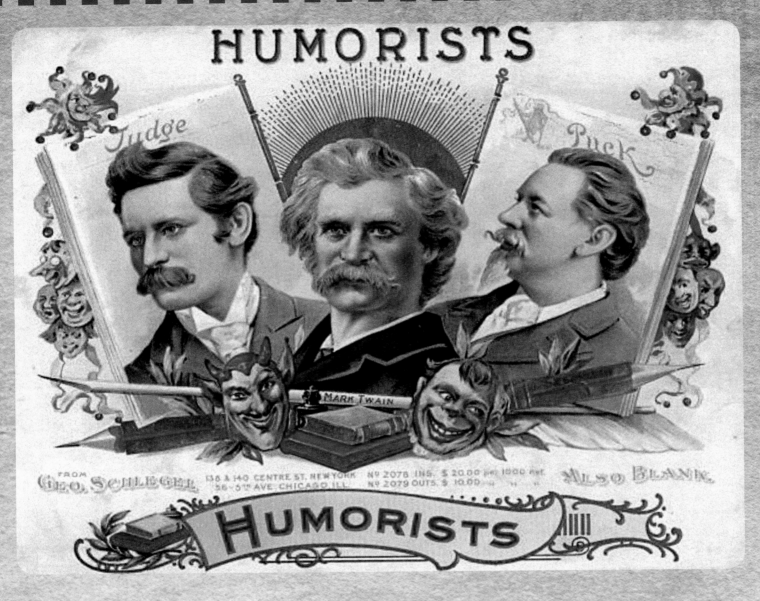

Benjamin Franklin had his apple a day, but here's a man who had a different formula for longevity.

Mark Twain at 70

BACKGROUND

On February 3, 1905, Mark Twain, the 19th-century's most celebrated humorist, celebrated his 70th birthday. That was quite a feat, considering that the life expectancy at that time was only 47. At his lavish birthday party at Delmonico's restaurant in New York City, Twain gave a raucous speech on his secrets to longevity. Here are a few excerpts.

ON SLEEPING: "Since 40 I have been regular about going to bed and getting up. I have made it a rule to go to bed when there wasn't anybody left to sit up with; and I have made it a rule to get up when I had to. This has resulted in an unswerving regularity of irregularity."

ON EATING: "In the matter of

diet, I have been persistently strict in sticking to the things which didn't agree with me until one or the other of us got the best of it. For 30 years I have taken coffee and bread at eight in the morning, and no bite nor sup until seven-thirty in the evening. That is all right for me, but headachy people would not reach 70 comfortably by that road, and they would be foolish to try it. And I wish to urge upon you this—that if you find you can't make 70 by any but an uncomfortable road, don't you go."

ON SMOKING: "I have made it a rule never to smoke more than one cigar at a time. As an example to others, it has always been my rule never to smoke when asleep, and never to refrain when awake. I have stopped smoking now and then, for a few months at a time, but it was not on principle, it was only to show off."

ON DRINKING: "When others drink, I like to help."

ON MORALITY: "Morals are an acquirement—like music, like a foreign language, like piety, poker, paralysis—no man is born with them. But if you are careful with a moral, and keep it in a dry place, and disinfect it now and then, and give it a fresh coat of whitewash once in a while, you will be surprised to see how well it will last and how long it will keep sweet, or at least inoffensive."

ON BEING INVITED TO PARTIES: "If you shrink at

the thought of night and the late home-coming from the banquet and the lights and the laughter through the deserted streets, you need only reply, 'Your invitation honors me, and pleases me, but I am seventy—seventy—and would rather nestle in the chimney-corner, and smoke my pipe, and read my book, and take my rest, wishing you well in all affection.'"

ON THE BIG SEVEN-O: "The 70th birthday! It is the time of life when you arrive at a new and awful dignity; when you may throw aside the decent reserves which have pressed you for a generation and stand unafraid and unabashed upon your seven-terraced summit and look down and teach—unrebuked. You can tell the world how you got there.

"I have achieved my 70 years in the usual way: by sticking strictly to a scheme of life which would kill anybody else. It sounds like an exaggeration, but that is really the common rule for attaining old age. We can't reach old age by another man's road."

ELVIS PRESLEY PROPOSED TO GINGER ALDEN WHILE HE WAS SITTING ON THE TOILET.

99

The Odd, Odd World of Baseball Injuries

Major League ballplayers are big, tough, manly men who cannot be felled by any mere mortal destructive force...except for ice packs, donuts, sunflower seeds, and handshakes.

- Catcher Mickey Tettleton of the Detroit Tigers went on the disabled list for athlete's foot, which he got from habitually tying his shoes too tight.

- Wade Boggs once threw out his back while putting on a pair of cowboy boots.

- In 1993 Rickey Henderson missed several games because of frostbite—in August. He had fallen asleep on an ice pack.

- Ken Griffey Jr. missed one game in 1994 due to a groin injury. (His protective cup had pinched one of his testicles.)

- Atlanta pitcher John Smoltz once burned his chest. He'd ironed a shirt...while still wearing it.

- Sammy Sosa missed a game because he threw out his back while sneezing.

- While playing for Houston, Nolan Ryan couldn't pitch after being bitten by a coyote.

- Marty Cordova of the Baltimore Orioles went on the disabled list after burning his face in a tanning bed.

- Atlanta outfielder Terry Harper once waved a teammate home, then high-fived him. The act separated Harper's shoulder.

- Pitcher Phil Niekro hurt his hand...while shaking hands.

- Milwaukee's Steve Sparks once dislocated his shoulder attempting to tear a phone book in half.

- San Francisco Giants manager Roger Craig cut his hand "undoing a bra strap."

- To look more menacing, Red Sox pitcher Clarence Blethen took out his false teeth during a game and put them in his back pocket. Later, while he was sliding into second base, the teeth clamped down and bit him on the butt.

- When the San Diego Padres won the National League West in 2005, pitcher Jake Peavy jumped on top of the celebration pileup. He fractured a rib and had to sit out the playoffs.

• The Cubs' Jose Cardenal once missed a game because he'd been kept awake all night by crickets chirping outside his hotel room.

• Kevin Mitchell of the New York Mets hurt a tooth on a donut that had gotten too hot in a microwave. On another occasion, Mitchell pulled a muscle while vomiting.

• Carlos Zambrano of the Cubs was on the disabled list after being diagnosed with carpal tunnel syndrome. Cause of condition: too many hours spent surfing the Internet.

• Minnesota's Terry Mulholland had to sit out a few games after he scratched his eye on a feather sticking out of a pillow.

• San Diego pitcher Adam Eaton stabbed himself in the stomach with a knife while trying to open a DVD case.

• Florida pitcher Ricky Bones pulled his lower back getting out of a chair while watching TV in the team clubhouse.

• Outfielder Glenallen Hill has an intense fear of spiders. He went on the disabled list after

suffering multiple cuts all over his body. Hill had fallen out of bed onto a glass table while having a nightmare in which he was covered with spiders.

• Before the first game of the 1985 World Series, St. Louis outfielder Vince Coleman was fooling around on the field and managed to get rolled up inside the Busch Stadium automatic tarp-rolling machine. Coleman's injuries caused him to miss the entire series.

"TWONGUE TISTERS"

Try to say these three times fast. And pay no attention to the person banging on the bathroom door, wondering what's going on in there.

"WHO WASHED WASHINGTON'S WHITE WOOLENS WHEN WASHINGTON'S WASHERWOMAN WENT WEST?"

"Imagine an imaginary menagerie manager managing an imaginary menagerie"

"LESSER LEATHER NEVER WEATHERED WETTER WEATHER BETTER"

"GIVE PAPA A CUP OF PROPER COFFEE IN A COPPER COFFEE CUP"

"I slit the sheet, the sheet I slit, and on the slitted sheet I sit."

"A thin little boy picked six thick thistle sticks."

"Many an anemone sees an enemy."

"SHAVE A CEDAR SHINGLE THIN"

"Which wicked witch wished which wicked wish?"

"We surely shall see the sun shine soon."

"ANY NOISE ANNOYS AN OYSTER BUT A NOISY NOISE ANNOYS AN OYSTER MOST."

"The epitome of femininity."

"Miss Smith's fish sauce shop seldom sells shellfish."

"WHICH WRISTWATCHES ARE SWISS WRISTWATCHES?"

"FRED FED TED BREAD, AND TED FED FRED BREAD."

"FLEE FROM FOG TO FIGHT FLU FAST!"

"THE BOOTBLACK BOUGHT THE BLACK BOOT BACK."

IN THE 1970S, 20% OF ALL ROAD ACCIDENTS IN SWEDEN INVOLVED A MOOSE.

103

More than three centuries after the end of the Salem witch trials, they continue to defy explanation. In the mid-1970s, a college undergraduate developed a new theory. Does it hold water? Read on and decide for yourself.

Salem: The Fungus Theory

ABOVE: The Personal Seal of the Chief Magistrate William Stoughton on the Warrant of Execution of Bridget Bishop.
OPPOSITE RIGHT: An engraving of 1863 depicts the Witch Trials at Salem...the inset shows Ergot Fungus in Barley.

Season of the Witch

In the bleak winter of 1692, the people of Salem, Massachusetts, hunkered down in their cabins and waited for spring. It was a grim time: There was no fresh food or vegetables, just dried meat and roots to eat. Their mainstay was the coarse bread they baked from the rye grain harvested in the fall.

Shortly after the New Year, the madness began. Elizabeth Parris, 9-year-old daughter of the local preacher, and her cousin, 11-year-old Abigail Williams, suffered from violent fits and convulsions. They lapsed into incoherent rants, had hallucinations, complained of crawly sensations on their skin, and often retreated into dull-eyed trances. Their desperate families turned to the local doctor, who could find nothing physically wrong with them. At his wit's end, he decided there was only one reasonable explanation: witchcraft.

Blame Game

Word spread like wildfire through the village: An evil being was hexing the children. Soon, more "victims" appeared, most of them girls under the age of 20. The terrified villagers started pointing fingers of blame, first at an old slave named Tituba, who belonged to the Reverend Parris, then to old women like Sarah Good and Sarah Osborn. The arrests began on February 29; the trials soon followed. That June, 60-year-old Bridget Bishop was the first to be declared guilty of witchcraft and the first to hang. By September, 140 "witches" had been arrested and 19 had been executed. Many of the accused barely escaped the gallows by running into the woods and hiding. Then,

sometime over the summer, the demonic fits stopped—and the frenzy of accusation and counter-accusation stopped with them. As passions cooled, the villagers tried to put their community back together again.

Unanswered Questions

What happened to make these otherwise dour Puritans turn on each other with such a destructive frenzy? Over the centuries several theories have been put forth, from the Freudian—that the witch hunt was the result of hysterical tension resulting from centuries of sexual repression—to

the exploitive—that it was fabricated as an excuse for a land grab (the farms and homes of all of the victims and many of the accused were confiscated and redistributed to other members of the community). But researchers had never been able to find real evidence to support these theories. Then in the 1970s, a college student in California made a deduction that seemed to explain everything.

In 1976 Linnda Caporael, a psychology major at U.C. Santa Barbara, was told to choose a subject for a term paper in her American History course. Having just seen a production

of Arthur Miller's play *The Crucible* (a fictional account of the Salem trials), she decided to write about the witch hunt. "As I began researching," she later recalled, "I had one of those 'a-ha!' experiences." The author of one of her sources said he remained at a loss to explain the hallucinations of the villagers of Salem. "It was the word 'hallucinations' that made everything click," said Caporael. Years before, she'd read of a case of ergot poisoning in France where the victims had suffered from hallucinations, and she thought there might be a connection.

The Fungus Among Us

Ergot is a fungus that infects rye, a grain more commonly used in past centuries to bake bread than it is today. One of the byproducts present in ergot-infected rye is ergotamine, which is related to LSD. Toxicologists have known for years that eating bread baked with ergot-contaminated rye can trigger convulsions, delusions, creepy-crawly sensations of the skin, vomiting...and hallucinations. And historians were already aware that the illness caused by ergot poisoning (known as St. Anthony's Fire) was behind several incidents of mass insanity in medieval Europe. Caporael wondered if the same conditions might have been present in Salem.

They were. Ergot needs warm, damp weather to grow, and those conditions were rife in the fields around Salem in 1691. Rye was the primary grain grown, so there was plenty of it to be infected. Caporael also discovered that most of the accusers lived on the west side of the village, where the fields were chronically marshy, making them a perfect breeding ground for the fungus.

The crop harvested in the fall of 1691 would've been baked and eaten during the following winter, which was when the fits of madness began. However, the next summer was unusually dry, which could explain the sudden stop to the bewitchments. No ergot, no madness.

She Rests Her Case

Caporael continued to research her theory as she pursued her Ph.D., publishing her findings in 1976 in the journal *Science*, which brought her support from the scientific community and attention from the news media. Caporael has been careful to say that her theory only accounts for the initial cause of the Salem witch hunts. As the frenzy grew in scope and consequence, she's convinced that the actual sequence of events probably included not only real moments of mass hysteria but also some overacting on the part of the accusers (motivated as much by fear of being accused themselves as by any actual malice toward the accused).

The toxic weed the devil's trumpet, *Datura Stramonium*, breaks open its seed pods

Other Possibilities

Caporael's theory remains one of the most convincing explanations for what started the madness that tore apart the village of Salem, Massachusetts, in 1692...but there are others.

ENCEPHALITIS LETHARGICA

Historian Laurie Win Carlson compared the symptoms of the accused in Salem (violent fits, trance or coma-like states) with those experienced by victims of an outbreak of *Encephalitis Lethargica*, an acute inflammation of the brain, between 1915 and 1926. The trials were likely "a response to unexplained physical and neurological behaviors resulting from an epidemic of encephalitis," she says.

JIMSON WEED

This toxic weed, sometimes called devil's trumpet or locoweed, grows wild in Massachusetts. Ingesting it can cause hallucinations, delirium, and bizarre behavior.

THE GRAND CANYON MULES

Mules have been hauling people and cargo up and down the Grand Canyon for more than a century. Here are some fun facts about these industrious pack animals...

● Mule trips into the Grand Canyon are so popular that reservations are taken as many as 23 months in advance—and trips always sell out.

● For day-trippers, it takes about 2-1/2 hours to get down the 10-mile Bright Angel Trail to Plateau Point, a good stopping point along the canyon route. But if you want to go all the way to the canyon floor, it will take a full day.

● President Teddy Roosevelt took a mule ride down when he visited in 1903. He was one of the first public figures to do so.

● Mule rides aren't cheap. A one-day ride down and back is about $140—but it includes a boxed lunch!

● The first person to offer mule rides was Captain John Hance, the first white settler in the Grand Canyon. He began his business in 1887. Today, private companies are licensed to offer the rides.

● The mules have a nearly perfect 100-year safety record—an impressive feat considering the steep switchbacks and crumbling shale on the trails.

● To ride to the bottom of the canyon on a mule, you must weigh less than 200 pounds, be taller than 4 feet 7 inches, not be pregnant, and speak English well enough to understand your wrangler's commands.

● Mules are not just for fun in the Grand Canyon. Five days a week, the U.S. Postal Service uses mule trains to deliver mail to Supai, Arizona, in the Havasupai Indian Reservation, located at the bottom of the canyon. Mules carry all forms of mail, including letters, food, and even mattresses. They haul an average of one ton of cargo down the canyon each day.

Ever wonder what inspired your favorite songs? Here are a few inside stories about some legendary hit tunes...

Behind the Hits

ABOVE: Elton in 1973
TOP RIGHT: Cover of the double album *Goodbye Yellow Brick Road*, 1973
OPPOSITE TOP: Katy Perry, out for the evening
OPPOSITE: Cover of the 12" vinyl single of Frankie Goes To Hollywood's "Relax"

Elton John: "Bennie and the Jets"

Elton John's lyricist Bernie Taupin wrote the song about a fictional glam rock band—it was a satire of the cocaine-fueled excesses of the 1970s music industry. But after recording the song, John and his band thought the song was bland, so producer Gus Dudgeon added in applause, whistles, and hand claps to make it sound more like a "live" performance. Released on John's 1973 album *Goodbye Yellow Brick Road*, it wasn't intended to be a single, but when an R&B station in Detroit surprisingly started playing "Bennie and the Jets," MCA Records decided to release it. John thought the song was "too weird" and predicted it would flop. He was wrong—it went to #1 on the pop chart.

Beck: "Loser"

In 1994 when Beck (real name: Beck Hansen) was an up-and-coming musician, he was fooling around at producer Karl Stephenson's house. Beck started playing slide guitar, and Stephenson began recording. As Stephenson added a Public Enemy–style beat and a sample from Dr. John's "I Walk on Gilded Splinters," Beck attempted to freestyle rap—something he'd never done before. Frustrated at his inability to rap, Beck began criticizing his own performance: "Soy un perdedor" ("I'm a loser" in Spanish). Beck wanted to scrap it, but Stephenson thought it was catchy. Stephenson was right— "Loser" made Beck a star.

Katy Perry: "California Gurls"

In 2010 Perry was almost finished with her third album, *Teenage Dream,* when she decided that she needed one more track to fill it out. Her inspiration: Jay-Z's 2009 hit "Empire State of Mind," which celebrated New York City. "What about LA?" Perry asked her manager. She said it was time for a "California song from a girl's perspective." So she and her writing team got to work on "California Girls." Perry wanted a West Coast rapper to join her on the song, so she went to Wikipedia and typed in "West Coast rappers." From that list, she chose Snoop Dogg, who heartily agreed. Shortly before the song was released, the classic rock band Big Star's lead singer, Alex Chilton, died. So Perry's manager (who was a big fan) asked her to change the spelling as a nod to Big Star's 1974 song "September Gurls." So she did. Released in May 2010, "California Gurls" spent six weeks at #1, and Billboard ranked it first on their "Top 30 Summer Songs of All Time" list. (The Beach Boys 1965 hit "California Girls" was ranked 16th.)

Frankie Goes to Hollywood: "Relax"

FGTH were arguably the biggest group since the Beatles to come out of Liverpool, England. In 1983, as "Relax" climbed the charts, a deejay for England's Radio One read the lyrics as the song played. He was appalled and yanked the song off the air, calling it obscene. (The lyrics aren't explicit, just sexually suggestive.) Radio One subsequently banned the song and BBC Television banned the video, but that of course only increased demand—people wanted to hear what the fuss was about. Result: The song hit the top of the charts. It later became popular in American dance clubs and has since become identified as one of the seminal songs of the 1980s.

LL Cool J: "Mama Said Knock You Out"

LL Cool J (real name: James Smith) was suffering from a street-cred problem. After releasing the sensitive ballad "I Need Love," the talk in the rap world was that he'd "gone soft." Unsure how to respond in song when recording his fourth album in 1990, LL Cool J thought of his grandmother (not his mama), who often told him, "If a task is once begun, never leave it 'til it's done." He called his grandmother and told her about his problem. She told him to simply "knock out" the competition...but to keep his lyrics profanity-free. From that conversation, LL Cool J started writing "Mama Said Knock You Out," an aggressive rap song that addresses his critics. It went to #1, the biggest hit of LL Cool J's career.

The Power of Poo

What's brown and sounds like a cowbell? *DUNNNG!*

FIRE STARTER

The Bible may have been way ahead of its time. One line in the book of Ezekiel says, "Lo, I have given thee cow's dung for man's dung, and thou shalt prepare thy bread therewith." It's perhaps the earliest written mention of what we now refer to as *biomass*—any biological material that can be used as fuel, including waste that can be burned. The most plentiful form of biomass on Earth is animal excrement, which, in its basic dried form, is known as dung. And humans have been using it for centuries.

The most popular fuel dung comes from members of the bovine family: cattle, bison, yaks, and water buffalo, due to both their large size and the high content of undigested plant matter in their droppings. When dried, these piles of manure are easy to pick up, carry, and toss into a fire. In the mid-19th century, that's what American settlers traveling west did with the massive buffalo chips scattered along the way. Luckily for them, buffalo dung has 50%–75% the heating power of wood, which was much harder to come by on the prairie. Today dung is still used as a heating source in much of the world. In India, with its millions of impoverished people and millions of cattle, dried dung is known as *gobar* and is used to fuel ovens built in the ground. In the mountains of Tibet, yak dung is used for both cooking and heating. In the Middle East, camels (which are not bovines) provide chips for fuel. And while it's not as common today as it was during the Incan empire, llama dung is used in many mountainous parts of South America.

WHAT CAN BROWN DO FOR YOU?

There's another way to convert dung into fuel—and it doesn't involve burning. The process, called *anaerobic digestion*, speeds up the decay of the dung inside a device called a *digester*. Digesters, like your intestines, produce a gas byproduct containing methane, except that digesters produce a lot more of it than you do—and it's about 60% methane, commonly referred to as natural gas. Anything that rots (sewage, garbage, dead things) can produce this methane biogas. And the gas can be used to heat homes and provide electricity.

By far, the most abundant source of biomass comes from the world's billions of farm animals—just one cow can produce up to 100 pounds of manure per day. Currently, most of that waste lands on the ground to rot on its own. As it does, it releases methane straight into the air—not a good thing, since methane is up to 21 times more harmful to the atmosphere than carbon dioxide. But when methane is collected and used as natural gas, it burns much cleaner than gasoline. Recently there's been a concerted effort on the part of dairy farmers to utilize this poo-power.

THE NUMBER TWO PROBLEM

Using dung as a heating source has some disadvantages. For one thing, stored droppings can generate heat as they decompose, spontaneously igniting a fire that's difficult to extinguish. Burning dung—whether by accident or on purpose—also generates a lot of acrid smoke, so indoor ovens must have good ventilation. Finally, dung is fecal matter, which means that extreme cleanliness is required to avoid illness. Still, handled properly, dung can provide vital fuel for cooking food and keeping warm.

KARATE WAS NOT INTRODUCED TO JAPAN UNTIL ABOUT 1917.

ABOVE: A typical anaerobic digester plant

PERSONAL FOWL

Experts say that before long, we may be filling our cars with fuel made from chicken poop...or pig poop, or even human poop, at a cost of about 10 cents per gallon and with better mileage. In recent years, large poultry and pig farms have begun to use dung for power. A plant in western Minnesota converts 700,000 tons of turkey droppings per year into electricity. Another plant in the Netherlands is expected to power 90,000 households by converting 440,000 tons of chicken waste per year. Hog farmers in the U.S. are building converters to tap their waste lagoons for methane. And dozens of waste treatment plants and landfills are taking steps toward utilizing this abundant power source. So while dung may not solve all of our energy needs, there's certainly a place for it as we search for alternative forms of fuel. And, since poop is a fact of life, it's an energy source that won't be going away anytime soon.

MORE STEEL IS USED IN THE U.S. TO MAKE BOTTLE CAPS THAN TO MAKE CARS.

Ask the Experts

Everyone's got a question or two they'd like answered—basic stuff, like "Why is the sky blue?" Here are a few of those questions, with answers from books by some of the nation's top trivia experts.

TURNING OVER A NEW LEAF

Q: *Why do leaves change color in the fall?*

A: "The carotenoids (pigments in photosynthesizing cells), which are responsible for the fall colors, are always present in a tree's leaves. During the growing season, however, those colors are eclipsed by the green of chlorophyll. Toward the end of summer, when the chlorophyll production ceases, the other colors of the carotenoids (yellow, orange, red, or purple) become visible." (From *The Handy Science Answer Book*, by the Carnegie Library)

GET A LEG UP

Q: *Why do male dogs lift their leg up to urinate?*

A: "It isn't to avoid 'missing' and squirting their legs by mistake. It's to mark territory. Most dogs are compulsive in their habits and have favorite 'watering holes.' By lifting a leg, the urine flows up and out much farther, extending the boundaries of the male's territory. From a dog's point of view, evidently, the bigger the territory, the better." (From *Why Do Dogs Have Wet Noses?* by David Feldman)

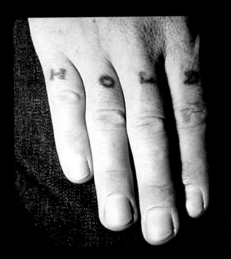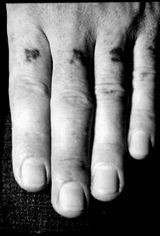

KNUCKLE UNDER

Q: *Why do our knuckles crack?*

A: "The bones in our fingers are separated by small pads of cartilage, and in between are small pockets of a thick liquid. When you bend your fingers, the bones pull away from the pads of cartilage and a vacuum forms. As the bending continues, the vacuum bubble bursts, making the cracking sound you hear. The process is very similar to what happens when you pull a rubber suction cup off a smooth surface." (From *Ever Wonder Why?*, by Douglas B. Smith)

STOP, POP, AND ROLL

Q: *How does quicksand work?*

A: "Not by pulling you down. Quicksand is nearly always found above a spring, which creates a supersaturated condition that makes the sand frictionless and unable to support weight. In addition, quicksand is airless, which creates suction as you struggle to get free. The most effective way to escape quicksand is to position yourself on top of it and 'roll' out." (From *The Book of Answers*, by Barbara Berliner)

SEEING THINGS

Q: *What are those little squiggles you see floating on your eyes when you look at the sky?*

A: "They're called 'floaters.' To some people they look like spots; to others, like tiny threads. They're not on your eyes, though; they're *in* your eyes. That's why blinking doesn't make them go away. Floaters are all that's left of the hyaloid artery. The hyaloid artery carried blood to your eye and helped it grow...when you were still inside your mother's womb. When your eyes were finished growing, the hyaloid artery withered and broke into pieces. But since these pieces were sealed up inside your eye, they had no place to go. You'll see them floating around the rest of your life." (From *Know It All!*, by Ed Zotti)

BOUNCING AROUND THE ROOM

Q: *Where does the force come from when you are thrown across a room after touching a live electrical connection?*

"Then the fearful truth flashed upon him. He was sinking in a quicksand!"

A: "It's not the electricity itself that throws you. The force comes from your own muscles. When a large electrical current runs through your body, your muscles are stimulated to contract powerfully—much harder than they can be made to contract voluntarily. The electric current typically flows into one arm, through the abdomen, and out of one or both legs, which can cause most of the muscles in the body to contract at once. The results are unpredictable, but given the strength of the leg and back muscles, the shock can send the victim flying across the room." (From *The Last Word: Questions & Answers*, edited by Mick O'Hare)

UNCLE JOHN'S WEIGHT-LOSS SYSTEM

Q: *Every time you fart, do you lose a little weight?*

A: "Actually, there is some reason to believe that after a good toot you weigh more—slightly. Two of the principal components of flatus are hydrogen and methane, which are both lighter than air. Thus it is conceivable that when you deflate, as it were, you lose buoyancy and add poundage. On the other hand, it is not clear what the ambient pressure of gas in the intestines is—a critical factor, since even a light gas under sufficient compression weighs the same as or more than air." (From *The Straight Dope*, by Cecil Adams)

AT SIX GALLONS PER PERSON PER YEAR, AMERICANS ARE THE LEADING CONSUMERS OF ICE CREAM.

113

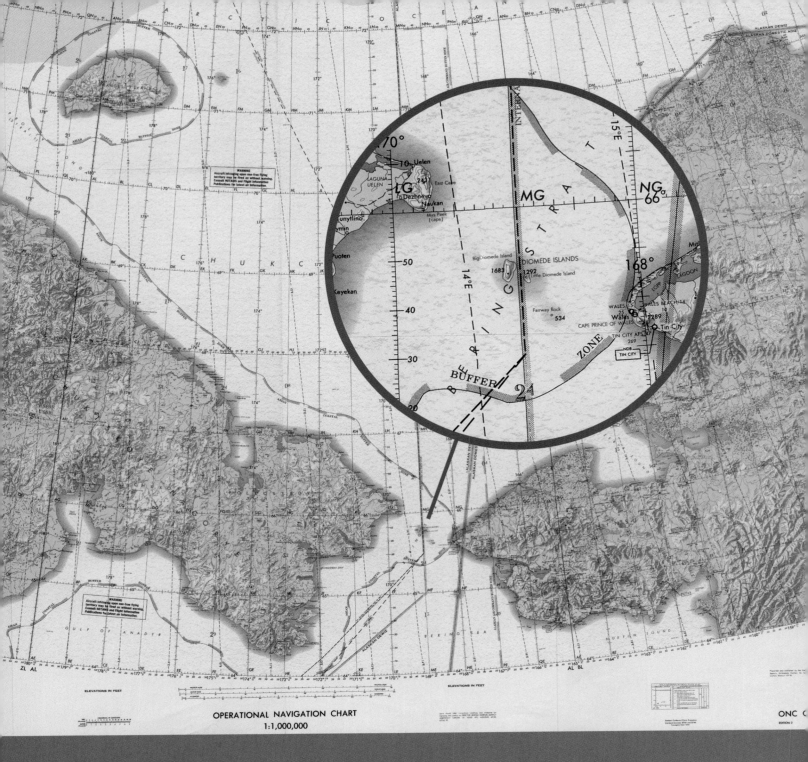

OPERATIONAL NAVIGATION CHART
1:1,000,000

PALIN COMPARISON

Q: *Can you really see Russia from Alaska?*

A: "Yes, but only the boring parts. Russia and Alaska are divided by the Bering Strait, which is about 55 miles at its narrowest. In the middle of the Bering Strait are two small islands: Big Diomede, in Russian territory, and Little Diomede, which is part of the United States. At their closest, these islands are a little less than two and a half miles apart, which means that, on a clear day, you can definitely see one from the other. If you stand on high ground on the tip of St. Lawrence Island—a larger Alaskan island—you can see the Russian mainland, about 37 miles away. It's not as if Alaskans can see into the heart of the Kremlin, though. The region you'd see is Chukotka, a desolate expanse of about 285,000 square miles with a population of about 55,000. That's an area roughly the size of Texas with a population the size of Pine Bluff, Arkansas." (From *Slate* magazine, "Can You Really See Russia From Alaska?" by Nina Shen Rastogi)

THERE ARE NO THUNDERSTORMS IN POLAR REGIONS. WHY? NOT ENOUGH WARM AIR.

How Insulting

IF YOU DON'T FIND THESE CLASSIC PUTDOWNS ENTERTAINING,
THEN YOU ARE A DOO-DOO HEAD.

"DON'T BE HUMBLE.
YOU'RE NOT THAT GREAT."
—GOLDA MEIR

"THERE'S NOTHING WRONG
WITH YOU THAT
REINCARNATION WON'T CURE."
—JACK E. LEONARD

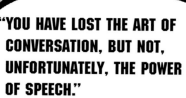

"YOU HAVE LOST THE ART OF
CONVERSATION, BUT NOT,
UNFORTUNATELY, THE POWER
OF SPEECH."
—GEORGE BERNARD SHAW

"I'M OLD? WHEN YOU WERE
YOUNG, THE DEAD SEA WAS
ONLY SICK!"
—MILTON BERLE

"YOU SHOW ALL THE
SENSITIVITY OF A BLUNT AXE."
—J. K. ROWLING

"YOU'RE A GOOD EXAMPLE
OF WHY SOME ANIMALS EAT
THEIR YOUNG."
—JIM SAMUELS

"YOU HAVE VAN GOGH'S
EAR FOR MUSIC."
—BILLY WILDER

"I NEVER FORGET A FACE,
BUT IN YOUR CASE I'LL
MAKE AN EXCEPTION."
—GROUCHO MARX

"IF YOU CAN'T BE A GOOD
EXAMPLE, THEN YOU'LL
JUST HAVE TO BE A
HORRIBLE WARNING."
—CATHERINE AIRD

THE FIRST TENNIS BALLS WERE STUFFED WITH HUMAN HAIR.

Who Discovered Uranus?

As early as kindergarten, we're taught that there are nine planets, but 200 years ago, even scholars were sure there were only six planets. Here's how we got the three new ones.

THE END OF THE SOLAR SYSTEM

People have known about Mercury, Venus, Mars, Jupiter, and Saturn for thousands of years. Early civilizations named the days of the week after each of these planets, plus the Sun and Moon. The Greeks watched them move through the night sky, passing in front of the stars that make up the constellations of the zodiac, and called them *planetes*—which means "wanderers."

As recently as the 1700s, people still believed that the planet Saturn was at the farthest extent of the solar system. That there might be other planets wasn't even a respectable idea. But as technology and science became more sophisticated, other members of the solar system came to light.

URANUS

In 1781 a self-taught astronomer, William Herschel, was "sweeping the skies" with his telescope. By March, he had reached the section included the constellation Gemini, and he spotted an object that appeared as a disk rather than a glowing star. Because it moved slightly from week to week, Herschel thought it was a comet. After a few months, however, he

LEFT: A 3D render of Uranus
OPPOSITE, LEFT: NASA image of Neptune
OPPOSITE, BELOW: 3D render of Pluto

decided the orbit was circular...and came to the shocking conclusion that it wasn't a comet, but an unknown planet. People were astonished.

No one since ancient times had named a planet. Herschel felt that it should be called "Georgium Sidus" (George's Star) in honor of his patron, George III—the king of England who ruled during the American Revolution. Some people wanted to name it "Herschel" after its discoverer. But one influential astronomer suggested "Uranus," after the Greek god of the heavens. That made sense, since this new planet was certainly the limit of the skies of the solar system. Or so they thought.

NEPTUNE

The newly-found planet had a slight variation in its orbit, almost as if something were tugging at it. Could there be another planet affecting Uranus? A century earlier, Isaac Newton had come up with laws describing the effects that the gravitational forces of planets have on one another. Using Newton's laws, two young scientists set out independently in 1840 to find the unknown planet whose gravitational forces might be pulling on Uranus. One of the scientists was a French mathematician, Jean Leverrier. The other was an English astronomer, John Couch Adams. Both hoped the unknown planet would be

where their calculations said they could find it.

Adams finished his calculations first, in September 1845. The following August, Leverrier completed his. Neither had access to a large telescope, so they couldn't verify their projections—and no one would make one available to them. Finally, Leverrier traveled to the Berlin Observatory in Germany, and the young assistant manager, Johann Gottfried Galle, agreed to help search for the planet.

That was September 23, 1846. That night, Galle looked through the telescope, calling out stars and their positions while a young student astronomer, Heinrich Louis d'Arrest, looked at a star chart, searching for the stars Galle described. Finally Galle called out an eighth-magnitude star that d'Arrest couldn't locate on the charts.

They had found the unknown planet! It had taken two years of research—but only a half hour at the telescope. The discovery belongs to both Adams and Leverrier, who had essentially discovered the new planet with just a pen and a new set of mathematical laws. The greenish

planet was named after Neptune, god of the sea.

VULCAN?

Leverrier was on a roll. He started looking for other planets and became convinced that there was one between the Sun and Mercury. He called his planet "Vulcan," the god of fire, because it was so close to the Sun. Leverrier noted that, like Uranus, Mercury experienced disturbances that caused it to travel farther in one point in its orbit. Since Neptune was one of the causes of similar pulls on Uranus, it made sense that another planet was affecting Mercury.

Leverrier never found Vulcan, but people believed it was there until 1916, when Einstein's general theory of relativity was published. Einstein gave a satisfactory explanation for the discrepancies in Mercury's orbit, so scientists no longer needed Vulcan. It thereby ceased to exist...until decades later, when Gene Roddenberry, creator of *Star Trek*, appropriated the planet and made it the home of Spock.

PLUTO

The discovery of Neptune did not completely account for the peculiar movements of Uranus. Once again, scientists considered the pull of another planet as a cause and set out to find "Planet X." Using the

telescope at his observatory in Flagstaff, Arizona, Percival Lowell searched for Planet X for 10 years. After he died in 1916, his brother gave the observatory a donation that enabled it to buy a telescope-camera. The light-sensitive process of photography allowed astronomers to capture images of dim and distant stars that they couldn't see, even with the aid of a telescope.

In 1929 the Lowell Observatory hired Clyde Tombaugh, a young self-taught astronomer from Kansas, to continue the search for Planet X. Lowell had suggested that the unknown planet was in the Gemini region of the sky. Using an instrument called the blink microscope, Tombaugh took two photographs of that area of the sky a few days apart and placed them side by side under the microscope. If something moved in the sky, as planets do, it would appear as a speck of light jumping back and forth as Tombaugh's eyes moved from one photograph to the other, looking through the microscope. That's just what happened. The observatory announced the discovery of the ninth planet on March 13, 1930. An 11-year-old girl, the daughter of an Oxford astronomy professor, chose the name Pluto—the god of the netherworld—for the new planet.

In 2006 Pluto famously lost its planetary status when it was determined to be a "dwarf planet," and not even the largest one. (That honor goes to a dwarf planet called Eris.) Pluto is, however, the largest object in the Kuiper belt—so it has that going for it, which is nice.

BAT MEAT IS A FOLK APHRODISIAC in parts of Indonesia and Malaysia. Bats are a fairly common food item there, so they're inexpensive in markets. Bats are served up like a Western romantic dinner—whole, like a lobster.

Don't have any Barry White CDs to get your partner in the mood?

ODD-PHRODISIACS

EXTRACTO DE RANA HAS BEEN SOLD FOR OVER A CENTURY IN THE OUTDOOR MARKETS OF LIMA, PERU. What is it? Frog juice, believed not only to increase sex drive but also to relieve asthma and fatigue. Here's how it works: A customer picks a live frog from a tank; the proprietor then kills, skins, and blends it with a mixture of white beans, honey, aloe vera, and maca, a plant-based stimulant (which is probably the real source of the increased virility).

NOT ALL APHRODISIACS ARE EDIBLE. One ancient Arabian formula calls for a man to catch and kill a vulture, chop up the meat, and mix it with honey and amalaka juice (an Asian berry). Rubbing his entire body with the meaty paste was said to enchant the ladies.

THE HOMIGLAS CULONAS, A SPECIES OF ANT NICKNAMED "THE BIG-BOTTOMED" ANT due to its wide mid- and end sections, is eaten as an aphrodisiac in Colombia. But only if it's a queen, and if its appendages are removed, and if it's roasted. It's believed to be so effective that it's a traditional wedding gift to Colombian newlyweds.

YOU MAY HAVE HEARD that soup made from the male organ of a tiger is considered an aphrodisiac in some cultures, and that sort of makes sense. A little more confusing: unhatched sea turtle eggs. It's unclear why, but they're consumed raw in Mexico. Their popularity (they're frequently stolen from American coastal areas) is thought to be one reason many sea turtle species are endangered.

IN NEPAL, SOME PEOPLE BELIEVE THAT DRINKING RHINOCEROS URINE increases sexual desire and male virility. It may be difficult to collect rhino pee, but it's so commonly regarded as an aphrodisiac that you can actually buy it in the gift shop of the Kathmandu Zoo—collected and bottled fresh daily by the staff.

Hi-Tech Toy Flops

Even if a toy is completely original and built around cutting-edge technology, it doesn't necessarily mean anyone will buy it.

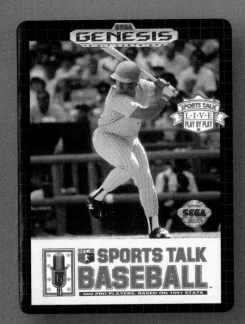

SPORTSTALK

By the late 1980s, kids (and adults) were buying baseball cards not just out of love of the game, but also as an investment. In 1989 LJN Toys tried to cash in on the craze with the Sportstalk—a handheld device, about the size of a Walkman, that "played" electronic baseball cards, each of which had a tiny vinyl record embedded on the back. Through the built-in speaker came two minutes of statistics about the player (voiced by Hall of Famer Joe Torre), along with radio calls of famous plays, and players reminiscing about their biggest moments on the field. It probably failed because it cost too much—$28 for the player and $2 per card. Toys "R" Us ordered half a million Sportstalks and sold fewer than 100,000.

JUICE BOX

In 2004 Mattel introduced the Juice Box, a personal, handheld, candy-colored video player for kids. But the Juice Box didn't play DVDs—kids (or their parents) had to buy the special $10 discs especially made for the device (titles included episodes of *Scooby-Doo* and *SpongeBob SquarePants*). To keep the device affordable (it retailed for $70), Mattel had to scrimp on technology: While regular video runs at 30 frames per second, Juice Box videos ran at 10 frames per second, producing a choppy image on a screen less than three inches wide, and in black and white. Industry experts say that despite its limitations, what ultimately forced the Juice Box off the market within a year of its introduction was the increasing popularity of built-in DVD players in cars and minivans.

VIRTUAL BOY

In the early 1990s, the next big thing in electronics was supposed to be virtual reality. Wearing a special helmet, a person would be able to inhabit lifelike imaginary, computerized worlds. But the only virtual-reality product ever released was a dud: Nintendo's Virtual Boy video game system. The $180 machine looked like a pair of binoculars perched on a tabletop tripod. There were two problems with the setup. First, it wasn't adjustable, resulting in lots of neck cramps; second, it was impossible to play with eyeglasses on. On top of that, the games weren't in color—that would have pushed the price to more than $500, so they were rendered in a fuzzy black, red, and blue display which created a 3-D effect. The image was so difficult to see

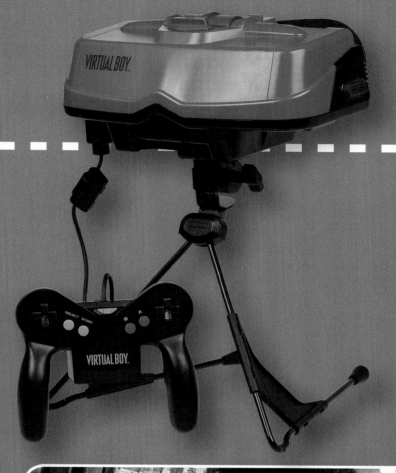

that headaches due to eye strain were common (the Virtual Boy had a built-in feature that made it turn off every 15 minutes to give players a chance to rest their eyes). Only 14 games were made for the system, including Virtual Bowling and Virtual Fishing. Only about 700,000 were sold, making it the biggest flop in Nintendo history.

CAPTAIN POWER

Televideo Interactive debuted in 1987 with Captain Power, the first of what was supposed to be a line of toys that interacted with TV shows. The toys were spaceships and military command centers that kids put in front of the TV during action sequences of *Captain Power and the Soldiers of the Future* broadcasts. The toys fired at the screen, and the screen fired back, causing the spaceship to light up, shake, and make noise. If an "enemy" from TV scored a "hit," it would eject the pilot figure from the spaceship.

The show itself was a live-action, high-budget production with lots of special effects...but it was a failure. Why? Because the show was no fun to watch without the toys (which cost upwards of $50), and the toys were no fun without the show, which featured a cast of no-name actors and aired in most markets in a seldom-watched 6:00 a.m. Sunday time slot.

KEITH RICHARDS SANG IN THE CHOIR AT QUEEN ELIZABETH II'S CORONATION.

121

Grip the Raven

You can find inspiration in the oddest places.

POE THING

On the third floor of the Philadelphia Free Library is a glass case displaying a stuffed crow. It's a raven, to be precise—the very bird considered by many scholars to have been the inspiration for Edgar Allan Poe's classic poem "The Raven." How this stuffed bird came to inspire Poe's poetry lies in the life and work of another great 19th century writer: Charles Dickens. Dickens had a talking raven named Grip as a pet. The bird delighted his family and friends with lines like, "Keep up your spirit!" "Never say die!" and

"Polly, put the kettle on, we'll all have tea!" Grip died in 1841 after eating lead paint off a wall, an event Dickens recounted in a letter to a friend: "On the clock striking twelve he appeared slightly agitated, but soon recovered, stopped to bark, staggered, exclaimed, 'Halloa, old girl!' and died."

RISING FROM THE ASHES

Dickens had the bird stuffed and set in a glass case. His novel *Barnaby Rudge*, published later that year, featured a talking raven named Grip. When the bird first appears in the book, someone asks, "What was that tapping at the door?" Someone else answers, "'Tis someone knocking softly at the shutter." Edgar Allan Poe was working as a reviewer for *Graham's Magazine* when *Barnaby Rudge* was printed in the United States. His review was favorable, except for one major flaw: the talking raven. Poe felt it could have been more "prophetically heard in the course of the drama." Four years later, Poe published his famous poem, with its lines "Suddenly there came a tapping...at my chamber door," and "Quoth the

OPPOSITE LEFT: Engraving of Charles Dickens
OPPOSITE, RIGHT: Engraving from an early edition of *Barnaby Rudge*, featuring Grip the raven

ABOVE: Edgar Allan Poe, c. 1845, the time of the publication of "The Raven"
ABOVE LEFT: An engraved illustration from the first edition
BELOW: Grip the raven as he is today, in the Philadelphia Free Library

Raven, 'Nevermore.'" The poem was an immediate success and secured Poe's lasting reputation in American literature.

FLY AWAY HOME

As for Grip, after Dickens' death the bird and case were sold at auction (the bird went for $210; the letter describing its death for $385), eventually ending up in the collection of Col. Richard Gimbel, the world's foremost collector of Poe memorabilia. By then Grip's association with Poe's poem had been well established by scholars. In 1971 Gimbel's entire collection, including the bird, was donated to the Philadelphia Library, where you can still see it today in the Rare Book department.

Let's Play Fireball Soccer

Bored by baseball? Fed up by football? Try these weird, weird sports instead.

Playing Fireball Soccer in Indonesia

Robot Camel Racing in the UAE

Wadloping in the Netherlands

Fireball Soccer

It's just like regular soccer, except the ball has been doused in gasoline and then set on fire. Invented in Indonesia, it's played by martial arts students trying to overcome their fear of fire (a healthy fear, if you ask us). Making fireball soccer even more difficult—they play it in bare feet.

Robot Camel Racing

Camel racing is the most popular spectator sport in the United Arab Emirates. The traditional choice for camel jockeys has always been children—they're small and lightweight. Until now. When human rights groups actively started to condemn the practice as a form of slavery, U.A.E. officials found an alternative: They hired several private high-tech labs to create a generation of robot jockeys. These humanoid robots are smaller and lighter than child jockeys and respond to commands via a remote control system mounted on the camel.

Wadloping

If you suffer from agoraphobia (a fear of open spaces), then you may want to avoid this sport. And if you don't like mud, it's even worse. It takes place in the Waddenzee, a shallow inlet separating the northern Netherlands mainland from the East Frisian Islands. Entrants leap off a dike on Holland's north coast into the knee-deep sulfurous mud and trudge across the Waddenzee to Simonzand Island, four hours away by foot. And in the middle of the race, you can't see any land, just mud as far as the eye can see. So many entrants have become lost and disoriented that they now have to race with a guide.

Shin Kicking

Also known as "purring" in Wales, here's how it's played: Two men stand face to face with their hands on each other's shoulders. At the signal, they start kicking each other's shins until one loses his grip

Chessboxing, Berlin 2008

Shin Kicking in Wales

Conger Cuddling in Lyme Regis, England

Quidditch at Middlebury College Vermont

on his opponent. (This sport has failed to catch on in other nations.)

Chessboxing

Inspired by a Serbian comic book, chessboxing is exactly what the name implies: chess and boxing. Opponents box for one round, then sit at a table adjacent to the ring and play a four-minute round of chess. Then they go back to boxing, then chess, until a winner is determined in either one event or the other.

Conger Cuddling

Since 1974, sports fans have flocked to the English village of Lyme Regis to watch two nine-man teams try to knock each other off of a wooden platform...by swinging five-foot dead eels at each other. (A conger is a type of eel.) In 2006 the contest was almost cancelled when animal-rights activists protested the event because "it's disgraceful to the memory of the eel." The contest was held—with rubber boat fenders instead of dead eels.

Quidditch

How exactly do you play this fictional sport—invented by J. K. Rowling for the Harry Potter book series—in which witches and wizards fly through the air on broomsticks, trying to throw a ball through a goal? And one of the balls—called the Golden Snitch—is actually sentient? In 2005 students at Middlebury College in Vermont modified the game so it can be played by Muggles (the non-magical). Rather than fly on broomsticks, the players run up and down a field holding broomsticks between their legs as they attempt to throw foam "bludgers" into the goal. The golden snitch is portrayed by a person dressed head to toe in yellow spandex who runs around the field erratically. More than 150 colleges now boast quidditch teams Players are not required to wear flowing wizard robes and pointy wizard hats...but most do anyway.

Oddballs

People are strange. Strange people are even stranger.

THE WOMAN WHO WENT NUTS

"Nuts are fresh tokens of primeval existence," said Elizabeth "the Nut Lady" Tashjian. She started collecting her "fresh tokens" in 1973 and never stopped for the rest of her life. The Nut Lady crammed her Connecticut mansion full of all kinds of nuts, things made from nuts, things that are used with nuts, and things that are inspired by nuts—including the "Nut Anthem," which she wrote herself. "Oh nutttts," she crooned, "have a bee-youtee-ful his-tory and lorrrre..." Her Nut Museum was quite popular with tourists, despite the fact that the Connecticut Department of Tourism removed it from its official guide in 1988, claiming the house was overrun with squirrels. The museum closed for good in 2002, and Tashjian passed five years after that. But in her 94 years on this Earth, she was able to spread the joy of her passion to countless others. One of her biggest accomplishments: She got to show David Letterman her nuts.

ABOVE: The Nut Lady stands by her own painting of nutcrackers, in 1972
LEFT: The Nut Lady's house in Old Lyme, Connecticut, the site of the Nut Museum

THE FIRST LETTER VANNA WHITE EVER TURNED ON *WHEEL OF FORTUNE* WAS A "T."

THE COLOR OF WRITING

Alexandre Dumas (1802–70), author of *The Three Musketeers* and *The Count of Monte Cristo*, always wrote his novels on blue paper, his poetry on yellow paper, and his non-fiction on rose-colored paper. Always. To do otherwise, he explained, was "unspeakable."

VAMPING

In order to be a vampire, you have to 1) sleep all day, 2) drink blood, and 3) be undead. Covering two out of three of those criteria are a married English couple—Vanian, 53, and his wife Ethereal Dark, 27—who call themselves "real-life vampires." (They're not quite undead yet.) And there are a few other vampire-y things they lack: "We don't sleep in coffins," explains Ethereal Dark. "We don't walk around with fangs, either." They do drink blood, though only a few drops a week, and only each other's. "Too much blood would make you vomit," explains Vanian, also noting the risk of infection from drinking a stranger's blood. Plus, to take blood from someone unwillingly, he says, would be "a form of assault." Also, they don't mind crucifixes or churches. And you can see their reflections. But other than all of those things, they're totally vampires! Why did the couple tell their story to the *Daily Mail* in 2014? "So people would be open-minded and accept us for who we are," explained Ethereal Dark. Vanian added, "Also, we don't sparkle."

SHE MUST REALLY LOVE CATS

According to *Guinness World Records*, the largest world's largest collection of cat memorabilia belongs to a French woman named Florence Groff. She reportedly owns "11,717 cat-related items, including 2,118 different cat figurines."

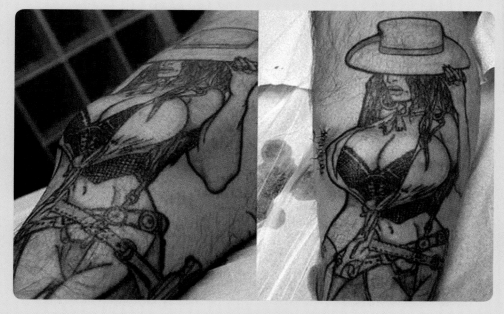

LEG WARMERS

Lane Jensen, an Alberta tattoo artist, has a tattoo of a large-breasted cowgirl on his left leg. In 2007 he decided his cowgirl didn't look buxom enough. So his tattoo got "breast" implants—dime-sized bags of silicone inserted into his leg under the tattoo. Two weeks later, Jensen lost a liter of lymphatic fluid from his leg—his body had rejected the implants. "I guess my girl wasn't meant to have 3-D breasts," he said.

ABOVE, LEFT: Alexander Dumas, circa 1855
ABOVE, RIGHT: Vanian and Ethereal Dark, vamping it up
BELOW: Lane Jensen's well-endowed tattoo

WORLD'S SHORTEST PLAY: SAMUEL BECKETT'S *BREATH*—35 SECONDS OF SCREAMING AND BREATHING.

127

COINED BY COMIC STRIPS

SECURITY BLANKET

ORIGIN: Pioneering child psychologist Richard Passman is given credit for identifying the phenomenon of children habitually clutching or carrying a favorite toy for comfort and security. Charles Schulz first used the concept in the June 1, 1954, *Peanuts* comic strip by giving Linus a blanket to carry everywhere he went. Linus called it his "security blanket." The term is now used by psychologists to define a child's (or anyone's) excessive attachment to a particular object.

"WE HAVE MET THE ENEMY AND HE IS US."

ORIGIN: After winning the Battle of Lake Erie in the War of 1812, Commodore Oliver Perry wrote in a dispatch to General William

Many common words and phrases were invented by cartoonists and first used in comic strips.

Henry Harrison, "We have met the enemy, and he is ours." Walt Kelly, author of the comic strip *Pogo*, reworded the phrase as "We have met the enemy and he is us," in the foreword to his 1953 Pogo collection *The Pogo Papers*. The meaning: Mankind's greatest threat is...mankind. The quote became better known when Kelly used it on a poster he was hired to illustrate for the first Earth Day in 1970.

THE HEEBIE-JEEBIES

ORIGIN: Billy DeBeck coined the term in his hugely popular 1920s comic strip, *Barney Google and Snuffy Smith*, about a community of backwoods hillbillies and

moonshiners. It first appeared in a 1923 strip where Barney tells someone to "get that stupid look offa your pan. You gimme the heeby jeebys!" It meant "a feeling of discomfort." Other phrases coined by DeBeck: "horsefeathers," "hotsie-totsie," and "googly-eyed" (after Barney Google, who had huge, bulbous eyes). The strip also gave us the nickname "Sparky," from the name of Barney's horse, Sparkplug. (Many young comic-strip fans were given the nickname "Sparky," among them, *Peanuts* creator Charles Schulz.)

MILQUETOAST

ORIGIN: "Milk toast" was a

OPPOSITE, FAR LEFT: Bill Holman's 1930s' *Smokey Stover The Foo Fighter*; OPPOSITE, TOP LEFT: *Peanuts*' characters Charlie Brown and Linus, who holds his security blanket; OPPOSITE, RIGHT: Walt Kelly's poster for Earth Day, 1970; TOP LEFT: Billy DeBeck, who coined the term "the Heebie-Jeebies" in 1923; LEFT: Harold Webster's Caspar Milquetoast, *The Timid Soul*; ABOVE: Al Capp originated the phrase "Sadie Hawkins Day" in his strip *Li'l Abner*.

simple dish (toast served in milk) frequently served at soup kitchens in the 1920s. Harold Webster named the main character in his late 1920s strip, *The Timid Soul*, Caspar Milquetoast. Thanks to the comic strip, by the 1930s the word "milquetoast" had become common slang to describe anybody who, like Milquetoast, was weak and timid.

SADIE HAWKINS DAY

ORIGIN: It's from Al Capp's *Li'l Abner*. One day a year in the comic strip's rural setting of Dogpatch, single women would chase the single men around. If they caught one, they got to keep—er, marry

him. The day got its name from Sadie Hawkins, the first woman in Dogpatch who caught a husband that way. High schools in the United States still hold "Sadie Hawkins Dances," to which the girls invite the boys.

FOO FIGHTER

ORIGIN: In Bill Holman's 1930s strip *Smokey Stover*, the title character rode around in a bizarre-looking two-wheeled fire engine (with a fire hydrant attached to it) that Smokey called a "foo fighter." The term was used by World War II pilots for any unidentified aircraft (including UFOs). The phrase became popular again in the 1990s

thanks to the hard rock band, the Foo Fighters. "Had I imagined that we would last more than a month and a half," confessed frontman Dave Grohl in 2014, "I might have named it something else. It's the dumbest band name ever."

Here Comes the Spammobile

You've heard of the Oscar Mayer Wienermobile; maybe you've even seen it in person. Here are a few more vehicles to watch for while Uncle John finalizes his design for the Pot Rod.

THE SPAMMOBILE

Looks Like: A blue bus with big Spam decals on each side that are supposed to make it look like a big can of Spam. What it really looks like is a city bus covered with Spam ads.

Details: The "Spambassadors" who drive the Spammobile crisscross the United States handing out free spample-sized Spamburgers (patties of Spam Lite, Less Sodium Spam, Smoked-Flavored Spam, Oven Roasted Turkey Spam, and regular Spam on tiny hamburger buns) to the public. Mmmmmm!

THE ZIPPO CAR

Looks Like: A 1940s-era black sedan, with the passenger compartment ripped out and replaced by two giant Zippo lighters, with their tops flipped open and neon flames sticking out.

Details: Zippo founder George G. Blaisdell had the first Zippo Car built onto a Chrysler Saratoga New Yorker in 1947. It cost him $25,000, which was a lot of money back then. But Blaisdell didn't have much to show for it—the car was so heavy that the tires blew out regularly. Rebuilding it onto a Ford truck chassis would have solved the problem, but the redesign made the car several inches taller than government regulations allowed. The estimate for fixing that problem was $40,000, so Blaisdell abandoned the project. Apparently he never even picked it back up from the Ford dealership that was hired to do the work.

The dealership eventually went out of business; no one knows what happened to the car, but it probably ended up at the wrecking yard. A replica of the original car was built in 1996 (hopefully with better tires).

THE ECKRICH FUNHOUSE

Looks Like: Eckrich makes sausages, and it's not easy being a sausage company in search of a promotional vehicle. Why? If you go with the obvious, a sausage shape, you'll just remind people of the competition—the Oscar Mayer Wienermobile. Having missed the wiener boat, Eckrich settled for a cartoon-looking house.

Details: They call it the Funhouse (it has windows with flower boxes filled with daisies that squirt water at unsuspecting passersby). There's nothing particularly sausagey at all about it, except maybe that most people eat their sausages at home. But, hey—Eckrich had to come up with something.

THE MEOW MIX MOBILE

Looks Like: A van converted into a crouching cat that looks like it's about to pounce. The cat comes complete with a motorized tongue that licks "whisker to whisker" 20 times a minute.

Details: A lot of promotional vehicles raise money for charity; Clawde the Red Lobster (an ad-mobile for the Red Lobster restaurant chain) supports the Special Olympics, for example. But the Meow Mix Mobile has a charity all its own: Meows on Wheels. "As the Meow Mix Mobile

travels around the country, it will be delivering Meow Mix brand cat food to people who have difficulty purchasing it themselves," the company's website says. "If you know any cat owners who are homebound, elderly or disabled, or for any reason have difficulty getting to the store to purchase food for their cats, we want to hear from you."

MORE ROLLING COMMERCIALS

THE MR. PEANUT HOT ROD

A motor home remade into a peanut-shaped race car, complete with a giant engine block sticking out of the "hood" and a giant Mr. Peanut sitting in the faux driver's seat. Why a hot rod? Mr. Peanut is "the Official Snack of NASCAR."

THE LIFESAVERS PEP-O-MINT CAR

One of the coolest vehicles of all, the 1918 Pep-O-Mint car looked just like a roll of Lifesavers on four of those old-fashioned wooden spoked wheels. The driver sat right in the middle of the roll; the O in Pep-O-Mint served as the left- and right-side windows.

THE HERSHEY'S KISSMOBILE

Looks like three big foil-wrapped Kisses (Regular, Almond, and Hugs) sitting on a giant Hershey's bar. The driver sits in the regular Hershey's Kiss (it has a curvy, kiss-shaped windshield); the other two kisses hold free samples.

The Tourist of Death

Here's a recipe for an Internet phenomenon: Begin with a major disaster, create an improbable image that cuts to the core of the disaster, and then distribute the image to a stunned and gullible public.

INBOX HORROR

Were you one of the millions of people who was e-mailed an eerie photograph in the weeks after the terrorist attacks of September 11, 2001? A young man wearing a black ski coat and knit cap is standing on the observation deck of the World Trade Center with Manhattan in the background. Behind him, a jet airliner is flying straight for the building, just seconds away from crashing into the floors below. The date stamp on the bottom right corner: "9-11-01."

By telling two conflicting stories—the blissfully ignorant tourist, and the hijacked plane that was about to take his life—the image perfectly captured the sense of security and complacency that Americans felt before the terrorists shattered it and "changed everything." The caption on the photo drove home the point even more:

This picture was from a camera found in the wreckage of the WTC, developed by the FBI for evidence and released on the net today. The guy still has no

name and is missing. Makes you see things from a very different position. Please share this and find any way you can to help Americans not to be victims in the future of such cowardly attacks.

WAIT A SECOND...

The photo was convincing enough at first...until people took a closer look at it. Why was the tourist wearing a coat and hat when the attack took place on a warm summer morning? Why was he on

the observation deck a half-hour before it opened? Why was the plane in the photo coming from the north, when it actually approached from the south? Oh, and why was it the *wrong kind of plane*?

But those inconsistencies didn't slow it down. According to columnist J. Scott Wilson: "In one day, I received no less than 150 copies of it from various readers, friends, and acquaintances. Despite the numerous impossibilities present in the

photo, folks just seemed to accept it at face value." But not everyone. Many wanted to know: Who was this guy? Who manipulated the photo? And why?

But before any answers were found, the image took on a life of its own all over the Internet. Several websites sprang up, such as TouristOfDeath.com and TheTouristGuy.com, featuring shots of "Waldo" (as he came to be known) showing up in other photos of historic disasters. There he was, posing in front of the Hindenburg as it went down in flames! And then in Tokyo, while Godzilla laid waste to the city! And

there he was back on the World Trade Center, but now, instead of a plane, he's about to be done in by the Stay Puft Marshmallow Man from *Ghostbusters*!

WHODUNNIT?

All the hype and spin-offs only added to the mystery of who this man in the photo really was. Over the next few weeks, commentators and pundits alike blamed everyone from bored students at MIT, to a "true-blooded American" attempting to stir up patriotism, to Osama Bin Laden sympathizers who wanted to gloat. And then, in early November, a 41-year-old

Brazilian businessman named José Roberto Penteado sent an e-mail to *Wired News*: "I believe that some friends planted my face onto that body." He said he'd never even been to New York and couldn't explain why someone would do it, but the guy in the photo looked just like him. Penteado became an instant celebrity. He appeared on several Brazilian talk shows and was featured in news stories all over the world. People approached him on the street and asked for his autograph, and Volkswagen's Brazilian subsidiary offered to buy the rights to the image from him and put it in a series of TV commercials. Suddenly, Penteado stood to profit...for doing absolutely nothing at all. There was one problem, though: Although he resembled the Tourist of Death, why didn't he have the original photo that his head was lifted from? And why was his jaw wider than the Tourist of Death's? And, when people really scrutinized it, Penteado's face appeared to have a different shape altogether.

Meanwhile, halfway around the world in Hungary, a group of friends knew for certain that Penteado was a fake, because they knew who the real fake was.

EXPOSED

Back in November 1997, a 21-year-old man named Peter Guzli from Budapest, Hungary, had taken a vacation to New York City. While sightseeing, his buddy snapped a few shots of him on top of the WTC. Nearly four years later, shortly after the attacks occurred, Guzli found himself drawn to that picture folder. On

a lark, he searched online and found an image of a plane (which was actually sitting on a tarmac in Houston, Texas, when the photo was taken) and then used Photoshop to cut the plane out of the picture and superimpose it over the background of his vacation shot. He added the fake time stamp and sent it to a few friends as a joke...never expecting that one of them would send it to his friends, who then sent it to their friends, and so on, and so on.

The more famous his doctored image became, the less Guzli wanted anything to do with it. He knew that a lot of shellshocked Americans would take offense at his attempt at dark humor. But then, when Penteado's fame began to spread, Guzli's friends urged him to come forward and claim the money for the VW commercial himself. Guzli refused, so his friends decided to do it for him. Two months after the picture first went viral, images with and without the plane were posted onto a Hungarian news site. From there,

the mainstream press got hold of the pictures, and the Tourist of Death finally had a name.

STAYING OUT OF DANGER

When Guzli was pressed for an explanation, he admitted that he "didn't have sleepless nights" over the incident, "but I certainly didn't want people to point their fingers at me on the street. I don't think this thing has to do with empathy or the lack of it. The people I intended it for all said they had a great laugh. That's all." When asked if he planned to profit from his fame, Guzli said he'd think about it. But after Volkswagen withdrew their offer (apparently realizing how tacky it would be to profit from such a horrific event), Guzli happily went back to anonymity. But that picture—recently named by several publications as one of the most powerful images of the 2000s—will live on in infamy, along with its hundreds of silly variations.

THERE ARE AS MANY MOLECULES IN A TEASPOON OF WATER AS THERE ARE TEASPOONS OF WATER IN THE ATLANTIC.

They might be fed up

One of our favorite bands, They Might Be Giants, issued this "things you may no longer say" list of overused phrases to their friends and crew. So if you roll with them, don't go there, or they'll throw you under the bus.

- "Too much information"
- "Off the hook"
- "That's what she said"
- "My bad"
- "Game changer"
- "I can't work under these conditions"
- "Playing the (whatever) card"
- "Throw someone under the bus"
- "Drinking the kool-aid"
- "LOL"

- "Phone tag"
- "Don't go there"
- "Crackberry"
- "It's all good"
- "It is what it is"
- "Talk to the hand"
- "Think outside the box"
- "Off the reservation"
- "Oh no you didn't"
- "I threw up a little in my mouth"
- "Give one-hundred and ten percent"

- "IMHO" (short for "In My Humble Opinion")
- "No worries"
- "Jumped the shark"
- "Voted off the island"
- "(Anything) on acid"
- "(Anything) from hell"
- "(Anything) on steroids"
- "Literally" (unless used in its correct context)"
- "That's how we roll"
- (The list itself is now on the list too.)

The Great Wall of... Florida

Why go all the way to Paris, France, to see the Eiffel Tower when you can visit Paris, Texas, and admire a 50-foot replica...wearing a bright red cowboy hat?

The Statue of Liberty, New York City
Replica: Paris, France
Details: France gave the original statue to the United States in 1886 to honor the friendship between the two countries. To show their appreciation, Americans living in Paris built a 35-foot replica in 1889. It stands on the Isle de Grenelle in the middle of the Seine River. But there's more: Between 1949 and 1951, the Boy Scouts of America donated about 200 eight-foot-tall copper Statue of Liberty replicas to towns across the U.S. (San Juan, Puerto Rico, and Cheyenne, Wyoming, each have one). The French have some as well: one in Barentin, made for a film; one in Colmar, birthplace of the original statue's designer, Frédéric Auguste Bartholdi; and one in Bordeaux.

The Great Wall of China
Replica: Kissimmee, Florida
Details: The original is 4,163 miles long and is considered one of the Seven Wonders of the World. The one in Florida isn't. This half-mile recreation is located at the Florida Splendid China Theme Park, built in 1993. It took 6.5 million bricks to construct. The Theme Park closed its doors in 2003 and has been left abandoned ever since.

The Leaning Tower of Pisa, Italy
Replica: Niles, Illinois
Details: Industrialist Robert Ilg constructed the 94-foot "Leaning Tower of Niles" in 1934 to honor the Italian "Father of Modern Science"—Galileo. Only half the size of the original, it matches the exact angle of the Pisa tower's distinctive tilt. Do the Italians approve? Yes—Niles and Pisa officially became "sister cities" in 1991.

The Hollywood Sign, Los Angeles, California
Replica: Palermo, Italy
Details: In 2001 Italian "post-studio" artist Maurizio Cattelan oversaw the installation of a giant, oversized replica of the famous Hollywood sign. "I had been working on icons," Cattelan explained of the piece. "The Pope, Adolf. I wanted to use one that would not be an icon, but a word. A word has more faces." Each of the nine letters is 75 feet high, and the sign measures 557 feet across (the original is only 450 feet across). It sits on Bellolampo Hill, overlooking Palermo's garbage dump.

Easter Island statues, South Pacific Ocean
Replica: Hunt, Texas
Details: Located in a field off Texas State Highway 39, these dimensionally accurate re-creations of the facelike statues of Easter Island were built by

local artisans Doug Hill and Al Sheppard. Bonus: If you visit, you'll get two for one—the statues share their space with a replica of another ancient monument, Stonehenge.

Washington Monument, Washington, D.C.

Replica: Pope's Creek, Virginia

Details: It's less than an hour from the actual Washington Monument, but if you're tired of the real thing you can always go here. It's part of the George Washington's Birthplace National Monument—Pope's Creek is where George was born—and although it doesn't have many relics from his childhood, it does have this 56- foot recreation of the monument (the actual one is 555 feet tall).

Eiffel Tower, Paris, France

Replica: Paris, Texas

Details: Paris, Texas, erected a 55-foot Eiffel Tower in 1993 in honor of its French namesake. When officials in Paris, Tennessee, heard about it, they built one 60 feet tall. Paris, Texas, fought back and made theirs five feet taller. Then, Paris, Tennessee, made theirs five feet taller. In 1998 Paris, Texas, put a bright red cowboy hat on their tower, making it a few inches taller. But neither beats the 540-foot replica in Las Vegas (or the 1,052-foot original in Paris, France).

"BLESS THIS HOUSE" AND "LOVE IS BLIND" ARE BOTH PHRASES FROM CHAUCER'S WRITINGS.

Uncle John has been itching to write about this subject for a long time.

Life's an Itch

WHY DO WE ITCH?

No one knows exactly why we itch, or how it works. "The itch," says Jeffrey Bernhard, of the Massachusetts Medical Center "is one of, if not the, most mysterious of all 'cutaneous intrusions.'"

Some scientists speculate that its function is to remove parasites and other foreign objects from the skin. Or it may serve as an "early warning system" for the body's borders. Sometimes itching is a warning of a serious disease.

Itching has a lot in common with pain—they even travel through the same kind of nerve cells (neurons). In fact, scientists once thought itching was a kind of pain. Now they're pretty sure itching and pain are two entirely separate functions.

Health experts divide itches into two different categories: sensory itches and allergic itches. They also say that scratching almost always makes itches worse.

SENSORY ITCHES

These are caused when special nerve endings in your skin called Merkel's discs (but referred to by doctors as "itch nerves") detect pressure on your skin. They immediately send nerve signals to the spinal cord, which sends them

on to the brain.

Your brain checks out the signals: If they're caused by something your body's used to—like clothes you wear all the time—it files the signals away in your subconscious. You don't even notice they're there.

But if the stimulus is new and unfamiliar—say you're wearing a new hat, or you have several days of new beard growth—your brain sends out a "foreign irritant" alert and makes you aware something's there. How? By making you itch—trying to get you to brush the irritant away.

At the same time, your brain is sending signals to the muscles in your hands and arms to start scratching. That's why you scratch even when you sleep.

Fortunately, your brain adapts to new sensations fairly quickly. So if the irritant hangs around for a while, the brain will calm down and start rerouting signals to your

subconscious. The irritant is still there, but the itch goes away.

ALLERGIC ITCHES

Allergic itching is what happens when a foreign body—e.g., medication or an insect bite—irritates your immune system. The immune system responds by releasing histamine, the chemical that is the body's main response to allergies. Histamine is the stuff that gives you rashes.

Histamine does several things to the nearby cells that makes it easier for them to fight off the allergen—it causes the blood vessels to dilate; it makes it easier for fluids to pass through the affected skin cells; and it stimulates nearby nerve endings.

In most cases, your body will get rid of the histamine naturally in 18 to 24 hours; antihistamine

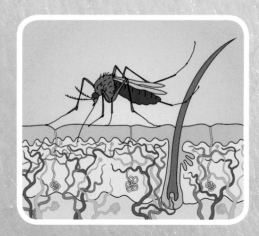

medications can do the same job in a couple of hours, but serious allergies can take much longer.

SCRATCH FEVER

Why do itches get worse when you scratch them? Because when you scratch, you irritate a second set of nerve endings—the ones that transmit pain. So even if you get rid of the original irritant, you've created a whole new one—you. Scratching also temporarily thickens your skin. "It sets up

what I call a hot spot," says Dr. Nia Terezakis, a New Orleans dermatologist. "Scratching thickens the skin, and when skin gets thicker, it itches more. You've got a nervous itch going. You stimulate the nerves to fire more and more." With allergic rashes, the problem is even worse. On top of irritating the nerve endings and thickening your skin, you also spread the histamine into unaffected cells—which makes the rash bigger.

SCRATCH FACTS

● Do you itch when you come in from the cold? That's because cold weather "numbs" your nerve endings... which makes them transmit signals more slowly. But when you get back

into a warm environment, your nerve endings spring back into action and flood the brain with itch signals. Your brain makes you feel itchy until it adjusts to the warmth.

● Wool is itchier than most fabrics because it stimulates two types of nerve endings at once: the pressure of the wool against your skin activates the itch nerves, and the individual fibers tickle the nerve endings that are wrapped around your hair shafts.

● No one knows why people itch so strongly at the base of the shoulder blades, the very place that's impossible to reach and scratch. "It's an intense itching that drives people crazy," says Dr. David R. Harris, a Stanford University dermatologist. "And no one knows why this occurs. We think it might be a peculiar reaction to the nerve fibers, but we don't know for sure."

● Chicken pox gets its name from the itch, not chickens. The ailment was originally called *gican pox* in Old English, which meant "itchy pox."

● It takes about three minutes from the time a mosquito bites you for the bite to begin itching.

● Everyone itches at least once a day. Even thinking about itching can make you itch.

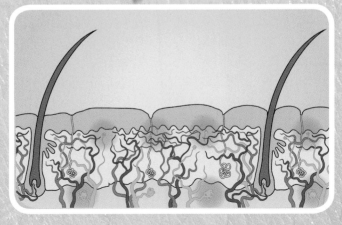

It's a perennial news story: some dictator is oppressing his people, plundering his country's treasury, and defying international law. Then suddenly he's out of power. You assume he's in prison. More likely, he's living in the lap of luxury...

Exile on Easy Street

Dictator: Augusto Pinochet, Chile

Reign of Terror: Pinochet came to power in a CIA-assisted coup in 1973. During his rule, tens of thousands of Chileans were tortured, killed, or "disappeared." Pinochet relinquished power amid growing opposition in 1990 but remained the commander-in-chief until 1998, when he became "senator-for-life."

Where'd he go? While visiting England in 1998, Pinochet was arrested by British authorities on charges of torture and genocide. During his house-arrest, he lived at Wentworth, an exclusive estate outside of London. Estimated cost: $10,000 a month. After a long legal battle, a British court ruled that he was too sick to stand trial. Pinochet went back to Chile, where he was arrested again, with more than 200 charges against him. In 2002 the Chilean Supreme Court ruled him unfit for trial and all charges were dropped. During his house-arrest in Chile, Pinochet got the same royal treatment he had in England: He lived on a baronial estate overlooking the Pacific Ocean.

Dictator: Alfredo Stroessner, Paraguay

Reign of Terror: He took over Paraguay in a military coup in 1954 and ruled for more than 35 years. (He was "reelected" eight times.) Stroessner was a participant in Operation Condor, a police action that tortured, disappeared, or executed hundreds of thousands of people in South America. And he helped turn Paraguay into a haven for Nazi war criminals.

Where'd he go? Stroessner was overthrown in 1989 and fled to neighboring Brazil, where he lived a quiet, comfortable life until he died in 2006 at age 93.

Dictator: Mengistu Haile Mariam, Ethiopia

Reign of Terror: Mengistu overthrew Emperor Haile Selassie in 1974 and turned to the Soviets for help in starting a Marxist regime. During the two-year campaign dubbed "the Red Terror," tens of thousands of "enemies of the revolution" were murdered. When families came to claim the bodies, they had to pay for the bullets that killed their loved ones before they could take them. After the fall of the Soviet Union in 1989, Mengistu lost support and was finally overthrown in 1991.

Where'd he go? He fled to Zimbabwe as a "guest" of President Robert Mugabe, where he still lives in a heavily guarded, luxurious mansion. Though he's formally charged with "crimes

against humanity" in Ethiopia, Zimbabwe refuses to extradite him.

Dictator: Jean-Claude "Baby Doc" Duvalier, Haiti

Reign of Terror: At the age of 19, he succeeded his father, "Papa Doc," as president-for-life. During his 15-year reign, tens of thousands of Haitians were tortured and killed. As Haiti turned into one of the world's poorest nations, Baby Doc stole an estimated $500 million.

Where'd he go? Although never officially granted asylum, Duvalier moved to France in 1986, taking the stolen money with him. He lived in a villa in the hills above Cannes, drove a Ferrari, and owned two apartments in Paris and a chateau. According to news reports, Duvalier went broke. How? He lost everything in his divorce from his wife, Michelle

Duvalier, in the mid-1990s. He returned to Haiti a year after the devastating 2010 earthquake, vowing to help "rebuild" the island nation. But Duvalier was charged with several crimes, and was still awaiting trial—while living in luxury during his house-arrest—when he died of a heart attack in 2014.

TOP LEFT: Augusto Pinochet, the Chilean Dictator arrested in 1998 during a visit to the UK, had previously been made welcome in Britain by Margaret Thatcher, when her Conservative government was in power.
TOP RIGHT: "Baby Doc" Duvalier, Haiti
ABOVE LEFT: Alfredo Stroessner, the Paraguay dictator, who helped turn his country into a haven for Nazi war criminals
ABOVE: Mengistu Haile Mariam of Ethiopia

DENTURES WERE ONCE MADE WITH TEETH PULLED FROM THE MOUTHS OF DEAD SOLDIERS.

141

What's Up, Chuck?

You may want to read this article on an empty stomach.

HURLER IN CHIEF

While on a 12-day trip through the western Pacific in 1992, President George H. W. Bush came down with an intestinal flu. He carried on with his schedule anyway, but he still wasn't feeling well at a state dinner in the home of Japanese Prime Minister Kiichi Miyazawa. Result: Bush threw up all over himself. The prime minister held Bush's head in his lap until the president had recovered sufficiently to walk to his limo for a speedy return to his hotel. (Bush wore a green overcoat given to him by a Secret Service agent to cover up the unsightly mess on his suit.) The incident inspired the birth of a new Japanese verb: *bushusuru*—to do a Bush, or "to commit an instance of embarrassing public vomiting."

TWO PUKEY LAWSUITS

● When Luiz Fernandes Peres was ready to settle his tab at the Taverna Pub Medieval Bar in Natal, Brazil, he noticed a "puke tax" had been added to his bill. The bartender explained it was because one of Peres's friends had thrown up in the bathroom. Angry, Peres sued the bar. "I consider this extortion," he told the local newspaper. The bar's owner defended the fee, saying they've been charging it to people who vomit on the premises for years.

● Austin Aitken was a regular viewer of NBC's gross-out game show *Fear Factor*. He had no problem watching people eat worms, but claimed a 2005 episode that had contestants eat rats chopped up in a blender made his blood pressure rise, made him dizzy and lightheaded, and ultimately, made him vomit. So he sued NBC for $2.5 million. "It's barbaric," he said, "some of the things they ask these individuals to do." The suit was thrown out of court.

NATURE SPEWS

● Hungry pigeons will eat human vomit.

● A shark vomits by thrusting its stomach out of its mouth and then pulling it back in.

● Flies spend 30% of their time throwing up...on your food.

● Rats are easy to poison because they cannot vomit. (Neither can horses or rabbits.)

● In 2002 paleontologists discovered 160-million-year-old fossilized dinosaur barf.

● Petrels are pigeon-size natives of

WHEN IN ROME

In ancient Roman times, throwing up was considered a status symbol. If you could afford to eat so much food that you made yourself sick, you were clearly better off than the lower classes. (Even Julius Caesar liked to vomit after a big dinner.) But contrary to popular belief, the Romans didn't vomit in vomitoriums. Why not? A vomitorium was actually a passageway in a theater or sports arena that people would "spew out of" when the play or event was over.

Antarctica that defend their nests by throwing up on predators. They have two stomachs: one for digesting food—mostly fish or shrimp—and another for storing a special orange oil. They can barf that orange goo a distance of three feet and sometimes farther. If you happen to be the target of the petrel's vomit, you'll stink of fish...for days.

YOU GOTTA THROW UP BEFORE YOU GROW UP

A 17-year-old boy in Olathe, Kansas, told his friends that he was planning to play a major prank on his Spanish teacher (the boy was failing the class). On the last day of school in June 2005, he walked up to the teacher and vomited all over him. A local judge found the teen guilty of battery. His punishment: four months of cleaning up the vomit of people who throw up in police cars.

A FEW MORE FACTS TO SPEW ON

● In competitive eating contests, anyone who vomits on the plate or table is disqualified.
● Why do you drool before throwing up? To protect your teeth from the acids in vomit.
● What's your *bilateral vomitation center*? The part of your brain that decides when to barf.

● Astronauts get "spacesick" so often that their toilet has a special setting for "vomit."

AND FINALLY, A JOKE

A man was flying home from a business trip when the flight attendant handed out freshly-baked brownies. The man wasn't hungry, so he decided to save the brownies for later, and he put them in the cleanest thing he could find—an unused vomit bag. After the plane landed, the man got up to leave and a flight attendant approached him. She asked, "Sir, would you like for me to dispose of that bag for you?"

"No thanks," he said. "I'm saving it for my kids."

FILL 'ER UP!

Air-to-air refueling is the aviation equivalent of threading a needle...at 10,000 feet and 300 miles per hour.

BACKGROUND

The first fuel transfer between planes in midair was a publicity stunt. On November 12, 1921, wing-walker Wesley May strapped a gas can on his back, stepped off the wing of a Lincoln Standard biplane and onto that of the Curtiss JN-4 "Jenny" two-seater biplane flying beside him, opened up the Curtiss's gas tank, and poured. The U.S. military's first attempt at air-to-air refueling was to dangle a 50-foot fuel hose with a shutoff valve from one biplane to another flying below. The passenger in the backseat of the lower plane had to grab the hose and hitch it to the fuel intake. By 1923 military fliers could keep their planes in the air for over 35 hours using this method, leading to the first non-

WONDER WOMAN'S BULLET-PROOF BRACELETS ARE MADE OF A METAL CALLED FEMINUM.

stop circumnavigation of the globe. In 1949 the *Lucky Lady II*, a B-50A "Superfortress" bomber, refueled in the air four times during its 94-hour trip around the world. The U.S. Air Force has more efficient methods today. Nonetheless, air-to-air refueling remains one of the trickiest and most dangerous maneuvers.

STEADY AS SHE GOES

The flying gas station that is an air tanker drags either a "flying boom"—a telescoping fuel pipe that hangs down like a bee's stinger behind the tanker—or a "probe and drogue," meaning the fuel hose has a small parachute, called a drogue, that keeps it from flapping around in the wind. A receiver plane flies in below and behind the tanker, guided by direction lights controlled by the boom operator on the tanker.

The drag from the extra equipment makes docking hard enough, but the midair interaction between two huge aircraft is much more difficult. Pilots have to compensate for the wake of the tail engine as well as for the turbulence created by the tanker aircraft itself. If the receiver aircraft approaches too quickly, it can find itself pushed up into the tail of the tanker. "These aircraft are not exactly nimble," says Lt. Col Kirk Reagan of the USAF. "It takes slow and steady movements and a lot of patience."

GASSED UP

Modern refuelers like the KC-135 "Stratotanker" and HC-130P "Hercules" can hold up to 100 tons of jet fuel, twice the weight

ABOVE: Soviet Military air refueling, March 1970
OPPOSITE: Three F-105 Thunderchief pilots guide their planes in a tight formation while refueling from an Air Force KC-135 Stratotanker "gas station," January 1966. The Thunderchiefs are on their way to bomb military targets in Vietnam.

of the plane. They can pump that fuel into another jet at 5,000 pounds per minute, making a refuel of a fighter jet a matter of seconds, not minutes.

Air-to-air refueling becomes a lot harder flying at high altitude with what pilots call a "combat load-out." "Lots of bombs and missiles equals more drag," says F-16 pilot Maj. Rob Redmond, USAF. Plus, "it can be disorienting flying through weather off the tanker's wing while waiting for your turn to get gas, and also while 'on the boom.'" He adds, with typical pilot understatement, "It is also nice when they stay out of the clouds."

Carrier-based tanker pilots also have to know how to "hawk"—to set the tanker in a flight pattern behind and well above a jet on its landing approach to the flight deck. This happens when a jet returning from a sortie is low on fuel and may not be able to circle back and try landing again. "If the pilot were to 'bolter,' that is, not land that time around," says Lt. Matt Powers, who worked as a flight officer on a carrier-based S-3 Viking tanker, "all he had to do to find us is look up. It's all about customer service."

NKAWTG

Although air-to-air refueling is one of the most dangerous midair flight operations, tanker pilots don't get as much recognition for their flying skills as fighter pilots. "As far from the tip of the spear as we airborne tankers may be," says Lt. Powers, "nothing is quite as satisfying as when the pilot who borrowed a few thousand pounds of gas from you comes to thank you in the ready room after the flight." As the air tanker motto goes, NKAWTG: Nobody Kicks Ass Without Tanker Gas.

SMART PHONE USERS BETWEEN 18 AND 24 SEND AND RECEIVE 48,000 TEXT MESSAGES A YEAR.

145

A lonely plastic bag blows across a parking lot. It tumbles down a hill and into a creek, where the water carries it downstream to a river. Down the river it goes until it's swept out to sea. Day after day it floats in the expanse until, there in the distance—another plastic bag! And another, and another...and millions of others. What is this strange place?

The Garbage Vortex

ALARMING DISCOVERY

In the late 1990s, a sea captain and ocean researcher named Charles Moore entered a yacht race in Hawaii. As he was sailing back home to California, he came upon an odd sight: "There were shampoo caps and soap bottles and plastic bags and fishing floats as far as I could see. Here I was in the middle of the ocean, and there was nowhere I could go to avoid the plastic."

Around the same time, oceanographer Curtis Ebbesmeyer was researching ocean currents by tracking debris that had washed up on beaches around the world. When he heard of Moore's discovery, he named it the Eastern Garbage Patch (EGP). Moore put together a team to survey the area in August 1998. Onboard the research ship *Alguita*, they pulled all sorts of strange objects out of the ocean:

an inflated volleyball dotted with barnacles, a picture tube for a 19" TV, a truck tire on a steel rim, and even a drum of hazardous chemicals. But most of what they saw was plastic...and something else. Moore described it as a "rich broth of minute sea creatures mixed with hundreds of colored plastic fragments—a plastic-plankton soup." But there was six times more plastic than there was plankton.

TROPIC OF PLASTIC

Just how large is the Eastern Garbage Patch? No one knows for sure—it's growing all the time, and the translucent plastic floats just below the water's surface. "It's one of the great features of the planet Earth, but you can't see it," said Ebbesmeyer. Estimates, however, say that it's larger than the state of Texas. And that's just on the surface. Much of the debris—up to 30%— sinks to the ocean floor and lands on top of

animal and plant life.

Just how fast is the EGP growing? In a survey conducted in 2007, Moore found that in less than a decade the "patch" had become a "superhighway of junk" running between San Francisco and Japan. He believes that the amount of plastic could now be 10 times higher than it was in 1998; some of the samples have as much as 48 parts plastic to 1 part plankton.

IN THE DOLDRUMS

How did all that garbage accumulate there? The answer is ocean currents. The EGP is located in an area known as the North Pacific Subtropical Gyre, about 1,000 miles from any landmass. The Gyre is formed by air and water currents that travel between the coasts of Washington, Mexico, and Japan. The clockwise currents form a vortex in the center, just as if a

giant soup spoon were constantly stirring it or, as Moore says, "the same way bubbles gather at the center of a hot tub."

The Gyre is part of the Doldrums—an area named by ancient sailors for its weak winds. For centuries sailors avoided it for fear of stalling there, and fishermen knew there was nothing there to catch but plankton or jellyfish. The Gyre has always accumulated marine debris such as driftwood, as well as "flotsam and jetsam"—stuff that washes offshore from beaches or falls overboard from ships and is caught by the currents and pulled into the middle, where it swirls continuously. But the difference in the last century is that the never-ending influx of trash has made much larger. A plastic bag that flows into the ocean from a California river will ride the currents for up to a year before finally making it to the EGP. And because ocean currents travel only about 10 miles per day, depending on where a object enters the ocean, it could float for much longer—even decades.

REVENGE OF THE NURDLES

Most garbage breaks down over time, but plastic is different. No one really knows how long it takes for plastic to biodegrade because, so far, none of it has. Instead of biodegrading, plastic photodegrades—the sun's UV rays cause it to become brittle, which breaks it down into small pieces... and then into minute particles that resemble tiny confetti.

Sailors call these plastic bits "mermaid tears," but the technical term is nurdles. They're light enough to float in the air (think of tiny packing peanuts and how impossible it is to keep them from spilling everywhere). Everything made out of plastic is made out of nurdles, and every year 5.5 quadrillion of them are manufactured around the world. Just how many end up in the oceans is anyone's guess, but it's a huge amount.

Moore has another name for nurdles: "poison pills." They absorb oily toxic chemicals called persistent organic pollutants, or POPs, which include DDT and PCBs. Though many of these chemicals were banned in the 1970s, they still linger in the environment and attach themselves to plastic debris. Japanese environmental researchers found that nurdles can absorb one million times their weight in POPs from surrounding water.

Even more troubling: The "poison pills" resemble plankton in how they seem to "swim" near the surface. Jellyfish and "filter feeder" fish that strain their food out of the water—and who have been eating plankton for eons—are now eating the nurdles instead. And then fish eat the nurdle-eaters. And then those fish are caught by fishing boats...which means there's a good chance you're getting more plastic in your diet than you realize. And not just plastic, but all of those toxic chemicals it absorbed.

THE SCOOP

But there is hope. In 2015 a 20-year-old Dutch engineering student named Boyan Slat unveiled his invention: a giant, floating buffer that uses existing ocean currents to collect the plastic bits. His organization, Ocean Cleanup, is currently obtaining the funding for a 62-mile long buffer that will be placed between Hawaii and California. Slat believes he can clean up half of the Pacific Garbage Patch within a decade. His critics have pointed out that it may be too little, too late—and Slat acknowledges that it's an uphill battle. "But considering the size of the problem," he says, "it is important to at least try."

CROCODILES SWALLOW STONES TO HELP THEM STAY SUBMERGED UNDER WATER.

147

Do you want to meet the Grim Reaper? Here's how.

You are more likely to die if...

...you take a multivitamin.

Studies are increasingly finding higher death rates for people, specifically women, who take multivitamins. Often, even healthier women—those who smoke and drink less, as well as those who aren't obese—are more likely to die if they take multivitamins.

...your doctor is older.

In one 2005 study, researchers found surgeons over the age of 60 tend to have higher death rates among patients than those aged 41 to 50, even though they tend to perform fewer procedures. Even younger, presumably less-experienced surgeons below the age of 40 tend to have comparable patient death rates to the 41-50 group. Another found that the higher the number of years since medical-school graduation, the higher the likelihood a cardiac patient would die in that doctor's care in the hospital.

...the nurse treating you has more patients.

One study found that risk-adjusted patient death over a 30-day period was 7 percent higher for each additional patient per nurse.

THE BIBLE CONTAINS THE PHRASE "HA, HA." (JOB 39:25)

...you have surgery during the wrong moon cycle.

In a 2013 study, researchers found that patients who had a type of heart surgery called aortic dissection repair had shorter hospital stays and were significantly less likely to die if they had their surgery during the waning full-moon period of the lunar cycle—that's just after a full moon.

...your doctor trained at an American medical school.

A study of cardiac patients in Pennsylvania found that those who were managed by foreign-born and foreign-trained doctors were less likely to die than those who studied in U.S. medical schools. The author of the study speculated that the difference was the result of primary care in the U.S. becoming less attractive to American medical school grads, and thus less competitive. By comparison, the foreign international medical school grads who manage to jump through the hoops required to come and practice in the U.S. are among the highest achievers worldwide.

...you're a patient at an overcrowded ER.

A study examined California hospitals that were routinely so overcrowded they diverted ambulances elsewhere. Patients at those overcrowded ERs were 5 percent more likely to die.

...you have an elective surgery on the weekend.

Researchers at the Imperial College of London analyzed millions of procedures that occurred between 2008 and 2011 and found that the day of the week you have an elective surgery affects your risk of death greatly. Monday is the best day to avoid the Grim Reaper, and the risk of death increases every day of the week that passes. The increased risk of death on the weekend? An astounding 82 percent.

MISS PIGGY HAD HER OWN PERFUME LINE, "MOI." KERMIT HAD A COLOGNE CALLED "AMPHIBIA."

149

Sometimes the circumstances of a famous person's death are as interesting as their lives. Take these folks, for example.

They Went Thataway

- - - - - - - - - - -

JASPER NEWTON "JACK" DANIEL (1846–1911)
Claim to Fame: The distiller who created Jack Daniel's Whiskey
Cause of Death: An unsafe safe
Postmortem: Daniel had a terrible time remembering the combination to his office safe

(no word on whether whiskey was a factor), and it was usually his nephew's job to open it. One morning, however, Daniel came in to work early and his nephew wasn't there. Daniel tried to open the safe himself and got so frustrated in the attempt that he kicked it, striking it so hard that he broke his toe. The toe became infected, and he developed septicemia, or blood poisoning, which killed him on October 10, 1911. Daniel's last words (according to the distillery): "One last drink, please."

ISADORA DUNCAN (1877–1927)
Claim to Fame:
One of the world's most famous modern dancers
Cause of Death:
Broken neck
Postmortem: On September 14, 1927, in Nice, France, Duncan climbed into the passenger seat of a

TOP: Jasper Newton "Jack" Daniel
ABOVE: Isadora Duncan

Bugatti race car wearing a long, red silk scarf. The scarf was a little too long: When the car started off, the tail end wrapped around the wheel and yanked Duncan out of the car, snapping her neck and dragging her for several yards before the driver realized what had happened.

Final irony: A day before she died, Duncan had told a reporter, "Now I'm frightened that some quick accident may happen."

TENNESSEE WILLIAMS (1911–83)

Claim to Fame: American playwright (*A Streetcar Named Desire*)

Cause of Death: He was capped.

Postmortem: Williams, 71, took a variety of pills the night he died in 1983, but that's not what killed him. He opened up a bottle of nose spray, used it, and accidentally dropped the cap in his mouth. Moments later, he choked on the bottle cap and died. It's likely that Williams was so full of drugs that his gag reflex was suppressed.

JOHN DENVER (1943–97)

Claim to Fame: American singer/songwriter ("Rocky Mountain High")

Cause of Death: Too short to fly his own airplane

Postmortem: Denver was a lifelong aviation buff and an experienced pilot. He learned to fly from his father, a former U.S. Air Force pilot who made his living training pilots to fly Lear Jets. Shortly before the crash, Denver, 53, bought an aerobatic plane known as a Long-EZ and was still getting used to flying it. According to the report released by the National Transportation Safety Board, he needed an extra seatback cushion for his feet to reach the foot pedals, but when he used the cushion he had trouble reaching the fuel tank selector handle located behind his left shoulder. The NTSB speculates that Denver took off without enough fuel. When one of his tanks ran dry and the engine lost power, he accidentally stepped on the right rudder pedal while reaching over his left shoulder with his right arm to switch to the other fuel tank, and crashed the plane into the sea.

Final Irony: Denver's first big success came in 1967, when he wrote the Peter, Paul, and Mary hit "Leaving on a Jet Plane."

TOP: Tennessee Williams
ABOVE: John Denver

Once again, the BRI answers the question:
Where did all this stuff come from?

Random Origins

THE POLITICAL SPECTRUM

The French Legislative Assembly met for the first time during the French Revolution on October 1, 1791. Like legislative bodies today, the group of 745 lawmakers and representatives grouped themselves according to their political affiliation. For no reason in particular, the more liberal members sat to the left of the speaker and the conservatives sat to the right. Today, "left wing" and "right wing" are still used to denote those same political affiliations.

The White Wedding Dress

Throughout history, most women got married in whatever dress they had available, no matter the color. But in 1840, when England's Queen Victoria married Prince Albert, she wore a white gown. Although Victoria wasn't the first royal to wear a white dress, she was the first whose wedding photos were widely published. Suddenly, women all over England wanted to emulate the queen. Those who had the money chose elaborate white dresses for their weddings, and soon, wearing white at a wedding became associated with wealth and status—which made it popular among the rich and desirable for common folk.

HIGHWAY DIVIDERS

One day in 1917, Dr. June Carroll of Indio, California, was driving down a dangerous stretch of desert highway. "My Model T Ford and I found ourselves face to face with a truck on the paved highway," she recalled. "It did not take me long to choose between a sandy berth to the right and a ten-ton truck to the left! Then I had my idea of a white line painted down the center of the highways of the country as a safety measure." She asked the local authorities to paint a line on the road, but they wouldn't, so Carroll painted one herself. Then she started a letter-writing campaign to the California Highway Commission. A few years later, the commission adopted the plan and added dividing lines to 3,500 miles of California roads and highways. The idea quickly caught on around the world.

CRUISE CONTROL

Ralph Teetor (1890–1982) was a prolific inventor who developed many car improvements. Ironically, he was sight-impaired and unable to drive, so his lawyer frequently offered to chauffeur him. The lawyer was a bad driver, though, prone to jerky starts and stops, which annoyed Teetor... and inspired him to invent a way to regulate the car's speed at a consistent level: cruise control. It was invented in 1945, but first offered as an option on 1958 Chryslers.

THE SODA STRAW

The first straws, made of parafinned paper, were introduced in 1888 by an inventor named Marvin Stone. They didn't catch on, however, because the hand-rolled tubes cracked easily and were unsanitary. Then in the early 1900s—not long after concessionaire Harry Stevens introduced hot dogs to New York Giant baseball games—he noticed that when fans drank from their soda bottles, they had to take their eyes off the game for a moment. So he hired a paper maker to roll some straws out of paper, and began including one with every soda he sold. It increased his sales and made straws a permanent part of American culture. In 1905 Stone's company came up with a machine to mass-produce them.

SCIENTISTS SAY: THE EASIEST SOUND FOR THE HUMAN EAR TO HEAR IS "AH."

153

CAUTION: SLOW CHILDREN

Kids just "act"—they often don't know any better. This can often lead to trouble...for us grown-ups.

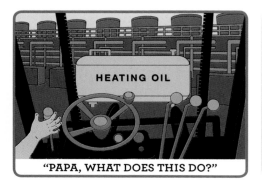

"PAPA, WHAT DOES THIS DO?"

"NOW I RINSE HIM WITH A FLUSH"

"I LIKE HEARING IT DING!"

SUPER GIRL

A four-year-old girl was visiting her father at the oil refinery in Baden-Württemberg, Germany, where he worked. While he was briefly distracted, the little girl climbed onto a forklift and released the brake, which started the machine rolling...and rolling... and rolling right into a 400-gallon tank of heating oil. The forklift punctured the hull, spilling about 130 gallons of heating oil onto the ground and into a sewer. "We're still not sure how the little girl released the brake. Four-year-olds don't have the kind of strength it takes to do that on a forklift," said a police spokesman.

WATERING HOLE

In May 2009, four-year-old Daniel Blair of London decided that his one-week-old Cocker Spaniel puppy needed his first bath. So he put the dog into the smallest pool of water he could find—the toilet. Once Daniel washed all the mud off the dog, he flushed the toilet...with the puppy still in it. Daniel immediately told his mother what he'd done, and she called a plumber who was able to locate the dog in an underground pipe 20 yards from the house. Amazingly, the dog survived.

MO MONEY, MO PROBLEMS

Madeline Hill runs a pub attached to her house in Sittingbourne, England. One night she was sitting in her kitchen counting up the night's cash earnings when she heard a knock at the door. She went to answer it, but first did what she always does with her cash if she's interrupted while counting it—she put it in the microwave. While Hill was out of the room, her 20-month-old son, Jordan, toddled into the room and pressed a bunch of buttons on the microwave, turning it on. The money, about $1,500, was burned to a crisp. (Hill doesn't put her money in the microwave anymore.)

Expand Your Vocabulary

Pepper your speech with these obscure but real words, and your kith will think you're perspicacious.

Ambivert: A person who's half introvert and half extrovert.

Backclipping: Shortening a longer word into a smaller one, like "chrysanthemum" to "mum."

Callipygian: Having shapely buttocks.

Furfurrate: What dandruff does when it falls from your scalp.

Genuglyphics: Painting or decorating a person's knees to make them more erotic.

Hypocorism: Baby talk.

Infix: A word placed inside another word to change its meaning, as in "fan-f*ck*ng-tastic."

Izzard: The name of the letter "z."

Kith: Your friends.

Lecanoscopy: The act of hypnotizing yourself by staring into a sink filled with water.

Liveware: People who work with computer software and hardware.

Otoplasty: A surgical procedure to fix ears that stick out.

Otorhinolaryngologist: An ear, nose, and throat doctor.

Pandiculate: To yawn.

Paradog: A military dog that's been trained to parachute out of airplanes.

Paranymph: The bridesmaid or best man at a wedding.

Perspicacious: Having keen mental perception and understanding.

Pica: A desire to eat nonfoods (like dirt).

Pilomotor reaction: What your hair does when it stands on end.

Pip: What an unhatched chick does to break through its eggshell.

Puwo: An animal that's half poodle and half wolf.

Taresthesia: The tingling sensation you get when your foot falls asleep.

Tautonym: A word consisting of two identical parts, like "tutu."

Ucalegon: A neighbor whose house is burning down.

Zoonoses: Diseases humans can get from animals.

Keith Urban Legends

And other fake stories about famous people.

LEGEND: Keith Richards once had his blood replaced with "clean" blood at a Swiss clinic to beat an addiction to heroin.

THE TRUTH: Richards has admitted to heroin addiction and has made several attempts to break it over the years. In 1973, some accounts say, he did receive some sort of dialysis-type treatment to "filter" his blood, but the idea of getting a "blood change" to treat an addiction isn't medically possible.

HOW IT SPREAD: Richards says he started the rumor himself: "Someone asked me how I cleaned up, so I told them I went to Switzerland and had my blood completely changed. I was just fooling around. I opened my jacket and said, 'How do you like my blood change?' That's all it was, a joke. I was sick of answering that question. So I gave them a story." Also, in his 2003 book *I Was Keith Richards' Drug Dealer*, onetime Richards friend (and drug dealer, by his account) Tony Sanchez also claims that Richards had his blood "changed."

LEGEND: When singer Mariah Carey was asked about the death of King Hussein of Jordan in February 1999, she confused him with basketball player Michael Jordan. "I'm inconsolable at the present time," she told CNN. "I was a very good friend of Jordan. He was probably the greatest basketball player this country has ever seen. We will never see his like again."

THE TRUTH: It never happened.

HOW IT SPREAD: The story appeared on an Internet chat site, falsely attributed to *USA Today* and CNN, and it spread from there.

LEGEND: John Denver was an Army sniper in Vietnam.

THE TRUTH: Denver never served in the Army or any other branch of the military. He was inducted in 1964, but he was classified 1-Y—not qualified for service—because he was missing two toes due to a lawnmower accident when he was a boy.

HOW IT SPREAD: Nobody knows exactly who started this one, but it began in the early 1970s. Similar stories have been spread about another "nice guy," Fred Rogers of *Mister Rogers' Neighborhood*. He wasn't a sniper, either.

LEGEND: Frank Zappa, in a "gross-out" competition, once ate a spoonful of feces onstage. Sometimes the claim is that he merely defecated onstage.

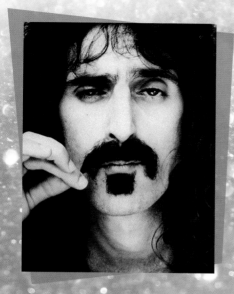

CLOCKWISE FROM BOTTOM LEFT: John Denver, Mariah Carey, Keith Richards, Frank Zappa, Keith Urban, Bono.

THE TRUTH: From *The Real Frank Zappa*: "For the record, folks: I never took a sh*t on stage, and the closest I ever came to eating sh*t anywhere was at a Holiday Inn buffet in Fayetteville, North Carolina, in 1973."

HOW IT SPREAD: "This legend originated in the mid-1960s," according to urban-legend investigators Snopes. com, "no doubt inspired by the eccentricities of Frank Zappa's music and appearance." In a 1993 interview in *Playboy*, Zappa called it "somebody's imagination run wild. Chemically bonded imagination."

LEGEND: Country-music singer Keith Urban, at a concert in North Dakota in July 2006, made all the Canadians in the audience leave—because their government hadn't supported the United States in the war in Iraq.

THE TRUTH: Urban played

at the North Dakota State Fair in Minot on July 21, 2006, but no credible reports have ever been found of him having asked any Canadians to leave. And several Canadians who were at the concert wrote to various Internet sites, saying that they hadn't been thrown out of the show.

HOW IT SPREAD: Via fake e-mails that made the rounds of the Internet sometime in late 2006. Here's a sample: "What an ass!!! No more Keith Urban for me!!! (or Garth Brooks) This big-shot western singer asked all Canadians to stand up at the Minot Fair. After everyone stood up, he asked them all to leave the stands because they were not helping out fighting with USA troops...Pass this around and see how his record sales do in Canada!"

LEGEND: U2 frontman Bono, while performing a show in Glasgow, Scotland, asked the crowd

for a moment of silence. Then he slowly clapped his hands for a few moments and said, "Every time I clap my hands, a child in Africa dies." An audience member then yelled out in a thick Scottish brogue, "Well, stop f*cking doing it, then!"

THE TRUTH: It was actually British comedian Jimmy Carr who said the famous line...in his comedy act. Carr was making fun of Bono and other celebrities who appeared in a 2005 charity commercial in which they said a child died from extreme poverty every three seconds—every time they snapped their fingers. Carr quipped, "I watched that, and couldn't help thinking, 'Well, stop clicking your fingers!'"

HOW IT SPREAD: Via hoax e-mails in 2006 regarding the concert in Glasgow—or New York, or London, or various other places. Even some newspapers fell for it and reprinted the stories, including Australia's *Sunday Mail*.

It's one of Michigan's most popular sporting events (after football, of course). It's done between 10 p.m. and 2 a.m. over a three-week period every spring, only when lake water temperatures are between 42°F and 44°F. What is it?

Smelt Dipping

FISH STORY

Rainbow, or Eastern American, smelt are small silver-colored fish that reside in the north Atlantic. They were transplanted to inland Michigan lakes in the early 1900s as a food source for larger lake fish. By 1936 the growing smelt population had found its way to the Great Lakes. Commercial fishermen in the area were not pleased, because smelt can clog nets and crowd out other species. But the many new smelt connoisseurs in Michigan could not have been happier.

Prime time for smelt dipping is mid-April to early May. Michiganders often plan smelt-dipping parties, getting groups of fun-loving folk together for a night in the dark, cold waters. Fortunately for nonanglers, no prior experience is necessary. All you need is a long-handled net, a bucket, warm clothes, and a flashlight. The smelt schools are so large that you merely need to run your net through the water and pull out a swarm of fish. Dump the catch in a bucket and repeat as necessary. Optional equipment: bonfire supplies and lots of beer.

GOOD EATIN'

What is the reward for all this effort? One of the sweetest, best-tasting fish you'll ever eat. And one of the safest. These youngsters haven't cruised the lakes long enough to absorb mercury or other nasty chemicals. But don't be greedy. You have to clean them before you can eat them, and it can be a chore if you grab too many.

Now that you have a big pile of

SHOW-OFFS: POLAR BEARS CAN EAT 50 POUNDS OF MEAT IN ONE SITTING.

smelt, what do you do with them? Put them on ice. These delicate critters can turn bad quickly. They also bruise easily, which reduces the quality of the fish, so don't overpack them in large containers. Dress the fish with a pair of scissors.

Many smelt dippers look forward to just one good smelt dinner a year, but any fish that you do not plan to eat right away can be frozen for up to six months.

OPPOSITE: The Rainbow Smelt (*Osmerus Mordax*)
ABOVE: The art of smelt-dipping
BELOW: Fresh smelt on ice

A POPULAR SMELT RECIPE

● Dip each fish in a mixture of one beaten egg, half a teaspoon of soy sauce, and half a teaspoon of garlic powder.

● Roll the fish in flour and cook briefly in a skillet with three or four tablespoons of hot, but not smoking, oil.

● Then let the feast begin!

WHEN BRAIN-DAMAGED PATIENTS GIVE BIZARRE ANSWERS TO QUESTIONS, THEY ARE CONFABULATING.

159

hat do you get when you combine a robe,
ravel, and delusions of grandeur?

Judges Gone Wild

THE LONG ARM OF THE LAW...N

n 1998 a Missouri judicial commission found Associate Circuit judge John A. Clark guilty of misconduct. The charge "most likely to be remembered," according to the National Law Journal: He sentenced defendants to community service and then allowed them to "do their time" by working in his yard.

JUDGE BREWSKI

While presiding over deliberations in a drunk-driving case, Lakewood, Washington, Municipal Court judge Ralph H. Baldwin disappeared into his chambers and returned a short time later with a 12-pack of beer. Then he invited the attorneys, jurors, and court staff to "stay for a cool one," but admonished them not to tell anyone. "I'll deny it if you repeat it," he said. Afterward, he brazenly carried an open container of beer to his car, telling onlookers, "I might as well drink and drive. I do it all the time anyway." Judge Baldwin later admitted that he made the statement but claimed he was joking and that the beer can was empty. "When I thought about it later, I thought, 'Oh, my God, you fool!'" he explained.

BRIBES AND MISDEMEANORS

While running for reelection in 2008, Philadelphia Traffic Court Judge William F. Singletary—also a church deacon—attended a "Blessing of the Bikes" motorcycle club gathering in a Philadelphia park. "If you all can give me $20," he said over the PA system, "you're going to need me in traffic court, am I right about that?...Now you all want me to get there." Video footage of the deacon's attempted bribe soon found its way to YouTube—and then to the authorities. Singletary was charged with four counts of misconduct and found guilty of all four, enough to cost him his judgeship.

THE LARGEST PRIME NUMBER KNOWN (SO FAR) IS 7,235,733 DIGITS LONG.

TAKING A BITE OUT OF CRIME

In 1997 Judge Joseph Troisi spent five days in jail after he bit defendant William Witten on the nose hard enough to make it bleed. The incident came about when Troisi—until then a "highly regarded member" of the West Virginia bench and former member of the state committee that investigates judicial misconduct—denied Witten's bail request, prompting Witten to mutter an insult under his breath. Troisi then "stepped down from the bench, removed his robe, and there was a confrontation," said state police captain Terry Snodgrass. Judge Troisi pleaded no contest to criminal battery, served his five days, and then resigned from the bench.

BANGING OUT SOME JUSTICE

When a boy charged with burglary went to the Wake County, North Carolina, Juvenile Court, Judge Don Overby sent the miscreant home to get his most-prized possession. The kid returned with a remote-controlled car, which he handed over to the court. Judge Overby then took a hammer and smashed it to smithereens. The judge has done this with other first time offenders as well. He says he got the idea after someone broke into his house and stole his CD player, his VCR, and $300 in cash. "I remember wishing these folks could feel the same sense of loss as I did," he said.

WORSHIP ME!

Elizabeth Halverson—a Clark County, Nevada, District Court judge—took the bench in January 2007. In her first few months on the job, the state's Judicial Discipline Commission received more than a dozen complaints about her behavior. They alleged that Halverson abused court staff with racial and religious slurs, sexually harassed a bailiff and made him feel like a "houseboy" by assigning him menial personal chores, hired a computer technician to hack into courthouse e-mail accounts, made false statements to the media about three other judges she believed were conspiring against her, fell asleep on the bench during two criminal trials, and ordered a clerk to swear in her husband so that she could question him under oath about whether he'd completed his chores at home. "Do you want to worship me from near or afar?" she reportedly asked one court employee. Six months into her judgeship, Halverson was suspended and charged with 14 counts of judicial misconduct. In 2008 she was removed from the bench for life.

Dysfunctional Erection

What weighs 40,000 tons, towers 555 feet over the nation's capital, has 897 steps, is made of 36,491 stones, and can boast with certainty that George Washington never slept there? The Washington Monument!

BEST LAID PLANS

Surrounded by 50 flags at the base, symbolizing each of the 50 states, the white marble obelisk is the jewel in the crown of the National Mall—but it took a surprisingly long time for the nation to get around to building it.

Immediately after the War for Independence, the Continental Congress made plans to honor General George Washington. As far back as 1783, there was a plan for an equestrian statue of Washington to be placed near the Capitol building—once the Founding Fathers figured out where the capital city was going to be. The capital moved several times, making it difficult to find a good spot for a tribute. After Washington died in 1799, lawmakers discussed erecting a monument in his honor; they settled on creating a tomb in the Capitol building. But Washington's heirs would not allow for his remains to be removed from his tomb at his home, Mount Vernon, in Alexandria, Virginia.

As the 100th anniversary of Washington's birth approached, there was another push to memorialize the first president. Congress allotted $5,000 in 1832 for a marble statue intended for the Capitol Rotunda. One problem: Artist Horatio Greenhough's creation—a 20-ton seated seminude figure—was too risque for Congress to get behind. (The statue ended up at the Smithsonian Institution in 1908.)

BY GEORGE

In 1833 George Watterson, a former Librarian of Congress, formed the Washington National Monument Society. Its purpose: to finally erect a fitting memorial. The society held a design competition that architect Robert Mills won. His original plan was a much more elaborate design than the current simple obelisk seen today. Mills wanted an even bigger obelisk surrounded by a colonnade (a long sequence of columns), which was to be interspersed with statues of other Revolutionary War heroes and capped by a classically inspired statue of a toga-clad Washington driving a chariot. There were even plans to entomb the remains of the heroes in underground catacombs. But money—and enthusiasm—were short-lived. In 1848 the Society decided to build the obelisk first and worry about the colonnade later. Excavation was begun later that year, and the cornerstone was laid on the Fourth of July.

STUMBLING BLOCKS

The Society encouraged all states and territories to donate memorial stones to be used in the interior walls of the monument. Donations poured in from other sources as well, including blocks from Native American tribes, businesses, and even foreign countries. Perhaps the most well known memorial stone came in the early 1850s from Pope Pius IX: a marble stone that had been part of the Temple of Concord in Rome. In 1854, however, members of the Know-Nothings (an anti-Catholic, anti-immigrant political party) stole the stone and allegedly threw it into the Potomac River.

THE EPIC OF GILGAMESH, THE EARLIEST KNOWN POEM, DATES TO THE 3RD MILLENNIUM B.C.

ABOVE: Architect Robert Mills's original winning design for the Washington National Monument
OPPOSITE: Panoramic view of the Washington, D.C., skyline showing the Washington Monument and the Jefferson Memorial

Donations to the society began to dry up in 1854, and Congress was reluctant to step in and help. The nation was embroiled in controversy over slavery; a monument to honor the Father of the United States seemed a folly to build when that very nation was in danger of being torn apart by civil war. The monument would stand unfinished for more than 20 years as the United States struggled to rebuild.

EXTREME MAKEOVER

In 1876 Congress appropriated $200,000 to resume construction. Plans for the colonnade were scrapped, and the size of the obelisk was changed to make it conform more to classical Egyptian proportions. Construction finally began again in 1879. The new architect, Thomas L. Casey of the U.S. Army Corps of Engineers, incorporated the original memorial

stones in the interior walls. The first to be placed was the Alabama stone. The last two stones were installed in 1982: the Alaska stone, which is made of solid jade; and another stone donated by the Vatican to replace the original one that was pilfered.

Why does the Washington Monument look like it's two different colors? Because it was left unfinished (at about 150 feet tall) for so long. Even though the same type of stone was used after

ABOVE: Despite using the same type of stone, after construction resumed, it had to be mined from a different quarry, hence the noticeable difference in the stone's color.

construction resumed, it had to be mined from a different quarry, and the white shade could not be matched exactly. If you look closely you can see the change in color about a third of the way up. The Washington Monument was opened to the public on October 9, 1888, and it typically receives more than 800,000 visitors each year.

LEFT: Comet Hale-Bopp during its transit close to Earth in 1997

OPPOSITE: This incredible picture shows a huge meteor hurtling to Earth during the annual Geminid meteor shower on December 14, 2009. Taken from the Mojave Desert area near Victorville under a very dark and mostly clear sky.

The Sky is Falling!

Mark this page and check it now and then. You might get to see several spectacular shows a year...and they're all free.

IT'S A PERSEID! IT'S A LEONID...

Do you know what a *meteoroid* is? It's a small, solid particle traveling through space. How about a meteor? It's the streak of light you see in the sky when a meteoroid hits the Earth's atmosphere and burns up. Most meteoroids are smaller than a grain of sand and burn up relatively quickly; some are larger—up to boulder size—and can cause "fireballs" to flare across the sky. Some even make it to the ground, at which point they're referred to as *meteorites*.

They're common, but several times a year they become much more common, in events known as "meteor showers," or "meteor storms." What's responsible for them? Comets.

Comets are relatively small solid objects in our solar system that, like the planets, orbit our Sun. Unlike the planets, whose orbits are fairly round, comets have elliptical orbits (long and narrow), traveling from way out in the solar system to its center at the Sun, which it circles very closely. Comets are made up of ice, dust, and rock, and as they

get close to the Sun, some of that ice turns to gas, and some of its dust and rock is ejected. That's what gives comets their big, glowing coronas—as well as their tails. After many millions of years, the entire orbital path of a comet becomes filled with debris...and then along comes us.

As the Earth makes its orbit around the Sun, it passes through several of those debris-filled comet trails. Some of that debris enters our atmosphere—and we see many more meteors than usual. That's how we get those fantastic shows.

THE NAME GAME

Meteor showers are named after constellations, and that causes a lot of confusion, since the meteors have absolutely nothing to do with those constellations. Here's the explanation:

● When you look up into the sky during a meteor shower, you can see many seemingly unrelated meteors in a wide swath of the sky, all of them moving in many different directions...but look more closely. If you could draw a line back from all the meteors you see, you'd find that they all go back to one point in the sky.

● All the debris fragments in a comet's path are naturally traveling the same direction, in parallel lines. As we view them as meteors from here on Earth, perspective makes those parallel paths appear to recede to a single point in the distance. This point of origin is known as a meteor shower's *radiant*.

● Because it occurs in the sky, the stars become a backdrop, and the radiants of different meteor showers fall "in front" of different constellations. In the case of the Perseid meteor shower, for example, which happens

every August, its radiant falls within the constellation Perseus—hence the name. The radiant of November's Leonid meteor shower is located in the constellation Leo.

● The confusion comes in because people long ago believed (and many still do) that meteor showers were somehow related to those constellations. They're not: Constellations are made up of stars billions and trillions of miles away; meteor showers actually occur in the Earth's atmosphere—just 50 to 75 miles above your head.

ABOVE: A Perseid meteor crossing the night sky

SHOWTIMES

There are dozens of viewable meteor showers during the year. Here's a list of some of the most intense ones. Put a copy of this page on the refrigerator so you won't miss any of the shows. Check an astronomy book or an online source to find out where the radiant constellations are going to be, dress appropriately—and enjoy.

JANUARY: Start off the new year with the Quadrantids, seen from about January 1–5. They're named after the constellation Quadrans Muralis, which isn't recognized anymore—modern star charts show the Quadrantids emanating from around the constellation Hercules. They regularly show as many as 130 meteors an hour (if weather conditions are good).

APRIL: The Lyrids are named for the constellation Lyra, they peak on April 21 or 22, and can show up to about 30 meteors an hour.

MAY: The Eta Aquarids peak on the night of May 5 and appear to emanate from inside the constellation Aquarius. They're

relatively mild: In the Northern Hemisphere you can see about 10 meteors an hour, in the Southern Hemisphere about 30—but once in a while those numbers climb. And the comet that left this trail: Halley's Comet, which orbits the Sun every 75.3 years.

JUNE: The Boötids arrive in late June, peaking on June 27—and you never know how many meteors are going to show up. Often it's very few—but sometimes it goes crazy, with more than 100 an hour. Bonus: The particles in this comet trail are moving at about 10 miles per second—not very fast in the comet debris world—making for slow, lazy meteors.

AUGUST: The Perseids last from around July 20 to August 22, peaking on the night of August 12th, when you can see from 50 to 80 meteors an hour. It's named for the constellation Perseus. In 1864 it became the first meteor shower positively associated with a comet

—the Swift-Tuttle, which orbits the Sun once every 156 years.

OCTOBER: In the early evening hours of October 9, 1998, millions of people in Japan looked up—and saw about 500 meteors an hour fill the sky for about two hours. They were the Dracobinids, named for the constellation Draco, and peak from October 8–10. NASA reports that in some years it can reach as high as 20,000 an hour. Also in October: The Orionids reach their highest output between October 20 and 22 and appear to emanate from the constellation Orion. These are some of the fastest meteors, zipping along at about 66 kilometers a second—often producing fireballs.

NOVEMBER: The Leonids are associated with Leo, and show up every year between November 13 and 21, with the peak generally on the 17th. They're known for their 33-year-cycles—the length of time their comet takes to make one orbit. Some years it causes meteor storms that are downright frightening: On November 12, 1833, an estimated 60,000 meteors an hour filled the sky above the eastern portion of North America for about four hours before dawn. Many people thought the world was coming to an end.

DECEMBER: The Geminids come between December 12 and 14. Their corresponding constellation is, of course, Gemini, and they're known for their multi-colored show—with white, yellow, blue, red, and green meteors—as many as 140 of them per hour—flying across the sky.

"Never tell your daughter about your sex life—or the lack of it. It's ugly to see pity in a daughter's eyes."
JOAN RIVERS

"Never esteem anything as of advantage to you that will make you break your word or lose your self-respect."
MARCUS AURELIUS

"Never fry bacon in the nude."
H. PETER MINER

"Never stand between a dog and the hydrant."
JOHN PEERS

"Never put a sock in a toaster."
EDDIE IZZARD

NEVER

UNCLE JOHN'S CREDO: NEVER FOLLOW THE ADVICE OF EXPERTS.

"Never try and teach a pig to sing: it's a waste of time, and it annoys the pig."
ROBERT A. HEINLEIN

"Never, ever go to bed with a man on the first date. Not ever. Unless you really want to."
CYNTHIA HEIMEL

"Never play cat and mouse games if you're a mouse."
DON ADDIS

"There are two things I've learned in life: you should never race a guy named Flash, and never bring a girl named Bubbles home to meet your mother. Both of which I've done, by the way."
BURT REYNOLDS

"Never mistake motion for action."
ERNEST HEMINGWAY

POPULAR FAST-FOOD SNACK IN JAPAN: *TAKOYAKI*, OR OCTOPUS DUMPLINGS.

167

It's time to reflect on the second-most important object in the bathroom.

MIRROR, MIRROR ON THE WALL...

POOLS OF LIGHT

How do mirrors work? Generally speaking, by reflecting light. Most objects don't give off any light of their own. They can only be seen because light from other sources—the sun, a candle, a lightbulb—hits them and bounces off, hitting their eyes. Not all of the light bounces, though. Some is absorbed by the object and some is transmitted through the object. The part that does bounce back is the reflection. Flat shiny surfaces like water, metal, and mirrors reflect light well because very little of the light is absorbed or transmitted—most of it is reflected.

When light hits a mirror, it bounces off in the opposite direction, but at the exact same angle it came from. It appears as if the image is coming from behind the mirror, but it's not—what we see is a virtual image.

THE FIRST MIRRORS

For centuries, mankind's only mirrors were pools of water or polished metal. The first glass mirrors were made by Venetian craftsmen in the 1300s. Their method: They covered the back of a piece of glass with an amalgam of tin and mercury, rubbed flat and smooth. A piece of wool cloth would then be laid on top of the mercury and pressed with iron weights for more than a week. Then the excess mercury would be drained off. This method remained a carefully guarded secret, and for centuries Venice had a monopoly on mirrors.

In 1665 the chief minister to Louis XIV of France went to Italy and—at the risk of death—bribed 18 Venetian mirrorsmiths to move to France. Soon after their defection, the French passed a law making it illegal to import Venetian mirrors. Three years later, a Frenchman named Louis Lucas beat the Venetians at their own game—he invented plate glass. Venetians only knew how to make blown glass, so each mirror started out as a bottle or cylinder which was slit open and flattened while still hot. The size of mirrors was therefore very limited.

But Lucas discovered how to pour molten glass onto an iron table where it could be flattened with an iron roller. Now mirrors could be made that were much larger. Soon France became famous for its mirrors. Louis XIV purchased 700 mirrors and lined an entire hallway at the Palace of Versailles with them in a stunning display.

UPON FURTHER REFLECTION

In 1835 German chemist Justus von Liebig discovered a way to make a better mirror. He invented a process for using silver as a backing instead of tin and mercury. He flushed the glass with silver salts and then covered it with a solution of silver nitrate. After being heated and left undisturbed for an hour, a chemical reaction caused the metallic silver to separate and adhere to the glass. Then it was coated with shellac and painted with a black backing. And that's how mirrors were made for the next 150 years.

In mirror making today, silver or aluminum is vaporized,

MAIN IMAGE: The Hall of Mirrors at the Palace of Versailles, Louis XIV's residence outside Paris
INSET, LEFT: German chemist Justus von Liebig
INSET, RIGHT: The world's largest mirrors are in the two Keck Telescopes in Hawaii.

then sprayed onto glass. For finer mirrors—such as those used in telescopes—aluminum, chromium, or gold are heated in a vacuum tank. When they reach the critical temperature, they "flash" into vapor, filling the tank with metallic gas. A film is then deposited on whatever material is inside the tank.

MIRROR LORE

● In the 1600s, the Dutch used to cover their mirrors with curtains when not in use, lest the reflectiveness be used up!
● In ancient China, reflective pieces of polished brass were placed over doorknobs so that evil spirits would scare themselves away.
● Ben Franklin mounted mirrors outside his second-story window so he could secretly see who was knocking at his door.
● The word "mirror" comes from the Latin *mirari*, meaning "to wonder at." It's also the root word for "miracle" and "admire."
● The world's largest mirrors (to date) sit inside the twin Keck Telescopes—the world's largest

telescopes—at the W. M. Keck Observatory in Hawaii. Each mirror is made of 36 hexagonal segments which work together as a single piece. Diameter: 33 feet.
● In olden days, some people thought that the reflection of the body in a shiny surface or mirror was an expression of the spiritual self, and therefore if anything happened to disturb that reflection, injury would follow. This was the origin of the superstition that breaking a mirror would bring seven years of bad luck.
● Trade secret: Building managers install mirrors in lobbies because people complain less about waiting for slow elevators when they're occupied looking at themselves.
● In 1994 Russian astronauts orbiting in the *Mir* spacecraft tried using mirrors to reflect sunlight into northern areas of their country in an attempt to lengthen the short growing season. It didn't work.
● Did you ever wonder if the mirror in the dressing room is a real mirror or a two-way mirror?

Here's a simple test: Place the tip of your fingernail against the reflective surface. If there's a gap between your fingernail and the image, it's a genuine mirror. However, if your fingernail directly touches the image, watch out—it very well could be a two-way mirror. Remember, though, that mirror technology is always changing, so no test is 100% foolproof.
● A vanity license plate that reads "3M TA3" was banned after someone looked at it in the mirror.
● A middle school in Oregon was faced with a problem: Some girls, who were just starting to use lipstick, would press their lips to the mirrors, leaving dozens of little lip prints. The principal called all the girls to the bathroom. She asked the custodian to demonstrate how difficult it was to clean the mirrors. He proceeded to take out a longhandled brush, dip it into the nearest toilet, and scrub the mirror. After that, there were no more lip prints on the mirrors.

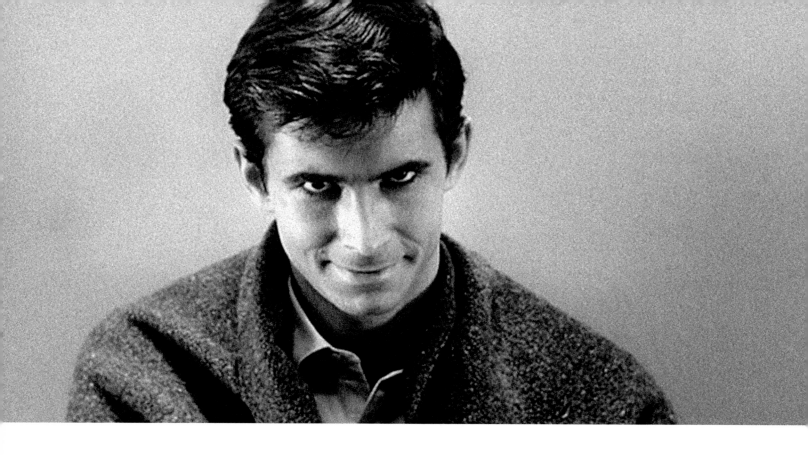

Ironic, isn't it?

There's nothing like a good dose of irony to put the problems of day-to-day life into proper perspective.

TOP: Anthony Perkins plays Norman Bates in the closing shot of *Psycho*.
ABOVE: Veteran actress Betty Lou Lynn during her sweater girl look in the 1950s

RURAL IRONY

Actress Betty Lou Lynn, 83, played Thelma Lou on *The Andy Griffith Show* in the 1960s. In 2007, after she was mugged two times, she decided to move away from Beverly Hills to Mount Airy, North Carolina. What could be safer than the friendly, small town that inspired Mayberry in the first place? Not long after Lynn moved there, she was mugged outside of a shopping center.

IRONY ON WHEELS

● In the early 1990s, in an effort to convince people to drive safely, British transportation officials placed dozens of signs along the notoriously dangerous A1 highway, displaying the number of road casualties over the previous year. In 2008 the signs were removed. Why? They were distracting drivers and—according to some officials—leading to more road casualties.
● While driving the WDJT news van out to Wisconsin's Big Muskego Lake on a Sunday afternoon in January 2007, Susan Wronsky thought she was traveling on an icy road. But she was actually driving on top of an iced-over

ALL SEA SLUGS ARE HERMAPHRODITES.

channel that ran parallel to the road. The vehicle broke through the ice and came to rest in the mud on the bottom of the five-foot-deep waterway. The van was totaled, but Wronsky escaped without injury. At the time of the accident, she was covering a story on how to drive safely in icy conditions.

UNSOLICITED IRONY

An anti-spam software company called SpamArrest had to issue this apology to its customers: "Recently, we have received some inquiries regarding a mailing we delivered to users of SpamArrest. Because of this, SpamArrest will not send unsolicited bulk e-mail again."

IRONY ON THE HIGH SEAS

In the chilly waters off Antarctica in 2007, two animal-rights activists were preparing to attack a Japanese whaling ship with a bottle of acid. But the attack had to be postponed when their ship got lost in the fog. They sent out a call for help, and a few minutes later the very whaling ship they were targeting came to their rescue. Once the activists were out of danger, they thanked the crew of the whaling ship. After an awkward silence, one of the activists said, "I guess we're back on schedule," and threw the acid onto the whalers' deck (two crewmen were injured). Then they jumped back on their boat and raced away.

DEATHLY IRONY

● A 22-year-old California skier stole a piece of padded yellow foam from a ski lift pole, dragged it up the hill, and used it as a

LEFT, TOP AND BOTTOM: The WDJT News van in trouble
TOP: The whaling ship *Nisshin Maru*, berths at a whaling festival in Kagoshima, Japan, 2008.
BELOW: It was Myra Davis's hand in the shower scene of *Psycho*.

makeshift sled. He crashed into the unpadded pole, hit his head, and died.

● Myra Davis was Janet Leigh's body double in the 1960 Hitchcock classic *Psycho*. It was Davis's hand that was seen in the famous shower scene in which Leigh's character is stabbed to death. On July 3, 1988, Davis was found strangled in her Los Angeles home, murdered by a 31-year-old "caretaker and handyman"...shades of Norman Bates.

Whisker Power

A cat's whiskers are a marvel of form and function.

- The scientific name for whiskers is *vibrissae*, and they're specialized sensory organs on a cat's body (mostly on his cheeks). On average, cats have 24 cheek whiskers—12 on each side of their face—that are arranged in four horizontal rows.

- Each whisker is double the thickness of an ordinary hair and is rooted in the cat's upper lip. Every root connects to 200 or more nerve endings under kitty's skin that transmit information directly to his brain.

- Cats use their whiskers to gain information about their environment. They can avoid bushes, sofas, and other obstacles with whisker power alone. Air currents create a tiny breeze as they move around an object. Cats feel this change with their whiskers and avoid objects in their path.

- Whiskers direct hunting cats to a successful pounce. In one experiment, a blindfolded cat was placed in an enclosure with a live mouse. When the cat's whiskers touched the mouse, the cat grabbed his prey and delivered a killing bite in one-tenth of a second.

- Once the prey is in the cat's mouth, muscles in his face allow the whiskers to curl forward and sense any movement that might mean the animal is still alive and possibly dangerous. Also, when cats crouch over an intended meal, they wrap their whiskers around the prey to make sure the animal is truly dead and safe to eat.

- The width of a cat's outstretched whiskers is usually the same as the width of his body. So cats use their whiskers to measure the diameter of holes or other openings to make sure they're wide enough to enter without being trapped. When kitty overeats and gains too much weight, though, his whiskers stay the same size. So a fat cat may misjudge the size of his body and get stuck in a hole—one good reason not to overdo the treats.

- Cheeks are the most well-known spots for whiskers, but cats also have them on the backs of their two front paws. These whiskers are shorter than the ones on a cat's cheeks and help him walk over uneven ground without stumbling. Paw whiskers also help cats determine the size and position of captured prey.

- Cats have whiskers over their eyes and on their chins, too. These are responsive to touch, but they aren't as important to a cat's survival as the cheek and paw whiskers are.

- A cat's whiskers should never be trimmed because without his whiskers to guide him, a cat can get disoriented in the dark.

- Whiskers are such an important part of a cat's physiology that the feline fetus develops whiskers before any other hairs. And when kittens are born, they're blind and deaf, but the touch sensors on their whiskers are fully operational.

THE LANGUAGE OF WHISKERS

Whiskers can also be used to communicate. Here are some tips for deciphering what your cat's whiskers are saying:

- A calm, resting, or friendly cat holds his whiskers out to the sides.

- An alert, curious, or excited cat's whiskers point upward.

- Backward-pointing whiskers often indicate that a cat feels defensive or is angry. So, you... human...the one with the kitty shampoo and bath supplies in hand: Back off!

VAUDEVILLE

PART I

If you've ever faked a soft-shoe or yelled out "One more time!" at the end of a song, you're doing vaudeville—America's favorite form of entertainment for half a century.

ABOVE LEFT: Antonio (Tony) Pastor, 1895
ABOVE: Tony Pastor's 14th Street Theater in Union Square, New York

BOWERY BOY

Although theater-going has been part of American cultural life since the 18th century, it was a pleasure reserved mostly for the upper classes, and found only in major cities like New York and Philadelphia. Most Americans lived in rural areas, with neither the time nor the money to attend shows on a regular basis. The Industrial Revolution changed all that: By the mid-1800s, more Americans were living in cities than on farms and, more importantly, they had extra money and one day off every week to spend it.

Tony Pastor was a New York entertainer and entrepreneur who produced raunchy variety shows in the city's working-class Bowery district. Pastor knew that the big money to be made in show business lay in getting the growing middle class into the theater. But few respectable New Yorkers, especially women and children, would be caught dead at Pastor's bawdy shows. So he created a new kind of variety show in a "clean"—meaning no sacrilegious language or overtly sexual content—family-friendly format. And he moved it uptown.

In 1881 Pastor opened the 14th Street Theatre in New York City's Union Square and launched a style of entertainment that dominated American theater for the next 50 years—vaudeville.

FAMILY FUN

Strictly speaking, vaudeville was a variety show: seven or eight

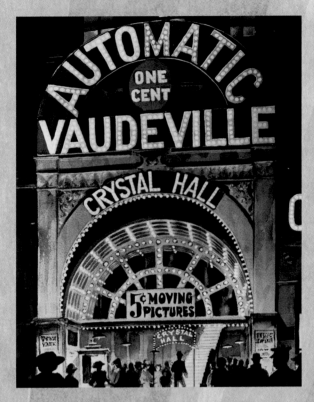

LEFT: With the coming of movies, customers could choose to watch vaudeville, or real moving pictures
ABOVE: Fred Allen (Left) and Jimmy Durante on set of *Sally, Irene, and Mary*

acts, featuring singers, sketches or routines by comedians and actors, and novelty acts like escape artists, high divers, quickchange artists, strong men, jugglers, and animal acts.

The origin of the name itself is obscure. It may be a corruption of the phrase *voix de ville*, French slang for "songs of the town," or it may have come from *vau-de-Vire*, a valley in Normandy that became known for satiric songs full of double-entendres written by street singers in the 15th century.

But Tony Pastor never called his shows "vaudeville." The term was given to the new form of entertainment by impresarios Benjamin Franklin Keith and Edward F. Albee. Keith and Albee were two of the most cutthroat producers in a business full of rascals and sharks. In 1883, using money they'd made with unauthorized productions of Gilbert and Sullivan operettas, they built a chain, or "circuit," of lavish theaters across the northeast. Then they stole Pastor's format, instituted the practice of playing two shows a day, and called it "vaudeville." Other producers jumped on the bandwagon, and soon there were other successful vaudeville circuits—the Pantages and Loew's, to name two—but Keith and Albee dominated the industry, gobbling up the other circuits one by one.

HULLY GEE!

Not only did Keith and Albee control the theaters, they also controlled the performers. Acts were required to uphold strict codes of behavior. Fred Allen, the radio superstar who started out as a juggler in vaudeville, recalled a warning sign posted backstage: "Don't say slob or sonofagun or hully gee [19th-century slang for "Holy Jesus!"] on the stage unless you want to be canceled peremptorily. If you are guilty of uttering anything sacrilegious or even suggestive you will be immediately closed and will never again be allowed in a theater where Mr. Keith is in authority."

They meant business. Acts that violated the rules were blackballed from the circuit. Keith and Albee eventually controlled the bookings in most of the 17,000 vaudeville theaters from coast to coast. Acts who didn't play by their rules didn't work.

BIRTH OF "BLUE"

Over time, as social conventions relaxed, the rules were bent, especially for big stars like Sophie Tucker and the Marx Brothers, who made pushing the envelope part of their act. But that process took years. In the meantime, Keith and Albee dutifully watched the Monday matinee of every new act. After the show, they wrote out terse instructions on what improper line or scene each performer was to cut before the evening performance. Those instructions were put in little blue envelopes, which would appear in the performers' mailboxes backstage. To this day, raunchy jokes and sketches are known as "blue" material.

For more about vaudeville, go to page 270.

13 Names for a 12-inch Sandwich

They're all basically the same: a long roll filled with layers of meat, cheese, tomatoes, onions, lettuce, and condiments. But what you call them depends on who you ask...and where they're from.

Hoagie

HOAGIE
Ingredients: Italian ham, prosciutto, salami, provolone cheese, lettuce, tomatoes, and onions on a long roll, with oregano-vinegar dressing
Origin: During World War I, Italian immigrants who worked in the shipyards at Philadelphia's Hog Island would eat these long sandwiches for lunch. A common meal in Italy, native Philadelphians took to them, first calling the sandwich a "hoggie" in reference to Hog Island, then later "hoagie." It became the official sandwich of Philadelphia in 1992, beating out the cheesesteak.

ZEP
Ingredients: Salami, provolone, tomatoes, onions, oregano, and oil
Origin: The name is short for "zeppelin" (because it's zeppelin-shaped). True zeps are found only within the city limits of Norristown, Pennsylvania, a small town 20 miles outside of Philadelphia. This sandwich also started with Italian immigrants.

SUBMARINE (OR SUB)
Ingredients: Boiled ham, hard salami, cheeses, lettuce, tomatoes, onion, maybe some garlic and oregano on Italian bread
Origin: This New Jersey sandwich was named by Dominic Conti, an Italian grocery store owner from the city of Paterson. In 1927 Conti went to see the _Holland I_, a submarine on display in Jersey's Westside Park. The sub reminded Conti of the biggest sandwich he sold in his store, so he borrowed the name.

ITALIAN
Ingredients: The same as a submarine
Origin: The only difference between this and the New York sandwich is geography; it's found mainly in the Midwest and upper New England.

CUBAN
Ingredients: Roast pork, ham, cheese, and a pickle on Cuban bread, grilled in a press until the contents are warmed by their own steam
Origin: In the Ybor City area of Tampa, Florida, this sandwich can be traced back to the 1880s, when many Cubans

immigrated there to work in the cigar factories. A real Cuban sandwich is almost impossible to find outside of Tampa or Miami. Why? Because Cuban bread contains lard, it must be made fresh daily, which makes it difficult to distribute.

HERO
Ingredients: Pork and other meats, provolone, usually with roasted peppers, vinegar, olive oil, and lettuce served on crusty Italian bread
Origin: It was also introduced to locals by Italian immigrants, but "hero" was the New York City name coined sometime late in the 19th century. According to legend, New Yorkers named it a "hero" because "it took a true hero to finish one in a single sitting."

PO'BOY
Ingredients: It can feature crawfish, shrimp, fried oysters, catfish, crab, deli meats, or meatballs on a baguette. Served "dressed" with lettuce, tomato, and mayonnaise, or "undressed," meaning plain
Origin: The po'boy was invented in

the Cajun section of New Orleans in 1929. Two brothers, Clovis and Benjamin Martin, took pity on striking transit workers (Benjamin was a former streetcar conductor) and gave these "po'boys" sandwiches made of leftovers from their restaurant. Shellfish was abundant and cheap at the time, and became the main ingredient. Today, any long sandwich served in New Orleans is considered a po'boy, even one with deli meats. However, outside of New Orleans, it usually refers only to sandwiches containing seafood.

DAGWOOD
Ingredients: Anything and everything readily available that can fit between two slices of bread. A true Dagwood is built to such a humongous size that it is nearly impossible to take a bite.
Origin: The only food that Dagwood Bumstead, husband of Blondie in the popular comic strip, knew how to prepare was a mountainous pile of dissimilar leftovers precariously arranged between two slices of bread. The sandwich became synonymous with the character and took his name.

GRINDER
Ingredients: Similar to a hoagie or a hero, but usually toasted
Origin: Italian immigrants set up sandwich shops near the East Coast shipyards during World War II. Their main customers were "rivet grinders," the men who ground rivets on warships, and the term passed along to the sandwiches. Today, this term is especially popular in Michigan and the upper Midwest.

WEDGE
Ingredients: Various meats, very thinly sliced, stacked, folded, and cut in half with the halves served at a 90-degree angle
Origin: Not only the name of a sandwich, it's also the name of a delimaster's illusionary trick of manipulating thinly sliced meats to make portion sizes look larger than they really are. This sleight-of-hand has been handed down through generations of deliworkers, primarily in Westchester County, north of New York City.

ROCKET, TORPEDO, AND BOMBER
Ingredients: Similar to a hoagie or a submarine
Origin: These are other working-class names for working-class sandwiches. Like the grinder, they were named for the immigrant workers who built the rockets, torpedoes, and bombers during World War II. Coincidentally, many WWII-era bombers were erected using a new technique called "Sandwich Construction."

Santa Under Surveillance

You don't have to search the darkened skies on Christmas Eve for a glimpse of Santa's sleigh. The government is one step ahead of you.

SORRY, WRONG NUMBER

It all began in 1955 with a wrong number. In Colorado Springs, Colorado, a local department store ran a Christmas advertisement that featured a "Santa Claus Hotline." One problem: The phone number was wrong—it connected callers to the Continental Air Defense Command (CADC), not Santa Claus. The senior officer on duty that Christmas Eve, Colonel Harry Shoup, was a little flummoxed when he started receiving calls from kids asking for Santa. After he realized what was going on, Shoup informed the children that he was working for Santa and tracking his sleigh on the radar. Over the next few days, local news stations covered the story, and a holiday tradition was born.

YES, VIRGINIA, THERE IS A SANTA CLAUS TRACKER

The North American Aerospace Defense Command (NORAD), successor to the CADC, took over the tracking duties in 1957 and has been monitoring Santa's annual ride ever since. The U.S.–Canadian military organization monitors the air and space defenses of North America year-round from its location in Cheyenne Mountain in Colorado. But on December 24, attention turns to the fat man in the red suit. Why? Master Sergeant John Tomassi, deputy head of Santa Tracking Operations in

2004, says it's because "we want to make sure he gets around the world all right." So how does NORAD do it?

RADAR: NORAD's "North Warning" radar system comprises 47 installations that begin monitoring Santa as soon as he leaves the North Pole on December 24.

SATELLITES: Able to detect missiles by the heat their launches create, satellites track the infrared heat emitted by Santa's famous red-nosed reindeer. One veteran tracker claims that the more carrots Rudolph eats, the brighter his nose glows.

JET FIGHTERS: These escorts are F/A-18 Hornets (also called CF-18s), while in Canadian airspace, and either F-15 Eagles or F-16 Fighting Falcons, over the United States. Though NORAD estimates that Santa travels about 600 times the speed of light—300 times faster than these planes—he does slow down to wave to the pilots.

SANTA CAMS: Both mounted on NORAD fighter jets and positioned in various grounded locations around the globe, these digital cameras are able to catch video and still images of Kris Kringle.

If you're interested in checking on Santa's Christmas Eve progress, you can call them toll-free at 1-877-HI-NORAD, or you can track him online at **www.noradsanta.org.**

BELTS

Buckle up with a few of our favorite geographical (and astronomical) belts.

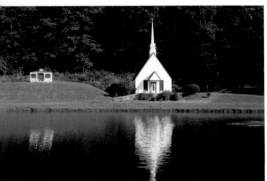

BELTWAY: A section of highway that loops the perimeter of a major city. In politics, it refers to the Capital Beltway, which surrounds Washington, D.C., and is used to describe the difference between political perceptions inside and outside of Washington.

BIBLE BELT: Nickname given to the American South, roughly from Florida north to Virginia and west to Oklahoma and Texas, where fundamentalist Christianity and church attendance are important aspects of local culture. The term was first used by *Chicago Daily Tribune* columnist H. L. Mencken in 1924.

BORSCHT BELT: Nickname for a region of the Catskill Mountains northwest of New York City, a popular vacation spot for wealthy New York City Jews from the 1910s until the 1970s. It was in the Borscht Belt resorts that scores of world-famous comedians got their start, including Henny Youngman, Milton Berle, Rodney Dangerfield, Lenny Bruce, and Sid Caesar.

SUN BELT: Nickname given to the American South and Southwest, from Florida and the Carolinas to Southern California, a region that's several degrees warmer year round than the North. The term was coined by author Kevin Phillips in his 1969 book *The Emerging Republican Majority*. (According to Phillips, anyway.)

STROKE BELT: Nickname given to a region in the American Southeast, particularly Tennessee, Georgia, and the Carolinas, that has an unusually high rate of death by stroke.

BELT: A town in central Montana, population 633, named after nearby Belt Butte, a mountain that appears to have a belt of rocks around it.

KUIPER BELT: A massive ring around our solar system that orbits the Sun far beyond the planets, the Kuiper belt is nearly two billion miles wide and contains hundreds of thousands of balls of ice known as KBOs (Kuiper Belt Objects). Pictured on the opposite page is an artist's rendition of Sedna, a dwarf planet discovered in 2004. With a diameter of 1,000 miles), Sedna orbits the Sun more than 80 billion miles away. And astronomers have only recently started studying the biggest belt in the solar system, so who knows what other fascinating KBOs are waiting to be discovered.

THIS PAGE, TOP TO BOTTOM: The Capital Beltway in Washington, D.C.; Church, West Virginia; View from Artists' Ledge of Kaaterskills Clove in New York's Catskills Mountains; La Jolla cove beach, San Diego, California

WEIRD ANIMAL NEWS
Strange tales of creatures great and small.

THEY'VE GONE NUTS!

A pack of vicious squirrels attacked and killed a dog in the village of Lazo in far eastern Russia in 2005. The dog had been barking at the squirrels when they attacked en masse. The squirrels ran off when people intervened, witnesses told the BBC, "some carrying pieces of flesh" in their mouths.

IT'S BETTER THAN WHAT THEY USUALLY THROW

Researchers at the Furuvik Zoo in Gavle, Sweden, realized there was a problem with their chimpanzee, Santino, when visitors complained that the animal was throwing rocks at them. The scientists looked at video footage and discovered, much to their dismay, that Santino

had actually planned the attacks. They found hidden stashes of rocks and concrete chunks all around his enclosure. When visitors came close, Santino unloaded. (The zoo keeps a close eye on him now.)

LOUNGING LIZARDS

A rare deep freeze hit the Florida Keys in early 2008 and fooled the native iguana population... into hibernation. Hundreds of the lizards fell out of trees and lied motionless on the ground, prompting concerned Floridians to take the stiff animals into their homes to warm them up. Bad idea: "When they warm up, they go back to being a wild animal," explained a local veterinarian. The iguanas (some as long as five feet) started thrashing about the houses,

causing extensive damage and in some cases, they bit people.

DOG GONE

"It was like something out of *The Wizard of Oz*," said Agnes Tamas, whose dog was blown away by a storm in Gesztered, Hungary, in 2010. Tamas, 57, could see the roofs being ripped from nearby houses when she ran to her cellar. She'd hoped her dog would be safe, but to her horror, she watched as his doghouse was swept up into the air and blew out of sight—with the pooch still inside! After the storm passed, Tamas searched and searched but could find no signs of her dog. A few days later, a man found the animal...20 miles away. Tamas was reunited with her dog, whom she renamed Lucky. (The

ONLY 2% OF AMERICANS ARE NATURAL REDHEADS.

doghouse, however, was never found.)

CHEETAH SCENTS

Biologists have long known that big cats are attracted to cologne and perfume, so they performed an experiment at the Bronx Zoo to find out which one the cats like the most. (The findings will help the scientists set scented remote camera traps.) Cheetahs were given several scents to smell, and the ferocious felines' favorite fragrance: Calvin Klein's Obsession for Men. According to zoo curator Pat Thomas, "The big cats would literally wrap their paws around a tree and just vigorously rub up and down. Sometimes they would start drooling, their eyes would half close, it was almost like they were going into a trance."

UNEASY RIDER

On a cold day in March 2005, Torri Hutchinson was driving along Highway 15 in Idaho when she noticed another driver gesturing frantically and shouting at her. Hutchinson was nervous—maybe the man was a crazed killer, or maybe he was telling her that her ski rack was coming loose. Reluctantly, Hutchinson pulled over and locked her doors. The man stopped behind her, got out, and ran up, yelling, "Your cat! Your cat!" Then Hutchinson realized why the man was screaming. Her orange tabby—named Cuddle Bug—had been clinging to the car's roof since she'd left home. They'd made it almost 10 miles before the other driver finally got Hutchinson to stop. She thanked the man and then took Cuddle Bug home.

TWEETY MOUSE

Of all the animal hybrids that scientists could come up with, this is the cutest: a mouse that tweets like a bird. It happened in Japan in 2012 while scientists were crossbreeding mice and monitoring them for abnormalities. "We checked the newly born mice one by one," said lead researcher Arikuni Uchimura. "One day, we found a mouse that was singing like a bird." He added that he hoped his research would lead to the creation of a talking mouse. "I know it's a long shot," he said, "but I'm doing this with hopes of making a Mickey Mouse someday."

In the 1950s, Senator Joseph McCarthy had the nation believing that Red Agents had infiltrated the U.S. government. But were the real conspirators the Communists...or McCarthy and his allies?

McCarthy's List

THE GREAT DIVIDE

On February 9, 1950, Joe McCarthy, a rumpled, ill-shaven junior senator from Wisconsin, made a Lincoln's Birthday speech to a Republican women's club in Wheeling, West Virginia. No one—not even McCarthy—considered it an important appearance. Yet that speech made Senator Joseph McCarthy one of the most feared men in America. Waving a piece of paper before the group, McCarthy declared, "I have here in my hand a list of 205 names made known to the Secretary of State as being members of the Communist Party, who are nevertheless still working and shaping policy in the State Department."

Republicans had been calling Democrats Communists for years. But before this, no one had ever claimed to know exactly how many Communists were in the government. McCarthy's speech made headlines. By the time he had given a similar speech in Salt Lake City, Utah, and returned to Washington, newspapers from coast to coast had repeated the charges. The country was in an uproar. The McCarthy Era—an American Inquisition that ruined the lives of thousands of innocent citizens accused of being

Communists, Communist dupes, or Communist sympathizers—had begun.

SEEING RED

McCarthy's influence grew rapidly. As the chairman of the Permanent Investigations Sub-Committee of a Senate Committee on Government Operations, he presided over a witch hunt for Communists. Fear became his most potent weapon. According to Kenneth C. Davis in the

book *Don't Know Much About History*, "Many of those who came before McCarthy, as well as many who testified before the powerful House Un-American Activities Committee (HUAC), were willing to point fingers at others to save their own careers and reputations. To fight back was to be tarred with McCarthy's 'Communist sympathizer' brush.... In this cynical atmosphere, laws of evidence and constitutional guarantees didn't apply."

OPPOSITE: Senator Joseph McCarthy in the late 1940s

RIGHT, TOP TO BOTTOM: Gary Cooper on the stand at the House Un-American Activities Committee (HUAC) hearings, Washington, D.C., October 24, 1947; Danny Kaye, June Havoc, Humphrey Bogart, and Lauren Bacall sitting in the crowd at the House Un-American Activities Committee hearings on October 31st 1947; Members of the House Committee on Un-American Activities sit for an executive meeting, Washington, D.C., August 8, 1948. From left, future American President Richard Nixon, chief investigator Robert Stripling, U.S. Representatives John McDowell, committee chairman John Parnell Thomas, and F. Edward Hebert.

For four years, McCarthy was as powerful as anyone in Washington. He forced President Eisenhower to clear appointments through him; the president even instituted loyalty programs for those working for the government to prove that he, too, was tough on Communism.

WAS IT A CONSPIRACY? #1

Did McCarthy and his cronies actually believe that there was a Communist conspiracy, or was it just an attempt to gain power? Some suspicious facts:

● Early in 1950, McCarthy told friends he needed a gimmick to get reelected. He was in political hot water with voters because he had introduced no major legislation and had not been assigned to any important committees. Newspaper correspondents in Washington had voted him "worst in the Senate."

● According to Frederick Woltman, a friend of the senator, McCarthy had made up the number of Communists on the spur of the moment during his Lincoln's Birthday speech—and

had just as promptly forgotten it. Caught off-guard by the outcry, McCarthy and his advisors wracked their brains for some lead as to what he said in the Wheeling speech. But he didn't keep a copy, and he had no notes. And his aides couldn't find anyone who remembered the exact number.

● That may be why every time McCarthy counted Communists, he came up with a different number. The day after the Wheeling speech, he changed the number from 205 to 57 "card-carrying Communists." A week later, he stated before a Senate Foreign Relations subcommittee that he knew of "81 known Communists." The number changed to 10 in open committee hearings, 116 in an executive session, 121 at the end of a four-month investigation, and 106 in a June 6 Senate speech.

● Privately, friends say McCarthy treated the list of Communists as a joke. In the book *The Nightmare Decade: The Life and Times of Senator Joe McCarthy*, Fred Cook writes, "When he was asked, 'Joe, just what did you have in your hand down there in Wheeling?' McCarthy gave his characteristic roguish grin and replied, 'An old laundry list.'"

● McCarthy was able to keep up the charade for so long because he would attack anybody who questioned his accuracy. For example: When the majority leader of the Senate, unable to get a firm number from McCarthy, asked if the newspaper accounts of his Wheeling speech were accurate, McCarthy replied

indignantly, "I may say if the senator is going to make a farce of this, I will not yield to him. I shall not answer more silly questions of the senator. This is too important, too serious a matter for that."

WAS IT A CONSPIRACY? #2

Was top lawman J. Edgar Hoover a coconspirator—even though it meant he was breaking the law? (The FBI's charter prohibits it from getting involved in domestic politics.) Evidence suggests he was. In fact, without Hoover's

TOP: J. Edgar Hoover testifying before the House on Un-American Activities Committee, Washington, D.C.
ABOVE: McCarthy waving a transcript of a monitored call between Pvt. G. David Schine (L) and Army Secretary Stevens, during the Army-McCarthy hearings, June 7, 1954 in Washington, D.C. On the right is McCarthy's chief counsel, Roy Cohn.

covert support, McCarthy couldn't have kept up his attacks. More suspicious facts:

● McCarthy and Hoover were friends. They often dined together, and played the ponies frequently.

● According to Curt Gentry in his book *J. Edgar Hoover: The Man and the Secrets,* "On returning home from his speaking tour, McCarthy called Hoover and told him he was getting a lot of attention on the Communist issue. But, he frankly admitted, he had made up the numbers as he talked...and he asked if the FBI could give him the information to back him up." William Sullivan, who later became third in command at the FBI, protested that the Bureau didn't have sufficient evidence to prove that there was even one Communist in the State Department.

● Hoover—completely ignoring the FBI's charter—assigned FBI agents to gather domestic intelligence on his ideological enemies, poring over hundreds of Bureau security files to help support McCarthy's charges.

● According to Gentry, Hoover did even more: "He supplied speechwriters for McCarthy...[One Hoover aide] personally took McCarthy in hand and instructed him how to release a story just before the press deadline, so that reporters wouldn't have time to ask for rebuttals. Even more importantly, he advised him to avoid the phrase 'card-carrying Communist,' which usually couldn't be proven, substituting instead 'Communist sympathizer' or 'loyalty risk,' which required only some affiliation, however slight."

● As McCarthy's star rose, Hoover helped the senator pick his staff. In fact, McCarthy hired so many ex-FBI agents that his office was reportedly nicknamed "the little FBI."

LEFT: Carl Levin (far left) presented a petition to Sen. Joe Duff (far right) calling for the censure of McCarthy. The petition included the signatures of more than 700 students, faculty, and administrative personnel at Swarthmore. McCarthy's four-year crusade had motivated Carl Levin and some of his friends to begin a petition-drive urging the Senate to support McCarthy's censure.

● Hoover was concerned about McCarthy's reckless charges— but not because they were untrue. A Hoover crony noted: "I've spoken to J. Edgar Hoover about McCarthy. He said the only trouble with Joe is that he's not general enough in his accusations. He'll give some number like '275 Communists.' And then the FBI has to account for them. It makes the job a whole lot tougher."

McCARTHY'S DOWNFALL

When McCarthy began attacking President Eisenhower and the U.S. Army in 1954, Hoover sensed that his own job might be in danger and ordered the FBI aides to not help the senator further. Poorly prepared, McCarthy attempted to bluff his way through televised army hearings, but this time he failed. Most Americans saw him as a bully and a liar, and the press turned on him. In December 1954, McCarthy became the fourth member in history to be censured by the U.S. Senate. In May 1957, he died of alcohol-related ailments.

DISTURBING FOOTNOTES

Apparently, McCarthy depended on his coconspirators at the FBI for more than information—he also needed their silence. Curt Gentry's extensive research suggests that:

● Hoover had several fat FBI files on McCarthy that could have destroyed his career. Much of the information they contained eventually became known: that McCarthy was a boozer and a chronic gambler; that he had exaggerated and lied about his military record during World War II; that as a Wisconsin judge he had granted "quickie divorces" for a price; and that he had used campaign contributions to speculate on the stock market.

● Gentry adds that there was another, more secret file on McCarthy that only Hoover and a handful of other agents had ever seen: "It concerned McCarthy's involvement with young girls. Very young girls...Former close personal friends of the senator were quoted in the memorandum as cautioning other friends that they should never leave McCarthy with young children, that there had been 'incidents.'"

YOU HAVE A 1-IN-77 CHANCE OF DYING BY ACCIDENT AND A 1-IN-211 CHANCE OF BEING MURDERED.

187

THE VILLAINS SPEAK

HOLLYWOOD BAD GUYS ARE OFTEN THE MOST INTERESTING CHARACTERS IN THE MOVIES.

" Free will. It's like butterfly wings: once touched, they never get off the ground. No, I only set the stage; you pull your own strings. "

JOHN MILTON (AL PACINO) *THE DEVIL'S ADVOCATE*

" Pop quiz, hotshot: There's a bomb on a bus. Once the bus goes 50 miles an hour, the bomb is armed. If it drops below 50, it blows up. What do you do? What do you do? "

HOWARD PAYNE (DENNIS HOPPER) *SPEED*

Holly McClane: "After all your posturing, all your speeches, you're nothing but a common thief..."

" I am an exceptional thief, Mrs. McClane. And since I'm moving up to kidnapping, you should be more polite. "

HANS GRUBER (ALAN RICKMAN) *DIE HARD*

" You want this, don't you? The hate is swelling in you now. Take your Jedi weapon. Use it. I am unarmed. Strike me down with it! Give in to your anger. With each passing moment you make yourself more my servant. "

THE EMPEROR (IAN McDIARMID) *RETURN OF THE JEDI*

" This "Superman" is nothing of the kind—I've discovered his weakness already. He cares. "

GENERAL ZOD (TERENCE STAMP) *SUPERMAN II*

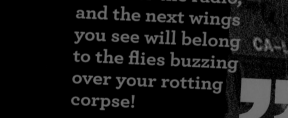

" Say a word about this over the radio, and the next wings you see will belong to the flies buzzing over your rotting corpse! "

CYRUS GRISSOM (JOHN MALKOVICH) *CON AIR*

" I'm a killer. A murdering bastard, you know that. And there are consequences to breaking the heart of a murdering bastard. "

BILL (DAVID CARRADINE) *KILL BILL, VOL. 2*

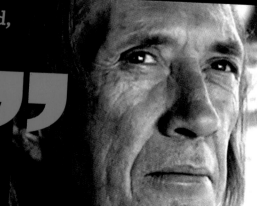

When Good Concerts Go Bad

For the poor fans who happened to attend these ill-fated shows, what transpired was no laughing matter. But for the rest of us, reading about them after the fact, it is.

BONO AND THE BIG LEMON

U2's 1997 tour featured a number of absurdly huge stage props. One of them was a 40-foot-tall lemon with a giant hatch door that members would emerge from to play encores. At a stop in Oslo, Norway, one night, the lemon wouldn't open. Engineers tried to get it open, stagehands tried to get it open, and U2 tried to get it open from the inside. Unable to loosen the door, the band instead went out through the lemon's back opening (where they came in), climbed down some stairs, and walked around the lemon to the stage, at which point the song ("Discotheque") was over.

TOP, CLOCKWISE FROM LEFT: Bono, Scott Stapp, Jewel

STAPP INFECTION

In December 2002, Scott Stapp, the singer for the rock band Creed, was on potent medication for a throat infection before a Chicago concert, but he still drank a bottle of whiskey before taking the stage. He mumbled through five songs, then went backstage to nap in his dressing room, thinking he'd performed a full concert. The band convinced him to come back out and continue singing... unfortunately, lyrics to songs they weren't playing. The show ended early—and four fans later sued Creed to get their money back. (The lawsuit was dismissed.)

A JEWEL IN THE ROUGH

Folk singer Jewel performed at a casino in Hampton, New York,

in May 2004. She played only five songs and spent the rest of the time making fun of people in the audience. Attendees say she insulted fans who were overweight or had bad teeth and said that drinkers and smokers were "sinners." For an encore, Jewel yodeled. One group of fans walked out of the show, demanded their money back, and drove by Jewel's tour bus, screaming obscenities at the singer.

NEITHER GRACEFUL NOR SLICK

Jefferson Starship toured Europe in 1978, but on the first night in Hamburg, Germany, lead singer Grace Slick refused to perform due to an upset stomach. The concert was rescheduled for the next night, and Slick prepared by reportedly drinking all of the alcohol in her hotel room's minibar before taking the stage. She spent the evening fondling the band's guitarist, Craig Chaquico, and then, in an insult to the German crowd, marched in a Nazi goose-step and gave the "Heil Hitler" salute. She then jumped into the crowd and stuck her finger up a man's nose. Slick said her behavior was "retaliation for World War II concentration camps."

EXCUSE ME, YOUR BIZKIT IS LIMP

Rap-metal band Limp Bizkit landed a spot opening for Metallica during a tour in 2003. But unfortunately, most of the

TOP: Grace Slick in 1978
CENTER: Fred Durst of Limp Bizkit
ABOVE: Fiona Apple in 2000

40,000 fans who came to a concert in Chicago were not there to see Limp Bizkit. Allegedly egged on by a local radio DJ, hundreds of fans pelted Limp Bizkit's lead singer Fred Durst with garbage, fruit, and coins. Some were even waving "Fred Sucks" signs. Durst retaliated by saying that the fans had the same "lousy aim as the baseball teams" in Chicago. At that moment, a fan threw a lemon, which struck Durst squarely in the crotch. Durst stopped the show and retreated to the wings, where he continued to yell at the crowd, yelling over and over, "Limp Bizkit is the greatest band in the world!" before a stagehand forcibly took his microphone away.

BAD APPLE

Fiona Apple was performing at New York's Roseland Ballroom in February 2000. Technical problems plagued the show, shutting off the singer's microphone several times. Apple flew into a rage: "You know, I just wanted to do real well in New York," she screamed, "but sh*t! I can't hear myself!" She played a few more notes of a song before stopping. "This song is dead," she yelled. "Just stop it! This is a nightmare!" Then she lashed out at all of the music critics in attendance: "If any of you give me a bad review, I'll f*ck*ng kill you!" Apple then began to cry, mumbled about how she needed to take a break, then left the stage. Concert over. No critics were killed.

A small British company put tracks on a tractor and changed agriculture—and war—forever.

Cat Tracks

ABOVE: Holt Manufacturing's Artillery Tractor in action with French Poilus at Vosges, on the Western Front, in the Spring of 1915
LEFT: David Roberts' Tracked Steam Tractor of 1903

MAKING TRACKS

In 1903 the British War Office offered £1,000 to the maker of a tractor that could haul 25 tons for 40 miles without stopping for fuel or water. The tiny agricultural manufacturer Hornsby & Sons (est. 1815) won with a tractor that went 58 miles. Chief engineer and manager David Roberts realized that if the British Army wanted to make full use of his 80-hp, 12-ton tractor, the machine could not get stuck in mud. By 1906 Roberts had come up with a novel chain track that he fitted onto the tractor. When British soldiers saw this rolling track in action, they dubbed the machine a "caterpillar." Two years later, the War Office purchased four chain-track tractors to tow artillery

pieces. Encouraged, Roberts worked to expand the caterpillar tractor's working applications, fitting it with wooden wheels for desert travel and boosting its top speed to 25 mph.

LOSING TRACK-TION

Hornsby & Sons wanted to share their caterpillar tractor with not only the army but also the general public. They commissioned a film to advertise it (the first commercial ever filmed). Audiences at the Empire Theatre of Varieties in London attended the premiere on April 27, 1908, and were impressed by the new vehicle. Unfortunately, soldiers in the Royal Artillery were not. One gunnery officer sniffed, "A team of eight horses in my opinion is far

superior under every condition." Roberts was devastated. When another officer suggested that they might be interested in the caterpillar if it could carry some kind of large gun protected by bulletproof armor, Roberts chose not to pursue it—a decision he would later regret. He only made one sale to the public and came to the conclusion that the caterpillar tractor was a loser. He decided to sell the caterpillar-track patent to cover Hornsby & Sons' losses.
  Enter C. H. Holt.

TRACK STAR

While Hornsby & Sons was developing engines and tractors in England, C. H. Holt Manufacturing was building wagon wheels and frames in

the United States. Founded in California in 1864, Holt quickly evolved into a large-scale farm equipment manufacturer, building 20-ton machines capable of hauling 50 tons. Holt tried to keep his heavy machines from sinking into deep mud by equipping them with tires seven feet in diameter and six feet wide. When that didn't work, he built redwood tracks for the tractors to ride on, which was cumbersome, time-consuming, and expensive. In 1909 he went to England to see what other farm-equipment manufacturers were doing to combat the mud problem. Holt saw the potential in the caterpillar tractor and snapped up the patent from Hornsby & Sons for a mere £4,000 pounds ($86,000 today). Holt also had the

foresight to trademark the name "Caterpillar."

Hornsby & Sons lost out due to bad timing—the British War Office decided within the year that they needed lots of caterpillar tractors to tow their heavy howitzers across the uneven fields of France and Belgium during World War I. They purchased 420 from Holt Mfg. for the hefty sum of $5,500 each ($118,000 today). By 1914 Holt had shipped 1,200 Caterpillar tractors to the English, French, and Russians, who sent them off to war. Most importantly, the Holt Caterpillar became the inspiration for the British tank.

Today, Caterpillar, Inc. is the largest manufacturer of construction and mining equipment, diesel and natural

ABOVE: U.S. troops move forward with British tanks during the advance on the St. Quentin Canal, France, 1918.

gas engines, and industrial gas turbines in the world, putting it at #66 on the 2010 Fortune 500 list.

STILL A-TRACK-TIVE

Although Hornsby & Sons missed the business opportunity of a lifetime when Roberts sold the Caterpillar patent, the company prospered with the Hornsby-Akroyd "hot bulb" engine. An early diesel engine designed by Herbert Akroyd Stuart, it was used to power tractors, locomotives, boats, submarines, and lighthouses for a generation. Hornsby-Akroyds powered the lights that originally lit the Statue of Liberty, Rock of Gibraltar, and Taj Mahal.

What goes up, must come down. And if it's a particularly rough flight, what goes down usually comes back up. Here's a collection of some of the strangest airplane stories that have ever taken flight.

Just Plane Weird

THE FOOD HERE IS TERRIBLE

In 1999 Northwest Airlines Captain Floyd Dean got a look at the meals being loaded onto the flight he was supposed to pilot from Detroit to Las Vegas...and decided he wanted something different. So he got off the plane—even though the Boeing 757 was scheduled for takeoff—and looked around the terminal for something better to eat. When he couldn't find anything he liked, he hopped in a cab and continued his search outside the airport, leaving 150 fuming passengers stranded on the plane for more than 90 minutes until he returned. Northwest fired the 22-year veteran on the spot for "abandoning his plane."

HEADING OUT

Chris Fogg was a flight nurse transporting a patient from Twin Falls, Idaho, to Seattle on a twin-engine Piper turboprop in June 2007. As they cruised at 20,000 feet, Fogg chatted with the pilot in the cockpit. All of a sudden, there was a loud popping noise, and then the window next to Fogg's right shoulder exploded... and he was partially sucked out of the window. Fogg's left arm and legs were still in the cockpit, but his head and right arm were outside battling 200 mph winds. The pilot put the plane in a steep dive down to 10,000 feet to equalize the pressure, and Fogg was able to pull himself back inside. They made an emergency landing in Boise 10 minutes later.

IN THE HOLE

On October 26, 1986, a violent explosion ripped through the rear toilet of Thai Airways flight 602 as it was preparing to land in Osaka, Japan. The plane landed safely...at which point investigators found a Japanese "Yakuza" gangster dangling head-first through a hole ripped in the floor by the explosion—his hindquarters badly injured by shrapnel—while two other Yakuza held on to his legs to keep him from falling onto the tarmac. The explosion is believed to have been caused when the Yakuza threw a hand grenade down the restroom trash chute so that it wouldn't be discovered when he went through customs.

got 2 go now time 2 land! kthxbye ☺

U MAD?

Only a few hundred feet from touching down in Singapore in May 2010, an Australian Jetstar Airbus carrying 167 passengers was forced to abort the landing and circle the airport for another attempt. Why did the plane have to abort? Because the landing gear wasn't down. Why wasn't the landing gear down? Because the pilot was distracted. Why was he distracted? According to SkyNews, he was sending a text on his phone. The plane landed safely and the pilot was suspended pending an investigation. OMG!

THE MOD SQUAD

In 1965 Braniff Airlines announced "The End of the Plain Plane." As part of Braniff's makeover, the airline hired fashion designer Alexander Girard to oversee every aspect of design for the company. Girard came up with a multi-colored fleet of jets: orange, beige, lemon, turquoise, ochre, and two shades of blue. The complementary interiors had seven different color schemes, using 56 different Herman Miller fabrics in red, green, orange, blue, yellow, and grey. The flight crews' ultra-mod uniforms, designed by Emilio Pucci, were plum, lavender, and orange, complete with colorful boots. Flight attendants were even given clear plastic bubble helmets to protect their hair in case of rain. (Two decades later, the crew uniforms on *Star Trek: The Next Generation* resembled the cut and style of the original Braniff designs.)

HIGH ANXIETY

"Imagine your adrenaline is being excited by the roar of the 747 engines as you thunder down the runway. Just after lift-off, there's a sudden hush from those massive engines. Your heart is in your mouth, pumping as it had never done before." Those are the opening lines from a book called *One Obsession, Two Obsession, Three Obsession, Four*, written by a former Qantas Airlines pilot named Bryan Griffin. Hired in 1966, the Australian pilot developed a compulsive urge to crash a plane, and it grew worse and worse as the years passed. A few times he even had to grab his own hand to keep it from shutting off the engines. "It's like it wasn't even my arm," he said. In 1979 Griffin finally informed his bosses of his urges but, amazingly, they cleared him to fly. Then a psychiatrist diagnosed him with severe obsessive compulsive disorder, anxiety, and depression. But still, Qantas cleared him to fly. Fortunately for passengers, in 1982 Griffin quit. He spent the next 28 years working odd jobs, seeing psychiatrists, writing his book, and filing lawsuits against Qantas. In 2010 a judge finally ruled that airline officials had "exacerbated" Griffin's condition by continuing to let him fly and awarded him $160,000.

THE WORLD'S RAREST BLOOD TYPE, A-H, IS FOUND IN FEWER THAN A DOZEN PEOPLE WORLDWIDE.

DEFENDANT: Judge, I want you to appoint me another lawyer.
JUDGE: And why is that?
DEFENDANT: Because the public defender isn't interested in my case.
JUDGE (TO PUBLIC DEFENDER): Do you have any comments on your defendant's motion?
PUBLIC DEFENDER: I'm sorry, Your Honor, I wasn't listening.

Court Transquips

- - - - - - - - - - - - - - - -

These were actually said, word for word, in a court of law.

JUDGE: Is there any reason you could not serve as a juror in this case?
JUROR: I don't want to be away from my job for that long.
JUDGE: Can't they do without you at work?
JUROR: Yes, but I don't want them to know it.

PROSECUTOR: Could you point to someone in this courtroom, or maybe yourself, to indicate exactly how close to a hair color you are referring to?
WITNESS: Well, something like hers (points at the defense attorney) except for more cheap bleached-blond hair.
PROSECUTOR: May the record reflect, Your Honor, the witness has identified Defense Counsel as the cheap blonde.

JUDGE TO DEFENDANT: You have a right to a trial by jury, but you may waive that right. What do you wish to do?
DEFENDANT: (Hesitates.)
LAWYER TO DEFENDANT: Waive.
DEFENDANT: (Waves at the judge.)

JUDGE: Mr. E., you're charged here with driving a motor vehicle under the influence of alcohol. How do you plead, guilty or not guilty?
DEFENDANT: I'm guilty as hell.
JUDGE: Let the record reflect the defendant is guilty as hell.

DEFENSE ATTORNEY: Are you sure you did not enter the 7-Eleven on 40th and N.E. Broadway and hold up the cashier on June 17 of this year?
DEFENDANT: I'm pretty sure.

PROSECUTOR: Did you observe anything?
WITNESS: Yes, we did. When we found the vehicle, we saw several unusual items in the car in the right front floorboard of the vehicle. There was what appeared to be a Molotov cocktail, a green bottle...
DEFENSE LAWYER: Objection. I'm going to object to that word, Molotov cocktail.
JUDGE: What is your legal objection, Counsel?
DEFENSE LAWYER: It's inflammatory, Your Honor.

JUDGE: The charge here is theft of frozen chickens. Are you the defendant, sir?
DEFENDANT: No, sir, I'm the guy who stole the chickens.

LAWYER: Could you briefly describe the type of construction equipment used in your business?
WITNESS: Four tractors.
LAWYER: What kind of tractors are they?
WITNESS: Fords.
LAWYER: Did you say 'four?'
WITNESS: Ford. Ford. Like the Ford. It is a Ford tractor.
LAWYER: You didn't say 'four,' you just said 'Ford?'
WITNESS: Yes, Ford. That is what you asked me, what kind of tractors.
LAWYER: Are there four Ford tractors? Is that what there is?
WITNESS: No, no. You asked me what kind of a tractor it was and I said Ford tractors.
LAWYER: How many tractors are there?
WITNESS: Four.

LAWYER: Have you ever been convicted of a felony?
DEFENDANT: Yes.
LAWYER: How many?
DEFENDANT: One, so far.

Admit it: At some point in your life, you said something really stupid that you wish you could take back. Think of the bright side—at least you're not famous enough for your idiotic utterance to end up in print! (Our condolences if you are.)

DUH!

"You mean, like a book?"
JUSTIN TIMBERLAKE, when asked what was the best thing he had read all year

"He treats us like men. He lets us wear earrings."
TORRIN POLK, University of Houston receiver, on his coach

"You get to meet important people from all walks of life, from Joe DiMaggio to Barry Bonds."
MICHAEL BOLTON, on the advantages of being famous

PREMATURE INFANTS ARE FIVE TIMES MORE LIKELY TO BE LEFT-HANDED.

"Stand up, Chuck, and let 'em see ya."
JOE BIDEN, to Sen. Chuck Graham, who is confined to a wheelchair

"It's kind of boring for me to have to eat."
KATE MOSS,
supermodel

"Sometimes they write what I say and not what I mean."
Baseball player **PEDRO GUERRERO,** on sportswriters

"It's clearly a budget. It's got a lot of numbers in it."
GEORGE W. BUSH

"Today's a big day in America. Only 36,000 people lost their jobs, which is really good!"
SEN. HARRY REID

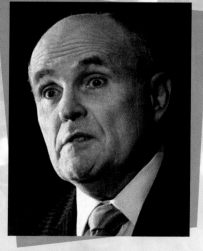

"I'm probably one of the four or five best-known Americans in the world."
RUDY GIULIANI, to British reporters

A TYPICAL CARROT HAS TO TRAVEL 1,838 MILES TO REACH YOUR DINNER TABLE.

The universe works in mysterious ways.

Amazing Coincidences

FREAKY PHONE CALL

In 1992 Sue Hamilton, a British office worker, needed to call her co-worker, Jason Pegler, when the fax machine broke. She found his number on a bulletin board, dialed it, and he picked up. "Sorry to ring you at home, Jason," she said. "I'm not at home," he replied. "I was walking past a phone booth when it rang." Instead of dialing Pegler's phone number, Hamilton had accidentally dialed his employee number—which happened to be the same number as the phone booth he happened to be walking past.

SHOULD HAVE STAYED HOME

In 1865 Robert Todd Lincoln was invited to attend a play with his parents. He arrived late to find that his father, Abraham Lincoln, had been assassinated. Fifteen years later, in 1881, President Andrew Garfield invited Robert to join him on a train trip. Moments before Robert boarded the train, Garfield was shot and killed. Twenty years later, in 1901, President Robert McKinley invited Robert to a public event. Seconds before Robert arrived, McKinley was shot. Having finally learned his lesson, Robert promised not to accept any more presidential invitations.

ESTRANGED INHERITANCE

In 1858 a poker player named Robert Fallon was caught cheating and was shot dead in a San Francisco saloon. No one wanted his $600 (money won by cheating was considered unlucky), but they had no problem winning it back. So they plucked a young man from the street to take the dead man's place. He obliged...and started winning. When a police officer arrived to investigate the killing, he seized the original $600 to give to Fallon's next of kin. The young man then said to the cop, "His name was Fallon? So's mine!" It turned out that the new player was Fallon's next of kin—his son. He hadn't seen his father in seven years. (He kept the money.)

FRONT PAGE NEWS

A blurry photo of a man stealing a wallet in a store ran on the bottom of the front page of the December 14, 2007, edition of Idaho's *Lewiston Tribune*. Above it was an unrelated photo of a man painting a business. Some readers noticed that both men were wearing the same clothes... and could be the same man. He was, leading to his arrest.

NAME GAME

In 1911 three men—named Green, Berry, and Hill—were convicted of a murder. They were hanged at London's Greenberry Hill.

FRIENDS FOREVER

On June 24, 2005, veteran actor Paul Winchell died at age 82. He voiced the character of Tigger in Disney's Winnie the Pooh films. The next day, John Fiedler died at age 80. He was the voice of Piglet.

LEFT: A newsworthy coincidence
TOP: Friends forever—Tigger and Piglet
ABOVE: Paul Winchell from the 1950s. (He's the one in the center.)
BELOW: John Fiedler in an early episode of *The Twilight Zone*

OUI, OUI! IN FRENCH, DANDELIONS ARE CALLED *PISSENLIT*, WHICH MEANS "PEE IN BED."

201

THE
SPACE SHUTTLE
A TIMELINE

After 500 million miles traveled, the space shuttle was the longest-lasting program in U.S. space aviation history. Here's a timeline of the 30-year adventures of the *Enterprise, Columbia, Challenger, Discovery, Atlantis,* and *Endeavour.*

1977

Test-shuttle *Enterprise* makes its first flight on August 12. It was originally named *Constitution,* but a write-in campaign from *Star Trek* fans convinced NASA to rechristen it.

1981

On April 12, *Columbia* blasts off from Launch Pad 39A at Kennedy Space Center in Florida. Columbia orbits Earth 37 times before landing at Edwards Air Force Base in California.

1983

Columbia becomes the first shuttle to put parts of Spacelab into orbit. Spacelab is billed as "science around the world and around the clock."

1984

On February 7, Bruce McCandless II makes the first untethered spacewalk as he floats around *Challenger* on its fourth mission.

1985

Atlantis debuts October 3 on a classified mission, one of 10 commandeered by the Pentagon to conduct military research.

1986

An O-ring fails at liftoff and *Challenger* explodes 72 seconds later, killing all seven onboard, including the shuttle's first civilian astronaut, teacher Christa McAuliffe.

1989

After a 13-month grounding to address safety issues, *Atlantis* sends the *Magellan* probe on its way to map Venus. Five months later *Atlantis* sends the probe *Galileo* on its way to Jupiter.

1990

Discovery puts the Hubble Space Telescope into orbit in April.

1992

On its debut mission, *Endeavour* serves as home base to the first three-person spacewalk. Pierre Thuot, Richard Hieb, and Thomas Akers retrieve the Intelsat VI (F-3) satellite.

1993

On September 22, *Discovery* touches down at Kennedy Space Center at 3:56 a.m. in the first shuttle night landing.

1995

On June 29, *Atlantis* is the first American shuttle to dock with the Russian space station *Mir.* It is the 100th manned spaceflight controlled from Cape Canaveral.

1997

In May *Atlantis* brings Michael Foale up to the *Mir* station and Jerry Linenger back down, completing the first of many missions to exchange space station crew.

1998

Columbia pulls away from Spacelab for the last time, completing the 20th and final Spacelab mission. Parts of it are used to build the International Space Station (ISS).

2011
After 39 missions, *Discovery* retires in March; *Endeavour* follows in June after completing its 25th. *Atlantis* concludes its 33rd mission with a successful landing on July 21, 2011, marking the 135th shuttle mission and the end of NASA's Space Shuttle Program.

2009
Atlantis **completes the last of four shuttle missions** to fix the Hubble Space Telescope. NASA declares the repairs a success.

2008
The Space Station becomes even more international when *Endeavour*, *Atlantis*, and *Discovery* add sections made by space programs in Canada, Japan, and Europe.

2007
After sitting idle for five years, *Endeavour* is sent aloft to bring supplies and structural pieces to the ISS.

2003
During liftoff on January 16, *Columbia* has a malfunction with its foam insulation, which causes the shuttle to break apart on re-entry 16 days later. All seven astronauts are killed.

1999
On May 29, *Discovery* becomes the first shuttle to dock with the ISS.

1998
Endeavour **brings up NASA's** *Unity* **connecting module and** links it to the Russian *Zayra* command module already in orbit. *Unity* and *Zayra* are still part of the ISS.

When economists want to get a sense of how the economy is doing, they look at things like the prime lending rate, the unemployment rate, and the Dow Jones Average. It turns out that's not all they look at.

Underwear Economics

DOWN UNDER

Alan Greenspan was the chairman of the Federal Reserve from 1987 to 2006. He was one of the most influential economists of his day, and his grasp of how the American economy works was profound. He was also famous for keeping an eye on an economic indicator that, on the surface at least, didn't seem to have much to do with the economy at all: sales of men's underwear.

What interested Greenspan about men's underwear was that the sales figures rarely changed. For most men, underwear isn't something they treat themselves to when they feel like splurging; it's a purely utilitarian item. They buy it to replace underwear that has worn out. And since underwear wears out at a pretty steady rate, sales of new underwear are pretty steady too.

Greenspan noticed, however, that on occasion underwear sales did dip. When that happened, he interpreted it to mean that significant numbers of men were financially stressed enough that they had stopped replacing their worn-out shorts.

FIRST THINGS FIRST

How many people see you in your underwear? When funds are limited, most men will put off buying underwear—clothes that people don't see—before they stop buying shirts and pants that people do see, if for no other reason than to keep up appearances.

If they have kids, men will put off buying their own underwear before they'll stop buying things for their children. For this reason, men's underwear sales tend to lead many other economic indicators— they register signs of economic distress months before sales of other items begin to slow. That's why Greenspan liked to keep an eye on it: If the economy was losing steam, he'd see it in men's underwear first.

THIS, THAT, AND THE OTHER THING

Over the years, economists have developed theories based on a lot of other items besides men's underwear. For example:

Boxcars. A lot of freight is shipped by rail in the United States, and when the freight isn't moving, the unused boxcars are parked on railroad spur lines until the economy picks up and they're needed again.

Movie Tickets. As expensive as a trip to the multiplex is nowadays, it's still a lot cheaper

ABOVE: One of these objects is Alan Greenspan, Chairman of the Federal Reserve 1987–2006. Can you guess which one?

than a weekend at the beach. People who can't afford to take a vacation often compensate by going to the movies instead, causing ticket sales to rise in a recession.

Donuts. People who can't afford a full breakfast in a restaurant will often trade down to a donut and coffee. Hot dog sales do well in hard times for the same reason: In the 1930s, they were known as "Depression sandwiches."

Laxatives. When people are under stress and living on donuts and hot dogs...well, you figure it out.

Lipstick. Studies show that women who don't have the money for a new dress or new shoes will spend $15 or $20 on lipstick

instead. Belts, scarves, bracelets, and other fashion accessories that dress up old outfits also do well, as do home permanents and dye kits that offer a cheap alternative to hair salons.

Alligators. Most gators that end up as boots, handbags, and other designer goods are raised on farms. Sales of these items tend to crash during a recession (they're too expensive and too flashy in hard times), and the alligator population on these farms explodes.

Lightbulbs. When Jack Welch took the helm at General Electric

in 1981, the company made more than just lightbulbs, but he still swore by sales of bulbs as an indicator of where the economy was heading. "When people are affluent, they go to the store and buy what's called 'pantry inventory,'" he told an interviewer in 2001. "They'll buy a pack of six or a pack of eight, and they'll wait for the lights to go out. When times are tough, a light burns out, they'll go buy one to replace the one went out. There are probably a thousand better indicators, but that one's never been wrong."

THE RELIGION OF THE TODAS PEOPLE OF INDIA FORBIDS CROSSING BRIDGES.

205

OOPS!

Everyone loves tales of outrageous blunders, so go ahead and feel superior for a few moments.

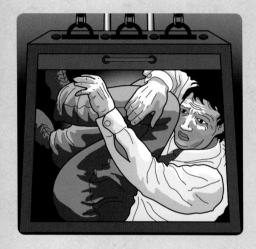

THE LOST WEEKEND

Somjet Korkeaw, a 42-year-old office worker from Bangkok, Thailand, was leaving work on a Saturday afternoon when he suddenly realized he'd forgotten something and had to return to his office on the 99th floor to get it. But the passenger elevators had already been turned off for the weekend and the stair doors were locked, so he decided to take a small cargo elevator (designed to carry food and documents). It was small, so he had to crouch into a ball to fit, but it was the only way back to the office. One problem: Korkeaw weighed 150 pounds, far too heavy for the lift to carry. Result: It got stuck between floors. He had to wait, bent over and crammed inside the little box, for more than 40 hours until the building reopened on Monday morning.

BIRD BRAIN

How much does Eric Torpy admire NBA legend Larry Bird? So much that when Torpy was sentenced to 30 years in prison for armed robbery and attempted murder in 2005, he said to the judge, "Why not make it 33?" (That was Bird's jersey number.) Equally bizarre: The judge granted Torpy's request. However, after serving the first few years of his sentence, Torpy wasn't happy with the situation anymore. "Now I wish that I had 30 years instead of 33," he said in 2011. "I've wisened up." Adding insult to injury, the story made the rounds in the press and Torpy was made fun of on *The Tonight Show*...which means that Larry Bird himself has most likely heard about it. "He must think I'm an idiot," said Torpy, who will be eligible for parole in 2033.

OUT-SQUIRRELED

A tourist at Montana's Glacier National Park wanted to take a picture of a squirrel that had scurried away into its rocky den. Trying to coax the animal out of its lair, the man dangled his only set of car keys in front of the opening. The squirrel darted out, snatched the keys right out of the man's hand, and disappeared back into the ground. Rangers tried to assist the frantic tourist, but the squirrel (and the keys) were nowhere to be found. The man had to call a locksmith out to the park and pay a hefty sum to get his car back on the road.

UNFRIENDLY FIRE

In July 2009, a French Foreign Legion commander ordered his troops to engage in target practice on a field near Marseille, in southern France. Bad idea: It was a hot, dry, and windy day, and the guns fired tracer rounds—which burn, so the soldiers can see where their shots land. Each round started a little fire...and all the little fires became one big fire (France's largest in three years, forcing the evacuation of 300 homes in a nearby neighborhood). The Foreign Legion apologized and explained that there are rules in place not to use incendiary devices on hot days, but for some reason, the commander ignored that rule. (Reportedly, the same thing nearly happened the year before.) Said one homeowner: "I've lost my home, my car, and all my possessions. My family is now living in a gym, and it's all because of these ridiculous soldiers."

HOG HEAVEN

In January 2011, Australia's *Morning Bulletin* reported a story of seemingly biblical proportions after cyclone Yasi caused severe flooding in the northeast part of the country: "There have been 30,000 pigs floating down the Dawson River since last week." Over the next few days, at least three other newspapers printed the *Bulletin*'s report verbatim. Apparently no one at any of the press offices questioned that incredible figure. Readers, however, had a tough time believing it and challenged the papers. A little digging revealed the truth: When *Morning Bulletin*'s reporter originally interviewed pig farmer Sid Everingham about the flood, Everingham didn't say "30,000 pigs"—he said "30 sows and pigs." The newspapers all printed corrections.

"Green, I love you green. Green wind. Green branches."
FEDERICO GARCIA LORCA

"Green is the prime color of the world, and that from which its loveliness arises."
PEDRO CALDERON DE LA BARCA

"Green is my favorite color, except for flesh."
TOM ROBBINS

"Green in nature is one thing, green in literature another. Nature and letters seem to have a natural antipathy; bring them together and they tear each other to pieces."
VIRGINIA WOOLF

"Green is my favorite because it's the color of my wife's eyes, grass, trees, life, and money."
CASPER VAN DIEN

"The road to the City of Emeralds is paved with yellow brick."
L. FRANK BAUM

"It is the color closest to light. In its utmost purity it always implies the nature of brightness and has a cheerful, serene, gently stimulating character. Hence, experience teaches us that yellow makes a thoroughly warm and comforting impression."
GOETHE

"There are painters who transform the sun into a yellow spot, but there are others who, thanks to their art and intelligence, transform a yellow spot into the sun."
PABLO PICASSO

"Orange is the happiest color."
FRANK SINATRA

"Orange is red brought nearer to humanity by yellow."
WASSILY KANDINSKY

"Beauty, to me, is about being comfortable in your own skin. That, or a kick-ass red lipstick!"
GWYNETH PALTROW

"Out of the ash I rise with my red hair / And eat men like air."
SYLVIA PLATH

"It was always my nickname when I was a little girl. My friends named me Pink because I was the only girl in my clique."
PINK

What's in a Color?

"Sit in reverie and watch the changing color of the waves that break upon the idle seashore of the mind."
HENRY WADSWORTH LONGFELLOW

"No colors any more I want them to turn black..."
MICK JAGGER & KEITH RICHARDS

"The first of all single colors is white."
LEONARDO DA VINCI

"White is not a mere absence of color; it is a shining and affirmative thing, as fierce as red, as definite as black...God paints in many colors; but He never paints so gorgeously, I had almost said so gaudily, as when He paints in white."
G. K. CHESTERTON

"Gray is the color of all theory."
GOETHE

"The moon is essentially gray, no color. It looks like plaster of Paris, like dirty beach sand with lots of footprints in it."
JAMES LOVELL,
APOLLO 13 COMMANDER

"If the sight of the blue skies fills you with joy, rejoice, for your soul is alive."
ELEANORA DUSE

"Blue color is everlastingly appointed by the Deity to be a source of delight."
JOHN RUSKIN

"I never get tired of the blue sky."
VINCENT VAN GOGH

"Purple is black blooming."
CHRISTOPHER SMART

"I think it pisses God off if you walk by the color purple in a field somewhere and don't notice it."
ALICE WALKER, THE COLOR PURPLE

"I won't eat any cereal that doesn't turn the milk purple."
CALVIN, CALVIN AND HOBBES

"Mauve is just pink trying to be purple."
JAMES WHISTLER

"We were on the dark side of the Earth when we started to see outside the window this soft pink glow, which is a lot of little angry ions out there going very fast. We were hitting them very fast."
ROBERT CRIPPEN, SPACE SHUTTLE ASTRONAUT

"A profusion of pink roses being ragged in the rain speaks to me of all gentleness and its enduring."
WILLIAM CARLOS WILLIAMS

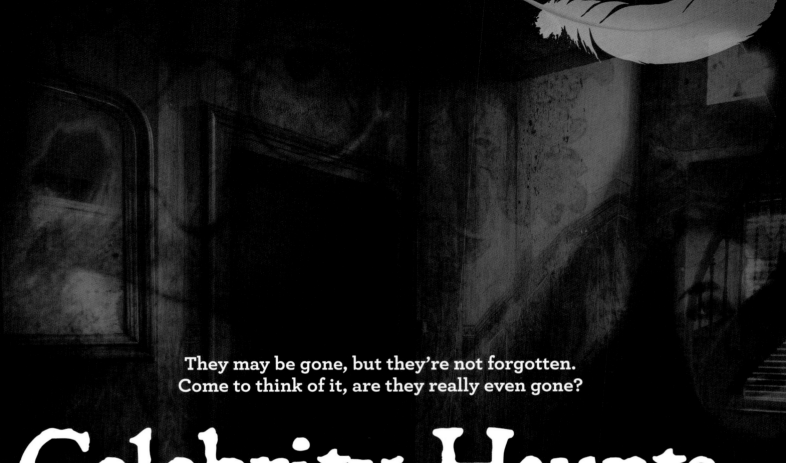

They may be gone, but they're not forgotten.
Come to think of it, are they really even gone?

Celebrity Haunts

BENJAMIN FRANKLIN (1706–90)

Franklin helped establish the American Philosophical Society in Philadelphia in the 1740s. His papers are housed there along with, according to some staff members, his ghost. Employees claim that Franklin hangs out in the library and likes to peruse its shelves. Aside from one nasty encounter with a cleaning lady, who claimed that he attacked her after hours, he's usually in high spirits.

KURT COBAIN (1967–94)

In the days following the Nirvana frontman's death by shotgun, fans gathered outside his Seattle home to pay their respects. But did Cobain join them? Some said they saw the singer's ghost watching them from the windows...and even from the roof. Six years later, in August 2000, a bartender in Essex, England, told reporters that Cobain's ghost had taken up residence in her laptop. She claimed that his face materialized on the screen one night, begged her for help, and then asked her to kiss him. She kissed the screen, and the image vanished. The laptop crashed and never worked again.

"MAMA" CASS ELLIOT (1941–74)

Actor and comedian Dan Aykroyd used to live in a Los Angeles home once owned by Mama Cass, lead singer of the Mamas and the Papas (who—despite the urban legend—did not choke to death on a ham sandwich). Aykroyd insists that she hasn't left the house. "Have I ever felt an unseen presence near me?" he wrote in

2010. "Damn right. In my bed no less!" Aykroyd said that, in addition to snuggling up with him, she would also "turn on the Stairmaster and move jewelry across the dresser." How did he know it's Mama Cass? "Because you get the feeling it's a big ghost."

MICHAEL JACKSON (1958–2009)

Shortly after the King of Pop's death, a TV crew from *Larry King Live* shot footage around Jackson's Neverland Ranch estate. When the show aired, several fans noticed something eerie: A shadowy figure seems to be walking from left to right across a hallway. CNN claimed the image was a shadow caused by a crew member walking past an off-camera light fixture, but viewers had a spookier explanation: It was Jackson's ghost. Since then, Jackson's image has been sighted dozens of times—everywhere from a Catholic school in Harare, Zimbabwe, to a reflection on the hood of a car in Stafford, Virginia.

JOHN LENNON (1940–80)

In 1995 the surviving members of the Beatles convened in a London studio to record a new song called "Free as a Bird," built on a vocal demo that Lennon had recorded in the 1970s. According to Paul McCartney, Lennon may have joined them. "There were a lot of strange goings-on in the studio— noises that shouldn't have been there and equipment doing all manner of weird things." Another sighting: Lennon once told his son Julian that should he ever die, he would visit him as "a white feather floating evenly across the room." About a year after Lennon's death, Julian Lennon reported that his father kept his word.

Fabulous Flops

Some folks have an eye for business, and some businesses have an "i" for idiot.

PUT A SOCK IN IT

Remember the Pets.com sock puppet? He appeared in 2000 in TV commercials for the online pet store and was wildly popular. He showed up on *Good Morning, America* and floated in the Macy's Thanksgiving Day parade as a 36-foot balloon. Unfortunately, Pets.com's concept—selling pet supplies over the Internet—wasn't as popular as the puppet. After little more than a year, Pets.com was gone...and so was $100 million in start-up funds.

Flop-Flip: And the sock puppet? He reappeared in 2002 in ads

LEFT: The sock puppet that flopped
RIGHT: The Flavr Savr tomatoes looked good... until you actually tried one.

for 1-800-BarNone, a company that offered loans to people with bad credit. He's even written an autobiography, *Me By Me*.

YOU SAY TO-MA-TO, I SAY TO-BLAH-TO

In 1994 a small biotech company called Calgene got FDA approval for the first genetically engineered whole food to hit the stores in the United States—the Flavr Savr tomato. It was genetically altered to delay ripening, which allowed growers to keep the plant on the

vine longer, shippers to keep it in the trucks longer, and grocers to keep it on shelves longer. It sounds good, but the tomatoes had problems: They didn't taste very good; crop yields were below expectations; and the machines used for packing them, built for still-green and firm tomatoes, mashed the Flavr Savrs to mush. After two years on the market, the original "Frankenfood" was pulled from stores. Calgene's loss: an estimated $150 million.

LEFT: Pfizer lost a whopping $71 million on its failed "fountain of youth" drug.
BELOW: Judging a can by its label—the controversial Power Master malt liquor said a bit too much.

HOPE SPRINGS ETERNAL

Pharmaceutical giant Pfizer Inc. spent 10 years and tons of money developing a "fountain of youth" drug designed to slow the aging process and keep people feeling young and vital well into old age. Initial research showed promise, prompting the company to pour even more money into the project. The reasoning was obvious: If it worked, the drug could make them millions, or even billions of dollars. In 2001 an independent testing lab performed a study that Pfizer executives expected would vault the drug toward FDA approval...but it didn't work out that way. The study actually concluded that people who took the "fountain of youth" drug had about the same results as those who'd taken sugar pills. By June 2002, the project had been canned. Cost of the decade of work: $71 million.

BEERZ IN THE HOOD

In June 1991, G. Heileman Brewing Company, makers of Colt 45, came out with a new beverage: PowerMaster, a malt liquor with a 5.8% alcohol content (the average American beer has 3.5%; most malt liquors have 4.5%). Black community leaders immediately protested, charging that the product was aimed specifically and irresponsibly at urban African Americans. For proof, they pointed to the billboard ads for the beverage that were popping up in black neighborhoods. The protests quickly spread around the country, and by July the Bureau of Alcohol, Tobacco and Firearms ruled that the "Power" in PowerMaster had to go. A beer's name, they said, cannot reflect the strength of its alcohol content (even though they had approved the name just a month earlier). Heileman was forced to pull

PowerMaster, at a marketing loss of more than $2 million.

Flop-flip: A year later, the brewer quietly introduced Colt 45 Premium, a malt liquor with a 5.9% alcohol content. The can was black with a red horse on it—the same design as PowerMaster.

FELT TIP FOLLIES

In late 2001, Sony Music came out with a "copy-proof" CD. It was a much-heralded step toward preventing the piracy of their artists' music, which they claimed hurt sales. Sony spent millions developing the technology and in the first few months of 2002 shipped more than 11 million of the discs. But by May the innovation proved to be a total flop. Word had spread like wildfire on the Internet that the high-tech copy-proofing could be thwarted... by scribbling around the rim of the CDs with an 89¢ felt-tip marker.

KALASHNIKOV PAT & THE HELICOPTER JAILBREAKS

Since 1986 there have been 11 helicopter-assisted jailbreaks from French prisons. Three of them involved the same man: Pascal Payet.

BACKGROUND: Pascal Payet, a.k.a. "Kalashnikov Pat," is one of France's most notorious criminals. In 1997 he was arrested for armed robbery and murder after an attack on an armored truck, during which he shot a guard 14 times. Payet was sent to Luynes Prison in southeast France to await trial.

1 **ESCAPE!** On October 12, 2001, a helicopter appeared above the prison exercise yard. A rope ladder was lowered, Pascal and one on other inmate climbed it, and the chopper flew off. The daring escape shocked French authorities and made headlines worldwide.

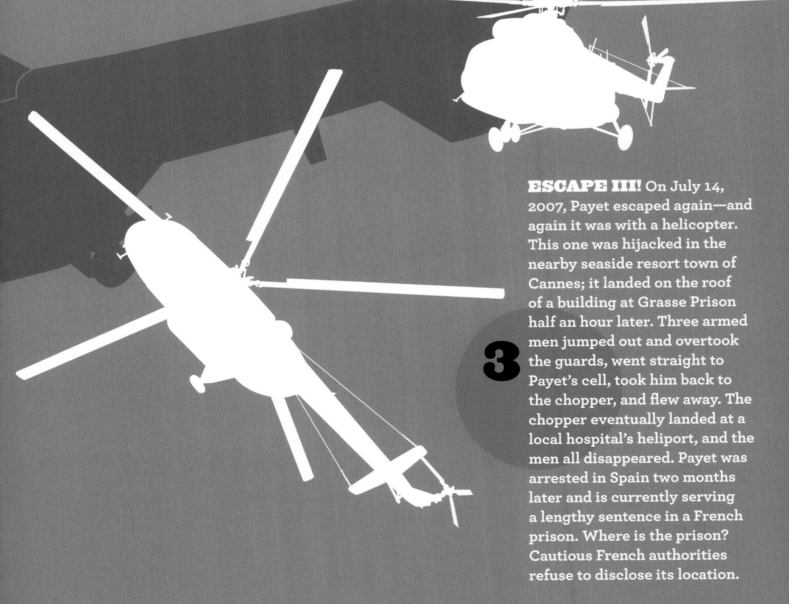

2 **ESCAPE II!** In May 2003, Payet was still on the loose when he and some associates decided to go back to Luynes Prison (in a hijacked helicopter) to pick up a few friends. Two of the men belayed commando-style down to the steel net that had been put over the exercise yard after Payet's previous escape, sawed a hole in it and dropped a ladder through, and three inmates, all cohorts of Payet, climbed up. The helicopter landed in a nearby sports stadium, and the men left in a waiting car. The three friends were recaptured a week later; Payet, some months later. In 2005 he was sentenced to 30 years in Grasse Prison in southeast France.

3 **ESCAPE III!** On July 14, 2007, Payet escaped again—and again it was with a helicopter. This one was hijacked in the nearby seaside resort town of Cannes; it landed on the roof of a building at Grasse Prison half an hour later. Three armed men jumped out and overtook the guards, went straight to Payet's cell, took him back to the chopper, and flew away. The chopper eventually landed at a local hospital's heliport, and the men all disappeared. Payet was arrested in Spain two months later and is currently serving a lengthy sentence in a French prison. Where is the prison? Cautious French authorities refuse to disclose its location.

U.S. BARTENDERS SAY THEY HEAR MORE COMPLAINTS ABOUT WORK THAN ANY OTHER SUBJECT.

215

Mythology for the Dogs

Do you want to hear about some classic canine folk legends?
Do you? Oh, yes you do! Oh, yes you do!

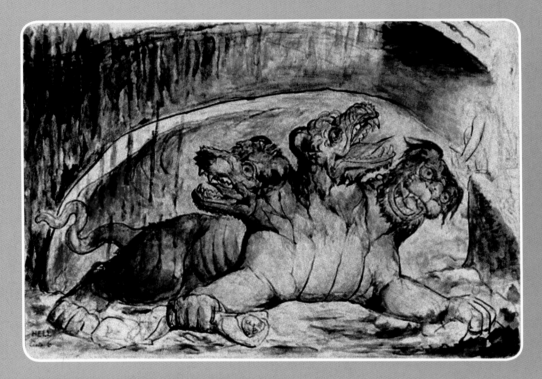

CERBERUS

This three-headed "Hound of Hades" guarded the Greek underworld and was the offspring of Echidna and Typhon, two serpentine beasts that also produced the Chimera (a creature made up of several animals) and Hydra (a sea serpent with many heads). In some legends, Cerberus sports as many as 100 heads, but three is the most common number. He was most famously featured in the story of the Greek hero Hercules, who had fallen from grace for killing his wife and children and had to participate in 12 tasks to save his soul. Capturing Cerberus and delivering him to the Mycenaean king Eurystheus was Hercules' final task. It was no easy feat; Cerberus wasn't supposed to leave the Underworld, and the living weren't supposed to go into it. The Underworld's rulers, Hades and Persephone, finally agreed to let him take Cerberus as long as he didn't hurt the dog. Hercules managed to wrestle the hound into submission and took him above ground. After showing Cerberus to Eurystheus (who was so frightened that he jumped into a storage jar), Hercules returned the dog unharmed to the Underworld.

PAN GU

This creation myth from southern China holds that the creator god, Pan Gu, is half man and half dog. He belonged to the earth god, King Gao Xin, whose biggest rival was another god named King Fang. King Gao offered his daughter's hand in marriage to anyone who could kill his adversary. Everyone was afraid of King Fang...except for Pan Gu, who went to the king's palace and ingratiated himself to his master's rival god.

Thinking that Pan Gu had abandoned his master, King Fang welcomed the dog and organized a banquet for him. But that evening, Pan Gu attacked King Fang and bit off his head. The dog carried the head back to King Gao, who was so pleased that he rewarded the good dog with a heaping plate of meat. But Pan Gu wasn't interested—he wanted the princess. King Gao refused to let a dog marry his daughter, and Pan Gu fell into a deep depression.

But the lovers had an idea: The king had a magic golden bell that could turn the dog into a man. If Pan Gu stayed beneath the bell and hid for seven days, he'd become human and be able to marry the princess. All went well until the sixth day, when the impatient princess peeked under the bell and interrupted the transformation process, leaving Pan Gu with the head of a dog and the body of a man. King Gao thought that was enough, though, and allowed Pan Gu to marry the princess. The couple moved to Earth—taking up residence in the remote mountains of southern China—and lived happily ever after. Their children became the ancestors of mankind.

FENRIR

Also called Fenrisulfr, this enormous wolf appears in Scandinavian mythology as the offspring of Loki (the Norse god of mischief) and Angrboda (a giantess). Fenrir's destiny, as prophesied in a Norse creation poem, was to devour the chief god Odin during the battle at the end of the world. When Odin found out about the prophesy, he brought Fenrir to live among the gods, who chained him, blinded him, and tried to trick him. Fenrir wouldn't fall for their tricks, though, and ultimately bit off one of the god's hands. The gods then chained Fenrir to a rock one mile underground.

Legend holds that when the mythic battle (called Ragnarök) at the end of the world begins, Fenrir will break free from his bonds and join the battle against the gods. The Scandinavians are still waiting.

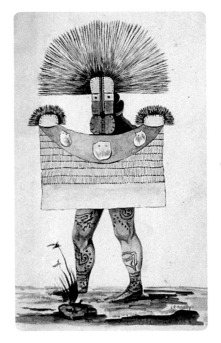

Weird, Weird

TABOO
Meaning: A behavior or activity that is prohibited
Origin: "Originally a Tongan word, tabu, meaning 'marked as holy.' The first taboos were prohibitions against the use or even the mention of certain things because of religious belief that to do so would invoke the wrath of the gods. The word gradually was extended in use to cover all sorts of prohibitions or bans based upon social convention." (From *Dictionary of Word and Phrase Origins, Vol. Ill*, by William and Mary Morris)

DWEEB
Meaning: A boring or contemptible person, especially one who is studious, puny, or unfashionable; a nerd
Origin: "The term has been in printed use since the early 1980s and may have originated in U.S. prep school slang, probably influenced by the words *dwarf*, *weed*, and *creep*." (From *The Oxford Dictionary of New Words*, edited by Elizabeth Knowles)

TATTOO
Meaning: A permanent mark on the skin made by ingraining an indelible pigment
Origin: "When Captain Cook sailed to Tahiti in 1769, he unwittingly introduced tattoos to sailors. Upon studying the island's inhabitants, Cook described how 'both sexes paint their bodys.' Cook called it 'tattow,' his rendition of the Tahitian term *tatau*. The word was derived from the Polynesian *ta*, 'to strike,' a reference to the puncturing of the skin 'with small instruments made of bone, cut into short teeth.'" (From *The Chronology of Words and Phrases*, by Linda and Roger Flavell)

BENJAMIN FRANKLIN GAVE GUITAR LESSONS.

Word Origins

SEEDY
Meaning: Somewhat disreputable; squalid
Origin: "During the seasons when rye, barley, oats, and other grains were being planted, a fellow who spent his days in the fields was likely to be covered with seeds. Once the derisive title entered common usage, it came to mean anything run-down—from shacks to individuals." (From *Why You Say It*, by Webb Garrison)

MUMBO JUMBO
Meaning: Confusing language; nonsense
Origin: "The earliest references used capital initials, as Mumbo Jumbo was said to be an African deity. Unfortunately, no one since the 18th century has reported any such deity in any West African tribe. It is possible that mumbo jumbo is a corrupt form of *nzambi*, Congolese for 'god.'

"Many explorers dismissed any native god as ignorant superstition. A religious belief in Mumbo Jumbo, a god supposedly invented to scare the womenfolk, was seen as even more nonsensical. Presumably this gave rise to mumbo jumbo in its modern sense of 'obscure or meaningless talk.'" (From *Take Our Word for It*, by Melanie and Mike Crowley)

DOODLE
Meaning: Scribble absentmindedly
Origin: "Comes from the German word *dudeln*, meaning 'to play the bagpipe.' The notion seems to be that a person who spends his time playing bagpipes would be guilty of other frivolous timewasting activities—like scribbling aimlessly on scraps of paper. Although the word has been around for several centuries, it did not come into widespread popularity in the United States until Gary Cooper used it in the famous film *Mr. Deeds Goes to Town* in 1936." (From *Dictionary of Word and Phrase Origins, Volume III*, by William and Mary Morris)

GHOST TRAINS

THESE TRAINS REALLY PUT THE BOO IN CABOOSE.

ONLY THE DEAD GET OFF AT KYMLINGE

Just outside of Stockholm, Sweden, there's an abandoned metro station on Line 11 known as Kymlinge. Construction on the stop was halted in 1976 when the town decided to turn the area above it into a nature preserve. In the years since, Kymlinge has become associated with its own ghost train. The *Silverpilen*, or "Silver Arrow," was built in the mid-1960s as a test model for the Stockholm underground and was the only train in the metro system to retain its silver color— all subsequent trains were green. Until it was scrapped in 1996, the *Silverpilen* was used only as a backup, and it was an unusual sight for passengers expecting to catch the usual green train.

But what's more shocking is that people continued to see the silver train long after it was scrapped: Witnesses have reported spotting the train, often late at night, in the abandoned tunnels. Sometimes the cars are empty, while other times ghostly passengers occupy *Silverpilen*'s spectral seats. Local legend claims that a few real commuters have inadvertently boarded the ghost train, where they disappeared for weeks or months at a time, only to return with no memory of where they'd been. Some were never heard from again, prompting the locals to say, "Only the dead get off at Kymlinge."

TRACK LIGHTING

Over the years, hundreds of people have reported seeing unusual lights along an abandoned rail line in St. Louis, Saskatchewan, despite the fact that the tracks themselves have long since been removed. Several years ago, Serge and Gail Gareau decided to entertain a couple of out-of-town guests by taking them to the spot where the lights had been most often seen. The foursome parked beside the former site of the tracks and waited. Suddenly a bright yellow light appeared in the distance with a smaller reddish glow beneath it. The lights hovered above the old track bed. When the friends drove in that

THE NATION'S MARTYR!

BORN Feb. 12, 1308.
MURDERED April 14, 1865.

But if this country cannot be saved without giving up that principle, I was about to say I would rather be ASSASSINATED upon this spot than to surrender it.
A. LINCOLN.
Feb. 22d. 1861.

direction, the lights vanished, only to reappear right behind them. Unnerved, the couples beat a hasty retreat.

The mayor of St. Louis, Emile Lussier, says the story of the lights dates back to an incident in the 1920s when late one night, while performing a routine check of the track, a Canadian National Railway engineer was struck and decapitated by his own train. The small reddish glow is said to be from the dead engineer's lantern as he searches for his missing head. The big white light is, of course, from the steam engine that killed him.

LINCOLN'S DEATH TRAIN

After Abraham Lincoln was assassinated in April 1865, a funeral train delivered his body from Washington, D.C., to its final resting place in Springfield, Illinois. Frequent stops were made along the way to allow mourners to pay their respects. At each halt clocks were stopped to commemorate the event. Several years later, a rail worker on the line between New York City and Albany (part of the death train's route) was clearing brush late one night in April when he reported a chilly wind, "like just before a thunderstorm," sweeping over the tracks. A "huge blanket of utter darkness" rolled over the man, snuffing out his lantern. Then a blue glow enveloped the tracks, followed by the bright headlight of a train. The man cowered against a tree

as a steam engine covered in black crepe emerged out of the darkness. A skeletal orchestra, led by a spectral conductor, played a dirge from a flat car behind the crewless engine. An identical train followed the first, except this time, in place of the phantom musicians, there was a single black crepe-covered coffin. Ghostly soldiers wearing blue Union uniforms stood at attention along the track and saluted the casket as it passed. The worker fled back to the Hudson Division station to find that the clocks were all running six minutes late. Ever since, every April brings reports of people hearing unexplained steam whistles, seeing mysterious plumes of smoke, and feeling chilly winds along the route of the train. To this day, some claim that watches and clocks still stop wherever it goes.

A COLUMN OF AIR ONE INCH SQUARE AND 600 MILES HIGH WEIGHS ABOUT 15 POUNDS.

221

Edited for Sensitivity

In the weeks after 9/11, the entertainment industry scrambled to remove any images of the World Trade Center or casual references to terrorism from new movies, music, and television. Here are a few examples.

● In September 2001, Jackie Chan was supposed to start filming *Nosebleed,* in which he was to play a World Trade Center window washer who uncovers a terrorist plot to blow up the towers. The movie was going to be filmed on location. It was scrapped entirely.

● Images of the World Trade Center were digitally removed from the background of episodes of *Law and Order, Friends,* and *The Sopranos.* (Interestingly, the 2003 miniseries *Angels in America* was shot after 9/11, but since it takes place in the 1980s, the towers were digitally reinserted for historical accuracy.)

● The first trailer for *Spider-Man* showed a group of criminals thwarted when Spidey traps them in a web and hangs their entangled helicopter between the two WTC towers. After 9/11, the trailer was immediately removed from circulation, as were posters that showed a reflection of the Twin Towers in Spider-Man's eye.

● *Party Music,* an album by the rap group the Coup, was delayed a month until October 2001 in order to redesign the cover. The original

LORRAINE BRACCO

OPPOSITE: The Twin Towers reflected in the eyepiece of Spider-man's mask

ABOVE: The Twin Towers as seen in Tony Soprano's side mirror as he drives from New York to New Jersey during the iconic opening titles of *The Sopranos*

version pictured two members of the group holding a detonator in front of the World Trade Center, engulfed in flames.

● In the original ending of *Men in Black II*, the World Trade Center towers split open and release a cloud of UFOs into the air, setting off a huge urban battle. After 9/11, a new sequence was produced.

● Microsoft deleted the World Trade Center from the New York skyline for its popular virtual pilot video game, *Flight Simulator*.

● The Arnold Schwarzenegger action movie *Collateral Damage* was originally supposed to hit movie theaters in October 2001,

but was delayed until February 2002. The plot: a firefighter travels to South America in pursuit of the terrorists that killed his family.

● Producers of the 2002 film version of H. G. Wells's novel *The Time Machine* cut a scene in which meteors rain down on New York City and cause mass destruction.

● The comedy *Big Trouble*, which climaxes with a nuclear bomb that threatens to explode a passenger airplane, was delayed from September 2001 to April 2002.

● The scheduled November 2001 opening of the Broadway musical *Assassins*, about the

men and women who had tried to kill American presidents, was postponed.

● Release of the crime drama *Heist* was moved a month forward to November 2001 because of a scene in which Gene Hackman's character outsmarts airport security and brings a bomb on a plane.

● Although it had already been released in early 2001, the rock band Jimmy Eat World changed the name of their album *Bleed American* to *Jimmy Eat World* after 9/11. Reason: The original title seemed lurid in light of terrorist attacks on American citizens.

LONELY PARROTS CAN GO INSANE.

How one small act of thievery turned a picture into a worldwide sensation.

The Mona Lisa Caper

The Louvre, 1911: the empty space where the *Mona Lisa* should have been hanging

NOW YOU SEE HER...

August 21, 1911. Louis Beroud, a painter, was setting up his easel in the Salon Carré, one of the Louvre's more than 200 rooms, directly facing the spot where the *Mona Lisa* smiled out at her admirers. Beroud was going to paint her as he had done many times before, but there was an empty space where the painting should have been.

When he asked a guard about it, he was told that it was in the photography room, where copies were made. Beroud waited three hours for the painting's return, but eventually, his patience gave out. He asked the guard what was taking so long. The guard checked again. When he came back, he sheepishly admitted that the *Mona Lisa* was...gone.

A STAR IS BORN

The most famous painting in the world today wasn't quite that famous at the turn of the 20th century—she was certainly revered among art aficionados. But news of the mysterious theft of the mysterious woman caught the public's collective imagination, transforming da Vinci's masterpiece from mere painting to cultural icon. All of a sudden, the *Mona Lisa* was a cottage industry: Her likeness showed up on posters, postcards, mugs... in nightclubs, silent movies, magazines...she was everywhere. Perhaps strangest of all: Record crowds showed up at the Louvre just to view the empty space where the painting had been hanging.

But where was the actual *Mona Lisa*? Theories abounded in France. Some thought it was an elaborate practical joke; others, a political ploy by the Germans to humiliate the French. Rumors even flew that it was the work of local Paris artists—Pablo Picasso among them. They were rounded up and brought in for questioning.

It took a week for the entire museum to be searched thoroughly. All that turned up was the painting's empty frame, found at the top of a staircase that must have been the thief's escape route. Months passed. Then two years. There was still no sign of her.

THE DA VINCI CODE

The big question: What would an art thief do with the painting? At the time, it was worth about $5 million— today, it's priceless. Even if a buyer were willing to spend that much, the painting was too high-profile to be passed along the art-theft network. It was too easy to trace. The crook would be caught.

The answer came on November 29, 1913. A wealthy Italian art dealer, Alfredo Geri, received a letter from a man who called himself Leonard Vincenzo. He offered to return the *Mona Lisa* to France...for a fee. Geri figured it was a hoax, but he was intrigued enough to set up a meeting at a hotel in Florence, Italy. Geri took along Giovanni Poggi, the director of Florence's Uffizi Gallery. The two men walked into the hotel room to find Vincenzo, a short, mustachioed Italian man who told them he'd been working in Paris at the time of the theft. Vincenzo reached underneath the bed and retrieved an object wrapped in red silk. Geri unrolled it, and Poggi verified its authenticity: It was the *Mona Lisa*.

The man on the left is Pablo Picasso; the man on the right is Vincent Peruggia. One of these men stole the *Mona Lisa*.

THE PATRIOT

Leonard Vincenzo didn't receive his ransom. Instead, he was taken to the police station, where he admitted his real name was Vincenzo Peruggia...and it was he who stole the *Mona Lisa*. On the morning of the theft, he explained, he entered the Louvre dressed in a painter's smock and went straight for the *Mona Lisa*. No one else was in the Salon Carré that morning, so Peruggia simply removed the painting from the four wall hooks and hid it under his smock—frame and all. When he reached the staircase, he removed the painting from the frame and walked out. The entire heist took about 20 minutes.

So why did Peruggia do it? "For the love of country," he said in court. "She belongs in Italy, where Leonardo painted her." (Peruggia also said he was upset with Napoleon for his various Italian conquests.) But his past criminal record of burglaries, along with a list of art dealers that police found (including Geri), convinced the judge that his motivations were less than patriotic. Peruggia spent seven months in jail. He went to his grave in 1927 still believing he was one of Italy's greatest patriots.

As for the *Mona Lisa*, she made a triumphant return to the Louvre. Today, she smiles out—from her nearly impregnable, climate-controlled, bulletproof glass case—at more than five million admirers each year.

IN 1993 SOTHEBY'S AUCTION HOUSE SOLD A 200-YEAR-OLD PIECE OF TIBETAN CHEESE FOR $1,513.

225

"Gloomy Sunday" is a ballad that's been covered by dozens of performers, from Billie Holiday to Björk. But some say it's more than just a sad song...it actually causes people to kill themselves. Or is it all just a coincidence?

The Suicide Song

Billie Holiday's rendition of "Gloomy Sunday" is arguably the most famous version of the suicide song, but even the altered lyrics couldn't quell the curse.

PIANO MAN

In 1933 Hungarian songwriter Rezso Seress was working as a piano player in a Budapest restaurant called Kispipa Véndegló. The 34-year-old was struggling to make it as a composer, but he hadn't published any songs yet. Then his girlfriend dumped him—because, she said, he was always depressed about his dismal music career. Seress grew even more despondent about the break-up, but he channeled his sadness into his songwriting. With the help of a lyricist named Laszlo Javor, Seress wrote a somber ballad called "Szomorú Vasárnap," or, in English, "Gloomy Sunday." The song was a lament about someone whose lover has died, leading the narrator to thoughts of suicide. Here's one translation:

Sunday is gloomy, my hours are slumberless. / Dearest, the shadows I live with are numberless. / Little white flowers will never awaken you, Not where the black coach of sorrow has taken you. / Angels have no thought of ever returning you. / Would they be angry if I thought of joining you? / Gloomy

Sinead O'Connor singing a sad version of "Gloomy Sunday."

Sunday. / Gloomy is Sunday; with shadows I spend it all. / My heart and I have decided to end it all. / Soon there'll be candles and prayers that are sad, I know. / Death is no dream, for in death I'm caressing you. / With the last breath of my soul I'll be blessing you. / Gloomy Sunday.

THE SONG REMAINS THE SAME

Seress added "Gloomy Sunday" to the repertoire of songs he played at the restaurant. Even though it had been gut-wrenching to write (and audience members were visibly saddened by it), Seress thought "Gloomy Sunday" was the best thing he'd ever written, and he made a serious effort to get it published by a sheet-music company. (In Europe in the 1930s, records were available, but songs were far more popular as sheet music to be played at home on the piano.) Seress sent the song to music publishers in Hungary, France, and England.

They all turned him down, and all for the same reason. As one of the rejection letters said, "It's the terrible compelling despair about it. I don't think it would do anyone any good to hear a song like that." Finally, in 1935, a music publisher agreed to release "Gloomy Sunday." The song became a moderate hit, providing Seress a modest income from the royalties. Things were beginning to look up.

IT'S GOT A GOOD BEAT AND YOU CAN DIE TO IT

According to the legend that has since sprung up around the song, trouble began in February 1936 when Budapest police investigated the first in a series of strange deaths. Joseph Keller, a shoemaker, was found dead with a suicide note consisting of the words "gloomy Sunday" and a request that his grave be decorated with 100 of the "little white roses" mentioned in the now-popular song.

After Hungarian newspapers reported the connection between the suicide and the song, morbid curiosity made sales of "Gloomy Sunday" sheet music and recordings skyrocket. But, eerily, so did the number of suicides allegedly related to the song:

● Two people were found in Budapest's Danube river, each clutching the sheet music of "Gloomy Sunday."

● As a band of Roma (Gypsy) street musicians performed the song, two people shot themselves.

● A man went into a nightclub and asked the band to play "Gloomy Sunday." They did, and he walked out into the street and shot himself.

● At a dinner party in a wealthy home, the song drifted from the party to the servants' quarters. Two maids heard the song and slashed each others' throats.

And, in perhaps the most bizarre twist, a Budapest woman who killed herself by drinking poison was later identified as Rezso Seress's ex-girlfriend—the inspiration for the song. Her suicide note consisted of two words: "Gloomy Sunday."

ILLEGAL DOWNLOADS

After 18 suicides were supposedly linked to the song, Budapest police took action. They asked musicians, orchestras, and radio stations to stop playing the song and ordered stores to stop selling its sheet music and recordings, effectively banning the song.

But even the ban didn't stop the deadly effects of "Gloomy Sunday." Fueled by the controversy over what the press had begun to call "the Hungarian Suicide Song," "Gloomy Sunday" became a bestseller all over Europe. And in the next few months, it was linked to even more suicides, including a shopkeeper

THERE ARE MORE CREATURES IN YOUR MOUTH THAN THERE ARE HUMANS ON EARTH.

227

Elvis Costello, yet another "Gloomy Sunday" singer

in Berlin who hung herself with the sheet music at her feet and a man in Rome who heard a beggar sing the song and then jumped off a bridge to his death.

ANARCHY IN THE U.S.

Curiosity about the song soon reached the United States, where a Hollywood songwriter named Sam M. Lewis composed an English translation (those are his lyrics at the start of this article). In 1936 the song was recorded by Hal Kemp and His Orchestra, one of the most popular bands of the era. It reportedly took 21 takes for them to cut the song because it upset the musicians. Unfortunately, the song's reputation had followed it from Europe, and an Ohio college student named Phillip Cooks reportedly became its latest victim: Accounts said that he listened to the song repeatedly, then took his own life in May 1936.

In 1941 Billie Holiday recorded the song—arguably the most famous version—which became a best seller in the United States and England. But her record label, fearful of more suicides, had hired Sam M. Lewis to add a third, more uplifting verse to the song. In it, the narrator says that the loss and despair were all just a dream, and that

everything's actually great. The happy ending didn't help—later that year, a New York typist killed herself, leaving a request that Holiday's version of "Gloomy Sunday" be played at her funeral. Because of all the hysteria over the song, BBC Radio in England would only play an instrumental version of "Gloomy Sunday."

One day in 1941, a London policeman heard that version being played repeatedly from an apartment window. When he investigated, he found an automatic phonograph playing the record on repeat next to a dead woman holding an empty bottle of pills. After that, the BBC banned all versions of "Gloomy Sunday," a ban that stayed in effect until 2002.

FATAL FAME

Ultimately, "Gloomy Sunday" was linked to nearly 100 suicides, a fact that troubled its songwriter, Rezso Seress, for years. He once told a reporter, "I stand in the midst of this deadly success as an accused man. This fatal fame hurts me. I cried all of the disappointments of my heart into this song and it seems that others with feelings like mine have found their own hurt in it." He never had another successful song, and became another "Gloomy Sunday" casualty

when he jumped out of a Budapest window to his death in 1968.

It's been debated for years: Did people really kill themselves because one incredibly sad song destroyed their will to live? Some say no, and point out that Europe in the 1930s was not a happy place. World War II was well underway for many countries, and just around the corner for others. Fascism was on the rise, and economic depressions had crippled the continent.

And Hungary, the birthplace of the "Suicide Song," had one of the highest suicide rates in the world in the 1930s. (It still does, for reasons that would probably take an army of psychiatrists to figure out.) The song hit a sensitive nation in a sensitive spot, at just the right time. And the suicides never reached epidemic proportions in other countries—though, unfortunately, the song's reputation undoubtedly helped its sales. After the 1940s, no other suicides were linked to the song until 1997, when Scottish singer Billy Mackenzie took his own life. His band, the Associates, had recorded "Gloomy Sunday" several years earlier. It was a distant coincidence, but the Gloomy Sunday conspiracy theorists took note.

CODA

Today the song remains a favorite of musicians, both for its haunting lyrics and melody and for its dark legend. It's been covered dozens of times in recent years by artists including Ray Charles, Lou Rawls, Branford Marsalis, Marianne Faithfull, Björk, Sarah McLachlan, Sinead O'Connor, and Elvis Costello.

Supersize Everything

Uncle John's books aren't the only things that have gotten larger.

TIPPING THE SCALES

The average American adult eats close to 1,700 pounds of food per year (about the weight of a compact car), which works out to 4.7 pounds per day. If that sounds like a lot, it is. In the last few decades, U.S. annual food intake has increased by 25 percent. Health officials cite this phenomenon as the cause of the "Great Obesity Epidemic." Of the average adult's annual intake, meat makes up 195 pounds, 57 pounds more than during the 1950s. Good news: Fruit and veggie consumption also went up. Bad news: So did grain products (flours, breads, cereals); Americans eat 200 pounds of them annually, 45 more than in the 1950s. And most of it is refined flours instead of healthier whole-grain products. Not surprisingly, nearly two-thirds of American adults are classified as overweight, up from less than half in 1980. And more than one-fourth today are classified as obese. Here are a few stories related to this epidemic.

HEAVY DUTY

Invented by the Great John Toilet Company (no relation to Uncle John), the Great John is the first toilet, says the manufacturer, made specifically for "modern Americans." Translation:

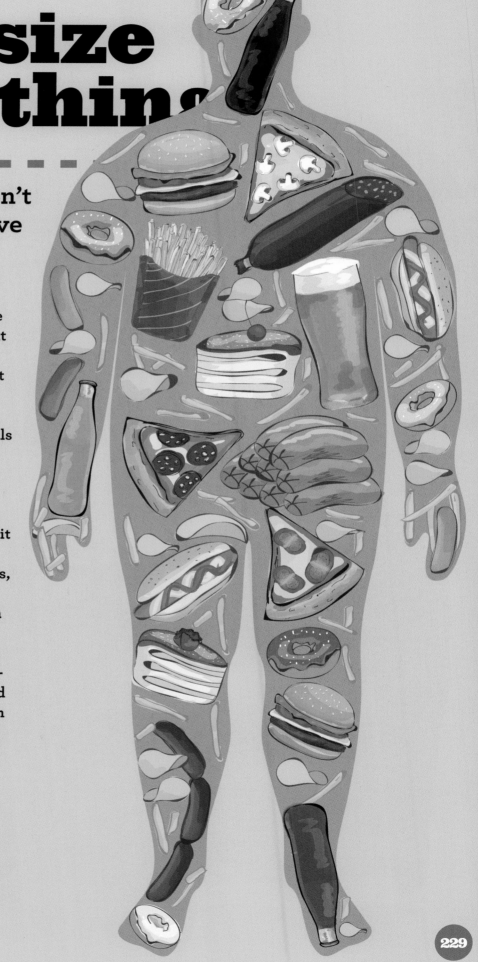

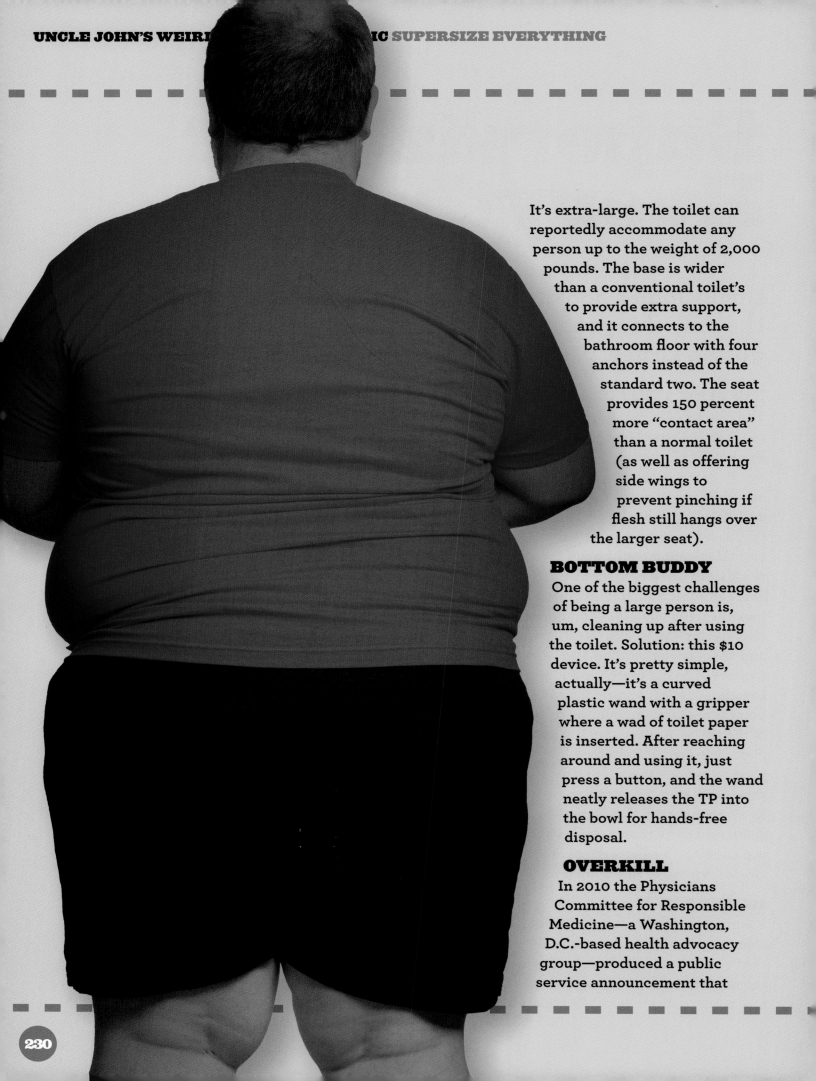

It's extra-large. The toilet can reportedly accommodate any person up to the weight of 2,000 pounds. The base is wider than a conventional toilet's to provide extra support, and it connects to the bathroom floor with four anchors instead of the standard two. The seat provides 150 percent more "contact area" than a normal toilet (as well as offering side wings to prevent pinching if flesh still hangs over the larger seat).

BOTTOM BUDDY

One of the biggest challenges of being a large person is, um, cleaning up after using the toilet. Solution: this $10 device. It's pretty simple, actually—it's a curved plastic wand with a gripper where a wad of toilet paper is inserted. After reaching around and using it, just press a button, and the wand neatly releases the TP into the bowl for hands-free disposal.

OVERKILL

In 2010 the Physicians Committee for Responsible Medicine—a Washington, D.C.-based health advocacy group—produced a public service announcement that

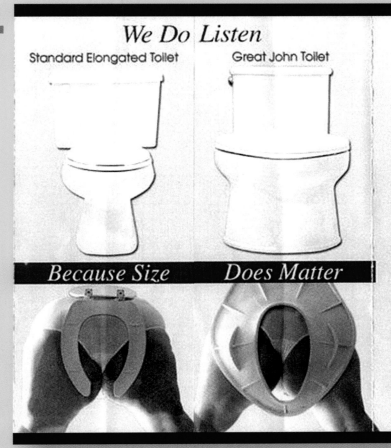

We Do Listen

Standard Elongated Toilet   Great John Toilet

Because Size   Does Matter

A new generation of products

The average size person has increased dramatically over the last century.

Most toilets made today are from designs dating back to the early 1900's.

For this reason GJTC engineers, medical doctors and artists took to the task of creating a NEW GENERATION of products satisfying today's needs.

The fruits of our research culminated in new designs... Great John products.

The Great John Company represents a group of people with years of experience in medical research and investigation fields, as well as experience related to the ceramic industry.

We are totally committed to the needs and concerns of obese and oversized people... *because we do listen.*

The **Great John®** *Toilet Co.*

5207 Maher Ave.
Laredo, Tx.
78045
Toll free: 1 (800) 456-0685
greatjohn@satx.net
greatjohn.com

The **Great John®** *Toilet Co.*

"The Only Toilet in the World for Big People"

depicted an obese man, dead on a table in a morgue, holding a hamburger. A woman cries over the body as McDonald's iconic "golden arches" logo appears, along with the tagline, "I was lovin' it." (It referred to McDonald's slogan, "I'm lovin' it.") The commercial, meant to agitate for healthier options on fast-food menus, aired twice in the D.C. area. When PCRM tried to air it in West Palm Beach, Florida, no station would touch it—they didn't want to get sued by McDonald's.

BABYFAT

In 2009 Colorado's Rocky Mountain Health Plans (RMHP) refused to cover Alex Lange because he had a preexisting condition: obesity. Alex's parents were furious. "He's only four months old," his father, Bernie, said to reporters. "He's breast-feeding. We can't put him on the Atkins diet or on a treadmill." Amid all the negative press ("RMHP Denies Healthy but Big Baby!"), the company explained that it had a relatively new process of determining which babies were most "insurable"—and at 17 pounds, Alex didn't make that list. RMHP has since changed its policy to insure any healthy baby, regardless of weight.

SPRAY OFF THOSE EXTRA POUNDS

Of all the odd weight-loss products out there, this is the oddest. It's called Clamor, and supposedly contains a chemical called Clarinol that can "shrink fat cells." Just spray Clamor

ABOVE: The Great John toilet
BELOW: Someone needs to stop feeding this guy.

on your food. It supposedly reduces fat on the food along with fat that's already inside the body. It comes in four flavors: butter, olive oil, garlic, and plain. So what is Clarinol? Clamor's maker says that it's a naturally occurring bacterium found in the stomach of cows. It's harvested from fried ground beef. And also it doesn't work.

DENTURES WERE ONCE MADE WITH TEETH PULLED FROM THE MOUTHS OF DEAD SOLDIERS.

231

"Your Dog Is So... Interesting Looking"

Pride in one's dog takes many forms. How about the world's ugliest?

SAM
WINNER
2003/4/5

ARCHIE
WINNER
2006

DOGGY DEAREST

Westminster it's not, but at the Sonoma-Marin County Fair in Petaluma, California, the World's Ugliest Dog contest has been entertaining visitors for over two decades. It started as a local summer attraction in 1988 but has garnered so much media attention over the years that now news cameras outnumber entrants, Internet voting climbs to the tens of thousands, and ugly aspirants travel from as far away as Florida to compete. (Winners get trophies, prize money, and the title, of course.) In 2006 suspense was especially high because Sam, the champion for three years running, had died at the age of 14, and the field was wide open for the 18 contenders. Here's a look at some of the ugliest winners ever to grace a dog show stage.

SAM

Award: World's Ugliest Dog (2003-2005)

Details: Probably the most famous ugly dog, Sam was a 13-pound Chinese crested who was so ugly that his owner, Susie Lockheed, was scared of him when she first brought him home. (He was also so ugly that Japanese TV reporters compared him to Godzilla.) Sam was acne-riddled, blind, warty, and hairless. He had crooked teeth, a fatty tumor on his chest, and a line of moles down his nose. But Lockheed loved him. Sam came to her as a rescue dog; his original owner lost her pet-friendly apartment and could no longer keep him. Early in their relationship, Lockheed was diagnosed with cancer. Sam slept with her, comforted her, and saw her through chemotherapy,

proving that judging an old dog on bad looks is never fair.

Cuddly side aside, he was plenty cranky, and had a fascination with his back leg. To Lockheed, it seemed that Sam believed there was an imaginary foe attached to his back leg. He'd snarl at it and bite, and whenever she gave him a treat, Sam would keep a close eye on that back leg to make sure it didn't steal the snack away.

ARCHIE

Award: World's Ugliest Dog (2006)

Details: In 2006, Archie (yet another Chinese crested) earned the title of World's Ugliest Dog. His owner, Heather Peoples, traveled all the way from Arizona to show off Archie's attributes at the fair. Unlike his predecessor, Archie does have hair—it sticks

PRINCESS ABBY WINNER 2010

GUS WINNER 2008

ELWOOD WINNER 2007

PEANUT WINNER 2014

up erratically all over his head. His tongue hangs out of one side of his mouth because he has no teeth to hold it in place. His naked, liver-colored belly resembles a sausage. And he's so ugly that the animal shelter where he was living (and where Peoples worked) gave Peoples $10 to take him away. It was supposed to be just a temporary thing, but Peoples says her husband fell in love with the beauty-impaired beast: "Now when we go out, my husband carries Archie in his arms like a baby."

Archie was the winner in a year fraught with scandal. The ugliest dog is crowned after an Internet voting campaign that lasts several weeks, but during the 2006 process, computer hackers infiltrated the contest's website and erased votes from some of the top dogs. Fortunately, contest organizers discovered the crime and remedied the situation: They started the voting over from scratch. In the end, Archie pulled past favorites Munchkin, Rascal, and Pee Wee Martini to take the crown.

ELWOOD
Award: World's Ugliest Dog (2007)
Details: This Chihuahua and Chinese crested mix took the top title after coming in second in 2006. He traveled all the way to California from New Jersey with his owner, Karen Quigley, who—despite the dog's new title—thinks Elwood is "the cutest thing that ever lived." Elwood's Internet voters, obviously, disagreed. With his dark, almost hairless body (Elwood does have a tuft of white fur atop his misshapen head) and a tongue that always droops from his mouth, Elwood is sometimes called "Yoda" or "ET"—affectionate nicknames, for sure.

Besides winning the title and taking home $1,000, Elwood is somewhat of a local celebrity back home in New Jersey, where he's a Good Will Ambassador for the SPCA. He and Quigley try to educate people about special-needs pets (from sick animals to ugly ones) and encourage residents to adopt homeless dogs and cats.

Quasimodo wasn't quite ugly enough at the 2014 contest; he came in second after Peanut.

Getting Dumped

What's sadder than a toy nobody wants? Millions of them.

FRED MacMURRAY

Disney

SON OF FLUBBER.

FLUBBER FLUBBED

"Flubber," introduced in the 1961 Disney film *The Absent-Minded Professor*, was a fictional gravity-defying ball of goop that could bounce and fly. To promote the 1963 sequel, *Son of Flubber*, Disney hired Hasbro Toys to release "real" Flubber. Hasbro's goop wasn't magical—the rubber/mineral-oil mixture was nearly identical to Silly Putty. But when more than 1,600 consumers later complained that Flubber had given them a rash, Hasbro recalled the toy. Thousands of pounds of the stuff were sent to a trash incinerator at a landfill in Rhode Island, but the Flubber wouldn't burn. It melted instead—and produced a giant black cloud over the landfill. What was left of the Flubber was sent back to Hasbro, who, with the government's permission, dumped it into the Atlantic Ocean. That didn't work, either—it floated back into Rhode Island's Narragansett Bay. Hasbro finally buried it on the grounds of a new warehouse in Pawtuckett, Rhode Island. A parking lot was paved over it, but employees say that on hot days, the Flubber still seeps up through the cracks.

E.T. THE ERRONEOUS-TERRESTRIAL

In July 1982, Atari paid $20 million for the rights to make a video game out of the year's biggest movie, *E.T.: the Extra-Terrestrial*. But for the game to be in stores by Christmas, it had to be finished by September 1—a deadline of just six weeks. The resulting game has been called one of the worst ever made (as E.T., the player walks around and avoids falling in holes). But based on the popularity of the movie, Atari manufactured more than five million cartridges. Only about a million sold; the rest were returned by stores to Atari and stored in a warehouse in El Paso, Texas. In September 1983, Atari sent 14 truckloads of unsold merchandise, the vast majority of which was E.T. cartridges, to a landfill in Alamogordo, New Mexico. To prevent theft, the games were flattened with a steamroller, then covered with a concrete slab. The landfill was excavated in 2013 by a documentary film crew, and one of the flattened cartridges is on display at the Smithsonian Institution in Washington, D.C.

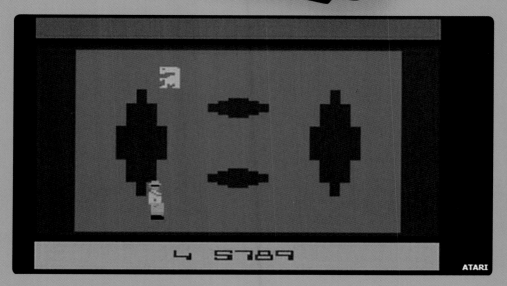

ABOVE: The yellow blob is supposed to be E.T. (we think).
BELOW: E.T.'s final resting place.

"I'd Like to Thank..."

About 99% of all acceptance speeches are boring. These excerpts celebrate the other 1%.

PAUL WILLIAMS

AWARD: The 1977 Oscar for Best Song, "Evergreen." The five-foot-tall songwriter walked up to the podium...

EXCERPT: "I was going to thank all of the little people, but then I remembered—I am the little people."

JUSTIN TIMBERLAKE

AWARD: International Album award ("Justified") and the International Male Solo Artist award at the 2004 Brit Awards

EXCERPT: "This is only my first record, so you guys stick with me. We've still got depression and drug addiction to go through."

JIM CARREY

AWARD: Golden Globe for Best Actor in a Comedy, *Man on the Moon* (2000)

EXCERPT: "I am now the Establishment I once rejected."

THE WORD MATTRESS ORIGINALLY MEANT "PLACE TO THROW THINGS."

NICOLE KIDMAN

AWARD: A star on the Hollywood Walk of Fame

EXCERPT: "I've never been so excited to have people walk all over me for the rest of my life!"

JESSICA YU

AWARD: The Oscar for Best Documentary Short Subject for *Breathing Lessons* (1997)

EXCERPT: "What a thrill! You know you've entered new territory when you realize that your outfit cost more than your film."

KANYE WEST

AWARD: At the 2006 MTV Europe Music Awards in Denmark, Kanye West was thrilled to win Best Hip-Hop Artist of the Year. But he was much less thrilled when his video, "Touch the Sky," lost the Best Video award to an obscure British band called Justice vs. Simian. As they were receiving their award, West crashed the stage.

TIRADE: "F*ck this! 'Touch the Sky' cost a million dollars! Pamela Anderson was in it! I was jumping across canyons and sh*t! If I don't win, this awards show loses credibility!" Backstage, West continued to fume: "I haven't seen their video. Possibly it could have been quite good, but no way better than 'Touch the Sky.' That is complete bullsh*t, I paid a million! Obviously it's not all about the money, but the response it got transcended everything, it really made great TV. It took a month to film. I stood on a mountain. I flew a helicopter over Vegas. I did it to be the king of all videos and I wanted to walk home with that award!"

DIANNE WIEST

AWARD: The Oscar for Best Supporting Actress for *Hannah and Her Sisters* (1987)

EXCERPT: "Gee, this isn't like I imagined it would be in the bathtub."

Dom Pérignon

No celebration would be complete without the aristocrat of wines, the bubbly beverage of love: champagne.

Drinking the Stars

BAD BUBBLES

Champagne, France, is the country's northernmost grape growing area. For centuries, Benedictine monks at the region's Abbey Hautvillers produced fine wines for the church's holy sacraments and Europe's nobility. The monks produced still wines (without bubbles)—rather, they tried to. But in the late 17th century, the abbey was having a problem with batches of unintentionally carbonated wine.

Usually, before wine is bottled, the grape juice has fermented, meaning that yeast on the grape skins has turned the fruits' sugars into alcohol. But grapes ripen slowly in Champagne's northern vineyards, and the monks had to harvest them late in the growing season. Winter cold sometimes halted the fermentation process—after the grapes had been crushed but before the wine went into bottles. Then when spring warmed up the wine, it finished fermenting, trapping carbon dioxide gas inside the glass bottles. This gas produced fizzing bubbles and built up pressure that could push out corks or even cause the bottles to explode. The monks called this phenomenon "mad wine."

BEES ARE BORN FULLY GROWN.

STAR STRUCK

In 1688 a monk named Pierre Pérignon became treasurer of the abbey, and his job included overseeing the wine operations. At first, he experimented with ways to prevent carbonation from fizzing up in the abbey's wine, but sometime during his 47 years at the monastery, he gained an affinity for the sparkling wine. According to legend, Pérignon was so enamored with the drink that, the first time he tried it, he called out to his fellow monks, "Come quickly, I am drinking the stars!"

Soon, Dom Pérignon tamed the mad wine into delicious champagne. He used rope and wire to keep the bottles corked and thicker glass bottles to prevent explosions. He also perfected champagne by blending multiple grapes from different vineyards to create the drink's signature taste and developed a method of producing a clear, straw-colored champagne from black grapes. Champagne soon became a favorite drink of English and French royalty.

BLUE-CHIP BUBBLY

Pérignon died in 1715 and was buried at his beloved Abbey Hautvillers. Today, his name and techniques are still attached to fine champagne. In 1794 wine trader Claude Moët bought the abbey and its vineyards. His family's company (which became Moët et Chandon in

The bubbly beverage may have reached its pop culture apex on Saturday *Night Live* when Christopher Walken offered "sham-pon-ya" to his unseen guest.

1832) continued to create the prestigious champagne. In 1921, to honor both the company's history and the monk many people call "the Father of Champagne," they named their finest vintage Dom Pérignon.

Considered by many wine critics (and brides and grooms) to be the best champagne in the world, Dom Pérignon has become a symbol of love and luxury. A gift bottle of 1998 Dom Pérignon (the champagne's finest year) can set you back about $140, and a special 1998 edition Dom Pérignon (presented in a gold-studded bottle designed by Karl Lagerfeld) goes for a whopping $1,915.

More Oddballs

ABOVE: John Albert Krohn donning his Colonial Jack outfit
ABOVE, RIGHT: A rare cover of Krohn's book

THE WALK OF COLONIAL JACK
BY J. A. KROHN

A Story of a 9,000 Mile Walk the Border of the United

PUSHING HIS LUCK

In 1908 John Albert Krohn—"Colonial Jack," an ex-newspaperman, decided to become the first person to push a wheelbarrow around the perimeter of the United States. Why'd he do it? For the money. Krohn figured he could sell aluminum souvenir medals along the way, and then sell the rights to his story when he made it home. "Sure, money is the root of all evil," he admitted, but "most of us need the 'root.'" Krohn left Portland, Maine, on June 1, 1908, and wheelbarrowed his way west to Washington State, then south to the Mexican border, then east to the Atlantic and north back to Maine. He covered 9,024 miles in 357 days, wearing out 11 pairs of shoes, 121 pairs of socks, and 3 rubber tires. TV and radio didn't exist, but he received plenty of news coverage and an enthusiastic response nearly everywhere he went; in some communities he was even "arrested" and sentenced to a meal and a bed at the best hotel in town. Krohn did write a book—no word on how well it sold—and then spent the rest of his life working in his garden.

URINE FOR A TREAT

In 1991 British artist Helen Chadwick came to Canada to create a series of 12 artworks: bronzed "Piss Flowers." She formed round piles of densely packed, fresh snow and then peed on them. Then she had a male friend "draw" (pee) a circular pattern on it. The

VINCENT VAN GOGH DIDN'T START DRAWING UNTIL HE WAS 27 YEARS OLD.

ABOVE: Helen Chadwick
ABOVE, RIGHT: Chadwick's "Piss Flowers" on display in London's Hyde Park and Serpentine Gallery

to determine the makeup of the ancient comet, and possibly learn the makeup of the solar system billions of years ago. But not everyone was happy with NASA and their "science." Marina Bai, a Russian astrologist, sued the American space agency for $300 million, claiming that the collision would change her horoscope. "It is obvious," Bai told Russia's *Izvestia* newspaper, "that elements of the comet's orbit, and correspondingly the ephemeris, will change after the explosion, which interferes with my astrology work and distorts my horoscope." (Case dismissed.)

FLIPPING OUT

A 17th-century German entertainer named Matthew Buchinger had a dazzling array of talents. He played 10 instruments (some of which he'd invented himself), sang, danced, read minds, was a trick-shot artist and marksman, bowled, did magic tricks, drew portraits and landscapes, and did calligraphy. Even more impressive: Buchinger had no arms or legs. He had finlike appendages instead of hands, and "stood" only 28 inches tall.

The multi-talented Matthew Buchinger

LAZTING IMPREZZION

By adding another "z" to his last name, Zeke Zzzyzus (formerly Zzyzus) regained his status as the last name in the Montreal phone book. His competition for the honor: "Pol Zzyzzo" and "Zzzap Distribution."

combined result looked something like a daisy. Then, before it could melt, Chadwick made a bronze casting of the snow, to create a lasting, one-of-a-kind sculpture. (She sold all 12 for $2,000 each.)

OUT OF ALIGNMENT

In July 2005, NASA sent a car-sized probe, dubbed Deep Impact, on a collision course with Tempel 1, a comet that passes Earth every 5.5 years. Scientists were hoping

Ethically Disabled

There are few things more pathetic than people pretending to be disabled—and few things more satisfying than catching them.

FUTBOL FAKERS

Their dream was to watch their country's soccer team play in a World Cup game in Germany in 2006, but the admission price was more than the three Argentinians wanted to pay. Determined to see the match, they found a loophole: Discounted seats were being offered to disabled people. So they somehow got themselves three wheelchairs and rolled into the match against Holland, claiming a handicapped viewing spot near the field. The ruse probably would have worked, too, if one of them hadn't gotten so excited after a play that he jumped out of his chair with his arms raised in the air. "A person near us thought there was a miracle happening," one of the fakers told reporters outside the stadium—which is where the three fans spent the second half of the game after security escorted them out (on foot).

PARALYMPIC FAKERS

The 2000 International Paralympics were a resounding success for Spain: The country won 107 medals overall, highlighted by the gold medal awarded to its intellectually disabled basketball team. A few months later, one of the players, Carlos Ribagorda, made this shocking admission: "Of the 200 Spanish Paralympic athletes, at least 15 had no physical or mental handicap." Ribagorda, a journalist for the Spanish magazine *Capital*, had joined the basketball team to expose the corruption. In the two years Ribagorda played for the team, no one ever tested his I.Q. Not only that, says Ribagorda, the team was told to slow down their game so they wouldn't attract suspicion. A subsequent international investigation concluded that only two members of the basketball team were intellectually disabled. In addition, as Ribagorda had discovered, some members of Spain's Paralympic track, tennis, and swimming teams were found to be only...morally handicapped.

LAWSUIT FAKER

In 2006 Las Vegas authorities suspected that wheelchair-bound Laura Lee Medley was taking them for a ride. After four separate

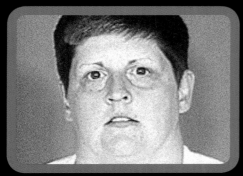

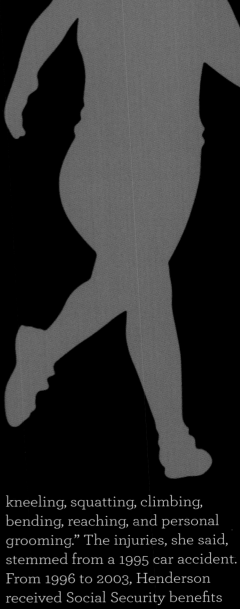

TOP, LEFT: Spain's "winning" Paralympic basketball team only had two honest players.
TOP, RIGHT: Dee Henderson (middle) during her glory days
ABOVE: Laura Lee Medley had to stand for her crimes.

lawsuits against four California cities over faulty handicapped access to public buildings, investigators smelled fraud. They tracked Medley to Las Vegas, where they arrested the 35-year-old woman—who was sitting in her wheelchair. Medley immediately began complaining of pain and begged for medical attention. Skeptical—but not wanting to doubt her if she really was in pain—police officers drove her to a nearby hospital. But moments after she was wheeled through the entrance, the "paralyzed" woman got up and started sprinting through the hospital corridors. She was quickly apprehended and cuffed. Medley was charged with four counts of fraud and resisting arrest.

BEAUTY PAGEANT FAKER

Dee Henderson was crowned Mrs. Minnesota International in a 1999 beauty pageant, thanks in part to the aerobic exercises she performed for the talent competition. Henderson owned and operated two businesses selling beauty pageant supplies, and was the director of three Midwest beauty pageants. Those are amazing accomplishments, especially considering the fact that at the same time, she was getting disability payments from the government. Henderson claimed she couldn't work, couldn't sit for more than 20 minutes at a time or lift anything heavier than her mail. She also had difficulty with "walking,

kneeling, squatting, climbing, bending, reaching, and personal grooming." The injuries, she said, stemmed from a 1995 car accident. From 1996 to 2003, Henderson received Social Security benefits totaling $190,000. But her case unraveled when a video taken by a private investigator showed her doing activities such as snorkeling and carrying heavy luggage (not to mention the aerobics). More damning evidence: an e-mail in which Henderson claimed she would "keep going and going and going and going" like the Energizer Bunny. She did keep going...to prison for 46 months.

More proof that this weird, weird world
of ours works in mysterious ways...

Amazing Luck!

HANGNAIL

Jan Madsen was fixing the roof of his home outside of Berlin when he tripped and started sliding toward the roof's edge. As he scrambled to grab onto anything that might prevent his fall, Madsen's nail gun accidentally went off and shot him through the knee. It was excruciatingly painful, but the nail pinned his leg to a wooden support beam and held him there until rescue workers arrived an hour later to free him.

BABY SAVES THE DAY

One afternoon in 1995 at the Kiddie Kove Nursery in Chicago, two-year-old Kolby Grinston reached up and innocently pulled the school's fire alarm. Teachers calmly filed their students outside as they had practiced many times before. Minutes later, as the children were waiting to return to their classroom, a car barreled through a red light and struck another vehicle, sending it across the nursery playground and crashing into the school. The car landed on top of a row of lockers, where the children would have been standing, hanging up their jackets and sweaters before their afternoon nap had Kolby not pulled the fire alarm.

HE WAS STUNNED

In the summer of 2000, Laurence Webbler took his eight-year-old grandson Josh on a fishing trip. The Texas native was looking forward to spending some quality time with Josh, but unfortunately, while they were out, he suffered a heart attack. As Webbler lost consciousness, Josh sprang

into action. He picked up the electronic fish stunner his grandpa had brought and jabbed him with 5,000 volts. "That was enough to get the old ticker going again," Webbler later commented.

HEAD CASE

It was bad luck when a 20-year-old Greek man accidentally shot himself in the head with his speargun while fishing off the island of Crete. A lifeguard found him floating in the water six hours later, the spear entering his jaw, going through his brain, and protruding from the top of his skull. But it was good luck when surgeons discovered that the spear had passed through one of the spaces in the brain that are nonfunctional—if it was just millimeters to the left or right he would have suffered serious brain injury or died. They removed it in

a three-hour operation that left the man with no brain damage and no health problems.

TAKE THE ZZZZZZ-TRAIN

A young woman was standing on a subway platform in Prague, Czech Republic, when she started bobbing back and forth as if she was falling asleep. Turns out, she was. As she fell forward, a man tried to grab her, but he was too late. She collapsed on the tracks mere seconds ahead of an approaching train. It skidded to a stop, and everyone expected the worst. Then they heard her calling for help. She was pulled up from between two train cars, then she brushed off her clothes and walked away. Amazingly, she'd landed directly between the tracks, and the train never even touched her.

Lucky Lohrke

Here's one of the most amazing, tragic, and surreal tales in baseball—and American—history.

BACKGROUND

Perhaps no one's ever deserved the nickname "Lucky" more than Jack Lohrke. As a ballplayer, he was a decent hitter and utility infielder for the New York Giants and Philadelphia Phillies from 1947 to '53. But Lohrke's most incredible achievement may have been just living long enough to play in the majors at all. Born in Los Angeles in 1924, he started playing minor league ball in 1942, when he was 18 years old. But then his life—along with those of thousands of other young men—was put on hold when he was called up to serve in World War II. And that's where this story begins.

BRUSH WITH DEATH #1: The Train

Riding on a troop train through California to ship off to war, Lohrke's railcar came off the tracks. Three men were killed in the horrific wreck while many of the survivors were severely burned by scalding water that rushed through the car. Lohrke walked away uninjured.

BRUSH WITH DEATH #2: The War

A year later, Lohrke survived the Battle of Normandy. Then he fought in the Battle of the

TOP LEFT: Lucky Lohrke in his prime, February 1947
TOP RIGHT: American GIs dig in at Bastogne during the Battle of the Bulge, Christmas 1944

Bulge, the deadliest campaign of World War II for American GIs, in which 19,000 U.S. servicemen were killed. On four separate occasions, the soldiers on either side of Lohrke were killed. Each time, he walked away uninjured.

BRUSH WITH DEATH #3: The Colonel's Seat

In 1945 Lohrke was sent home. Arriving in New Jersey, he boarded a plane for his flight back to California. Just as the plane was preparing to take off, a colonel marched onto the plane and took Lohrke's seat, forcing him to wait at the airport for the next transport. Less than an hour later, the plane crashed in Ohio. There were no survivors.

BRUSH WITH DEATH #4: The Phone Call

A year later, Lohrke was playing for the Double-A Spokane Indians in the Western International League. On a rainy day in June, the team's bus was negotiating Washington's Snoqualmie Pass through the Cascade Mountains on their way to a weekend series near Seattle. The Indians stopped for lunch at a diner in Ellensburg, and as they were preparing to get back on the bus, Lohrke was told he had a phone call. He thought that was odd, considering that he was in a small town in the mountains. But the team's owner had somehow tracked him down at the diner. And he had good news: Lohrke, who was on a hitting tear, had been promoted to the Triple-A San Diego Padres (then in the Pacific Coast League).

At first, Lohrke was ecstatic. But then he had to make a choice: Did he want to continue with the team to the Seattle area and take a train back to Spokane from there? Or could he make his way back home on his own? Lohrke thought about it...and chose to hitchhike directly back to Spokane. He bid his teammates farewell and watched them board the bus. About 30 minutes later, the bus skidded on the wet highway and crashed through a guardrail

before tumbling 350 feet down into a ravine, where the gas tank exploded. Nine players were killed, eight of whom were recent war veterans. To this day, it remains one of the worst disasters in the history of American sports. "I've often wondered how the Spokane owner knew we'd stop at that particular diner," Lohrke later said. "That was pure fate."

THE MIRACLE MAN

Although he was devastated by the loss of his teammates, Lohrke stuck with baseball and performed well enough in San Diego to make it the majors. As luck would have it, Lohrke was the third baseman on the 1951 New York Giants, the team that famously came back from a seemingly insurmountable deficit to win the National League pennant.

Lucky Lohrke retired from

baseball in 1953 and lived to be an old man. He died in 2009 at 85 years old.

ABOVE: American soldiers resting alongside the road behind the front line in Belgium, December 1, 1944

BELOW: Lucky Lohrke proudly displays his photo of the 1946 Spokane Indians. He outlived them all.

Here Speeching American

Let's face it: English can be pretty tough to grasp, especially if it's not your first language. Uncle John gives the authors of these signs and labels an "A" for affort.

IN A COPENHAGEN AIRPORT:
WE TAKE YOUR BAGS AND SEND THEM IN ALL DIRECTIONS.

IN A FINLAND HOSTEL:
IF YOU CANNOT REACH A FIRE EXIT, CLOSE THE DOOR AND EXPOSE YOURSELF AT THE WINDOW.

IN A JAPANESE HOTEL ROOM:
PLEASE TO BATHE INSIDE THE TUB.

IN AN AUSTRIAN SKI LODGE:
NOT TO PERAMBULATE THE CORRIDORS IN THE HOUSE OF REPOSE IN THE BOOTS OF ASCENSION.

OUTSIDE A RUSSIAN MONASTERY:
YOU ARE WELCOME TO VISIT THE CEMETERY WHERE FAMOUS RUSSIAN AND SOVIET COMPOSERS, ARTISTS, AND WRITERS ARE BURIED DAILY EXCEPT THURSDAY.

AIR CONDITIONER DIRECTIONS IN A JAPANESE HOTEL ROOM:
COOLES AND HEATES: IF YOU WANT JUST CONDITION OF WARM IN YOUR ROOM, PLEASE CONTROL YOURSELF.

WARNING LABEL ON CHINESE LINT-CLEANING ROLLER:
1. DO NOT USE THIS ROLLER TO THE FLOORINGS THAT MADE OF WOOD AND PLASTIC.
2. DO NOT USE THIS ROLLER TO CLEAN THE STUFFS THAT DANGEROUS TO YOUR HANDS SUCH AS GLASS AND CHINAWARE.
3. DO NOT USE THE ROLLER TO PEOPLE'S HEAD, IT IS DANGEROUS THAT HAIR COULD BE STICKED UP TO CAUSE UNEXPECTED SUFFERING.

FROM A MAJORCAN (SPAIN) SHOP ENTRANCE:
HERE SPEECHING AMERICAN.

IN A NAIROBI RESTAURANT:
CUSTOMERS WHO FIND OUR WAITRESSES RUDE OUGHT TO SEE THE MANAGER.

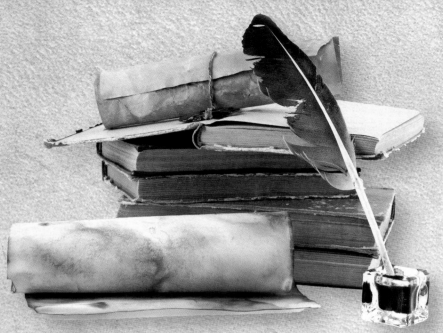

Getting the Last Word

These lines were taken from the actual wills of some pretty frustrated, but creative (and slightly looney) people.

DAVID DAVIS (1788): "I give and bequeath to Mary Davis the sum of five shillings, which is sufficient to enable her to get drunk for the last time at my expense; and I give the like sum to Charles Peter, the son of Mary, whom I am reputed to be the father of, but never had or ever shall have any reason to believe."

JOHN AYLETT (1781): "I hereby direct my executor to lay out five guineas in purchase of a picture of the viper biting the benevolent hand of the person who saved him from perishing in the snow. This I direct to be presented to him in lieu of a legacy of 3,000 pounds which I had, by a former will, now revoked and burnt, left him."

HENRY, EARL OF STAFFORD (England, 1719): "I give to the worst of women, who is guilty of all ills, the daughter of Mr. Gramont, a Frenchman, who I have unfortunately married, five and forty brass halfpence, which will buy her a pullet for her supper, a greater sum than her father can make her; for I have known when he had neither money or credit for such a purchase, he being the worst of men, and his wife the worst of women, in all debaucheries. Had I known their character, I would have never married their daughter, nor made myself unhappy."

Getting the Last Word

GARVEY B. WHITE (1908): "Before anything else is done, 50 cents is to be paid to my son-in-law to enable him to buy for himself a good stout rope with which to hang himself, and thus rid mankind of one of the most infamous scoundrels that ever roamed this broad land or dwelt outside of a penitentiary."

ELIZABETH ORBY HUNTER (1813): "I give and bequeath to my beloved parrot, the faithful companion of 25 years, an annuity for its life, of 200 guineas a year, to be paid half yearly, as long as this beloved parrot lives, to whoever may have the care of it; and if the person who shall have the care of it should substitute any other parrot in its place either during its life or after its death, it is my will and desire that the persons doing so shall be refused by my heirs the sum or sums they may have received from the time they did so; and I empower my heirs and executors to recover said sum from whoever would be base enough to do so."

PHILIP, FIFTH EARL OF PEMBROKE (England, 1700s): "I give nothing to my Lord Saye, and I make him this legacy willingly, because I know that he will faithfully distribute it to the poor. I give to the Lieutenant-General Cromwell one of my words which he must want, seeing that he hath never kept any of his own."

CAPTAIN PHILIP THICKNESSE (England, 1793): His will instructed that "my right hand to be cut off after my death and given to my son Lord Audley, and I desire it may be sent to him in hopes that such a sight may remind him of his duty to God after having so long abandoned the Duty he owed to a father who once affectionately loved him."

FRANCIS H. LORD (Australia, date unknown): To his wife: "one shilling for tram fare so she can go somewhere and drown herself."

JOSEPH DALBY (England, 1784): "I give to my daughter Ann Spencer, a guinea for a ring, or any other bauble she may like better. I give to the lout, her husband, one penny, to buy him a lark-whistle; I also give to her said husband of redoubtable memory, my farthole, for a covering for his lark-whistle, to prevent the abrasion of his lips; and this legacy I give him as a mark of my approbation of his prowess and nice honour, in drawing his sword on me (at my own table), unarmed as I was, and he well fortified with custard."

WILLIAM RUFFELL (1803): "To employ an attorney I ne'er was inclined. They are pests to society, sharks of mankind. To avoid that base tribe, my own will I now draw, May I ever escape coming under their paw."

Life Imitates Art

Countless movies and TV shows are inspired by real-life events. But when real-life events are inspired by fiction, that's when Uncle John takes notice.

THE BIRTH OF A NATION (1915)

Reel Life: *The Birth of a Nation* is considered one of the greatest American movies ever made—and one of the most racist. Director D. W. Griffith's classic tells the triumphs and travails of a white southern family before and after the Civil War. The film also uses cinematic techniques that were revolutionary for the time, such as tracking shots, extreme close-ups, fade-outs, extensive cross-cutting, and panoramic long shots.

Yet unfortunately, *The Birth of a Nation* offers an incredibly demeaning portrayal of African Americans. It depicts black northern soldiers (actually white actors in blackface) as sex-crazed rapists and glorifies the Ku Klux Klan for keeping former slaves "in their place" (i.e., away from the ballot box).

Real Life: The original Klan was a secret society founded after the Civil War to enforce white supremacy in the South. And it only lasted a few short years before dying out in the 1870s. But in the fall of 1915, following the release of *The Birth of a Nation*, a Methodist preacher named William Simmons decided to revive the Ku Klux Klan in Georgia. By the mid-1920s, the revitalized Klan boasted three million members across the United States, thanks in large part to the popularity of the groundbreaking silent film.

THE MANCHURIAN CANDIDATE (1962)
Reel Life: This Cold War classic features Laurence Harvey as a brainwashed U.S. soldier who finds himself at the center of an elaborate conspiracy involving Communists and conservatives. The goal of this conspiracy: to kill a presidential candidate.

TOP: Still images from the silent film *The Birth of a Nation*...which led the rebirth of the KKK

THE 1960S VW BEETLE WAS SO AIRTIGHT THAT IT COULD FLOAT.

To achieve this end, Harvey smuggles a rifle with a telescopic sight into a political rally where the man will be speaking.

Real Life: A year after the film was released, President John F. Kennedy was assassinated in Dallas, allegedly by former Marine Lee Harvey Oswald using a rifle with a telescopic scope. And in the decades that followed, speculation abounded that more than one person was involved in the shooting, that Oswald was a mere dupe, and that just like the movie, the president's murder was actually engineered by a shadowy cabal of extremists. To make things even weirder, *The Manchurian Candidate* co-starred Kennedy's buddy, Frank Sinatra, as a fellow soldier who unravels the assassination conspiracy. Following the film's release, a contractual dispute between Sinatra and the filmmakers forced *The Manchurian Candidate* to be

withdrawn from theaters and not shown to the public for decades. The suppression of the film only enhanced its reputation as an eerily prophetic political thriller.

DEATH WISH (1974)

Reel Life: This film stars Charles Bronson as a mild-mannered guy who turns into a pistol-wielding vigilante after his family is brutally assaulted by thugs. In one pivotal scene, Bronson is sitting by himself on a New York City subway car and is accosted by a mugger. Instead of handing over his cash, Bronson shoots the mugger and then casually walks out of the car.

Real Life: On December 22, 1984, Bernhard Goetz, a meek, self-employed electrical engineer, smuggled a five-shot .38-caliber revolver onto the New York subway. Goetz took a seat near a group of four young men. When one of the youths

ABOVE LEFT: Laurence Harvey in *The Manchurian Candidate*
ABOVE: Charles Bronson in *Death Wish*

approached him and demanded money, Goetz stood up, drew his gun, and shot all four of them. Goetz then pocketed his gun and walked off the subway. He later surrendered to police.

While Goetz appears to have been motivated by fear (he had been mugged previously), his actions eerily paralleled those of Bronson's character. Like Bronson in *Death Wish*, Goetz was seen by many as a hero, an "ordinary Joe" who lashed out in justifiable rage against deserving creeps. The outcome of the two men's actions, however, couldn't have been more different: At the end of *Death Wish*, Bronson is free and eager to impose lethal justice on a fresh batch of miscreants. Goetz stood trial for his crimes and although acquitted of attempted murder, he served eight months in jail for illegal gun possession.

When Uncle John learned that it was possible to do this, his first thought was, "Why would anyone want to hypnotize a chicken?" Good question. As Sir Edmund Hillary would say, "because it's there." (And it's a lot easier than climbing Mt. Everest.)

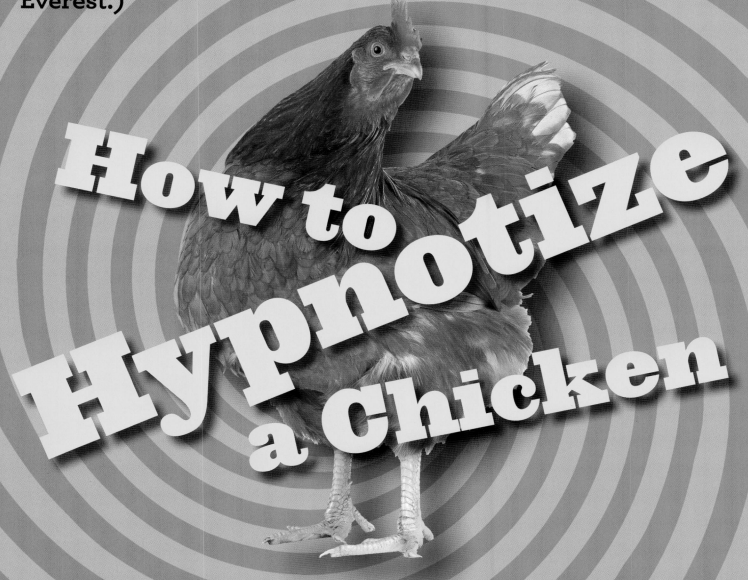

How to Hypnotize a Chicken

YOUR CHICKEN IS GETTING VERRRRY SLEEPY...

It wasn't very long ago that most Americans lived on farms, and lots of people knew how to hypnotize chickens. Not anymore—how many people can say they know anything about chickens, let alone how to hypnotize one? But if you ever get a chance to place a chicken under your spell, give it a try—it's fascinating to watch, harmless and painless for the chicken, and it provides an interesting insight into animal intelligence and behavior. (Who knows—you might even win a bar bet.) Turn the page to find out how.

ELVIS PRESLEY MADE JUST ONE TV COMMERCIAL: FOR SOUTHERN MAID DOUGHNUTS IN 1954.

253

INSTRUCTIONS

1

Techniques vary widely from place to place. Some methods call for laying the chicken gently on its side, with one wing under its body, holding it in place with one hand so that your other hand is free. Others say that turning the chicken upside down, lying on its back with its feet up in the air, is best. Either way, the disoriented bird will need a second to regain its bearings, but once it does it will not be bothered by being in this unfamiliar position.

2

Some hypnotists advocate placing a finger on the ground at the tip of the chicken's beak and drawing a line four inches long in the dirt extending out from the beak and parallel to it (picture Pinocchio's

nose growing). Trace your finger back and forth along the line for several seconds. Other practitioners say that drawing a circle, not lines, in the dirt around the chicken's head works best. Still others say all you need to do is stroke the chicken on its head and neck with your index finger. If one method doesn't seem to work, try another.

3

Whichever method you try, keep at it for several seconds.
That's about how long it takes for a chicken to go into a trance. Its breathing and heart rate will slow considerably, and its body temperature may even drop a few degrees.

4

You can now let go of the chicken. It will lie perfectly still

in a trancelike state for several seconds, several minutes, or even an hour or more before it comes out of the trance on its own. You can also awaken the chicken yourself by clapping your hands or nudging it gently. (The unofficial world record for a chicken trance: 3 hours, 47 minutes.)

5

If holding a chicken in one hand while hypnotizing it with the other proves too difficult, another technique calls for putting the chicken in the same position it goes into when it's asleep—with its head under one wing—and rocking it gently to induce a trance.

CHICKEN SCIENCE

Just as there are different theories as to which method of chicken hypnotism is best, so too are opinions divided as to what exactly is going on with the chicken when it is being hypnotized:

• The trance could be a panic "freeze" response, similar to a deer stopping in the middle of the road when it sees headlights.
• It may also be an example of *tonic immobility*, a reflex similar to an opossum's ability to go into a trancelike state when it feels threatened. Chickens roost in the branches of trees or other high places at night; the trance reflex, if that is indeed what it is, may help the chicken to remain perfectly still, silent, and (hopefully) unnoticed as foxes, raccoons, and other predators prowl below.

FRONTIER WOMEN

Most histories of the Wild West focus on men—cowboys, gunfighters, sheriffs—glossing over the fact that a lot of the era's women were just as powerful, influential, and hell-raising as their male counterparts.

CALAMITY JANE

(1852–1903) Claim to Fame: Soldier, caregiver, hell-raiser

Her Story: Born Martha Jane Cannery in Missouri, she was one of the most famous American women of the 19th century. Yet it's difficult to know for sure exactly what she actually did. Why? Because much of her legend comes from pulp-fiction writers, as well her own trumped-up autobiography. And then there were her days of touring with Buffalo Bill's Wild West Show, where Jane told many more tall tales about her rugged life. Here's some of what she claimed:

● She was married to Wild Bill Hickok and had his child.

● She was a scout for General Custer.

● She was a Pony Express rider.

● The name "Calamity Jane" was given to her by an army captain whom she rescued single-handedly in an Indian fight. Historians doubt these claims. But what makes Jane so interesting is that she could have told the truth and would still have been considered an amazing woman. Here's what is known:

● She was an expert horsewoman and sharpshooter.

● She often dressed as a man and fought Indians.

● A hard drinker who chewed tobacco (and cussed a lot), she was highly respected by the men she rode with.

● During a smallpox epidemic in Deadwood, South Dakota, in 1876, Jane nursed many of the sick back to health.

Most likely, Calamity Jane got her nickname simply because trouble seemed to follow her everywhere. In the end, alcoholism got the better of her—she died penniless at 51 years old.

NELLIE CASHMAN

(1845–1925) Claim to Fame: Humanitarian, entrepreneur, adventurer

Her Story: Cashman emigrated to Boston from Ireland with her sister and mother in the mid-1860s. An adventurer at heart, Cashman heard stories of the Gold Rush and decided to go west. She boarded a ship, sailed down the Atlantic coast to Panama, crossed the isthmus on a donkey, then set sail for San Francisco. But she didn't settle there—Cashman wanted to go where the action was, so in 1872 she moved to Nevada and worked as a cook in various mining towns while panning for gold. Using the little money she earned, she opened her first boardinghouse in Panaca Flat.

Once the boardinghouse was up and running, Cashman sold it, joined a group of 200 gold

PARIS HAS ABOUT 20,000 RESTAURANTS. NEW YORK HAS 23,000. TOKYO: 160,000.

255

LEFT: Nellie "Frontier Angel" Cashman
ABOVE: Libby Smith Collins

ABOVE: Pearl Hart

prospectors, and headed for Cassiar, British Columbia. She opened another boardinghouse there, then moved on to Victoria. But as a devout Catholic, Cashman's desire to help people was as strong as her love of adventure. Shortly after arriving in Victoria, she got news of a scurvy epidemic in Cassiar. She hired six men and hauled in 1,500 pounds of food and supplies—a trip that took 77 days, often through blizzard conditions. She nursed 100 men back to health and received the first of many nicknames, "Angel of the Cassiar." Other names given to her in time: "Frontier Angel," "Saint of the Sourdoughs," "Miner's Angel," and "the Angel of Tombstone."

All across the West, from Fairbanks, Alaska, to Tombstone, Arizona, Cashman was responsible for establishing restaurants, hotels, grocery stores, hospitals, and churches.

Charitable almost to a fault, she would sooner give a free meal to a hungry man than try to make a profit. Along the way, Cashman had many male suitors, but she turned them all down. When a reporter asked her why in 1923, she replied, "Why child, I haven't had time for marriage. Men are a nuisance anyhow, now aren't they? They're just boys grown up."

Cashman lived a long, hard life that never saw her slow down. She died at the age of 79—after contracting pneumonia on a 750-mile dogsled journey across Alaska.

MORE WILD WOMEN

LIBBY SMITH COLLINS

Like Nellie Cashman, Collins proved that a woman was capable of running a business. Her birthdate is unknown, but she came west with her parents sometime in the 1850s. After her

husband, a cattle rancher, fell ill in 1888, Collins took it upon herself to transport their herd from Montana to the stockyards of Chicago. She almost didn't make it: The railroad company wouldn't let her board—it was against regulations for an unaccompanied woman to ride on a train. Collins fought the rule, got it changed, and made a tidy profit in Chicago. She took the trip alone every year after that, earning her the nickname "Cattle Queen of Montana." A movie by that title was released in 1954, based on Collins's life and starring Barbara Stanwyck and Ronald Reagan.

CATTLE KATE

Born Ella Watson in 1861, Cattle Kate is more famous for the way she died than the way she lived: She was lynched by a vigilante mob in 1889 for alleged cattle rustling. After setting up a cattle ranch in Sweetwater Valley, Wyoming, Kate had tried to

STUDIES SHOW: IT TAKES 0.1 SECOND TO FORM AN IMPRESSION OF A STRANGER FROM HIS OR HER FACE.

ABOVE: Ella "Cattle Kate" Watson, lynched by the Wyoming Stock Growers Association.

register a brand with the state, but the Wyoming Stock Growers Association used their power to squash small-time ranchers. So Kate bought a brand from a neighboring farmer and began homesteading her land. This infuriated the big ranchers, who claimed ownership over the entire Sweetwater Valley. So a group of them took the law into their own hands and hanged Kate and her husband, Jim Averell. No one was ever tried for the crime.

PEARL HART

The only woman convicted of stagecoach robbery was Canadian-born Pearl Hart. She and a partner named Joe Boot held up a stagecoach in Arizona in 1899 (reportedly because Pearl needed money for her dying mother). They got caught, and newspapers ran with stories of the "Lady Bandit."

Hart gained even more notoriety from her disdain for authority: "I shall not consent to be tried under a law in which my sex had no voice in making!" She was sentenced to five years in prison in Yuma, Arizona, but served only three. She claimed that she was pregnant, so she was released early. After that, Hart was never heard from again.

ADOLF HITLER'S MERCEDES HAD A FALSE FLOOR TO MAKE HIM LOOK TALLER.

257

Anybody can eat a bunch of hot dogs, but it takes true commitment to be the world-record prune-eater.

Weird, Weird, World Records

COCKROACH-EATING

Ken Edwards (England) ate 36 in a minute in 2001.

A more extreme record holder is Travis Fessler (USA), who held 11 live cockroaches (each at least 2.5 inches long) for 10 seconds...in his mouth.

BROOM-BALANCING

Leo Bircher (Switzerland) holds the record for balancing a broom—on his nose—for a record time of two hours, one minute.

CHRISTMAS TREE-BALANCING

David Downes (England) balanced a seven-foot-tall tree on his chin for 56.82 seconds.

TYPING

In October 1987, Jens Seiler (Germany) typed 626 keystrokes, about 100 words, in a minute. More impressively, he typed the words backward.

BALLOON-STUFFING

Ralf Schuler (Germany) holds two records: 1) the most people stuffed inside a latex balloon—23, and 2) the fastest time to stuff someone (himself) into a latex balloon—37.1 seconds.

PRUNE-EATING

In 1984 Alan Newbold (USA) ate 150 dried plums in 31 seconds. (And then, presumably, a few hours later, Newbold set another record.)

WAITING

Jeff Tweiten and John Goth (USA) queued up to see *Star Wars: Episode II—Attack of the Clones* outside a Seattle movie theater on January 1, 2002...and stayed there until the film opened four and a half months later, on May 16.

MOST ANCIENT ROMANS LIVED IN APARTMENT BUILDINGS.

EXTREME HULA-HOOPING

In 2000 Roman Schedler (Austria) hula-hooped for 71 seconds straight. That may not seem very long, but he did it with a 53-pound tractor tire.

GUM-WRAPPER CHAIN

Gary Duschl (USA) has been purchasing gum and collecting wrappers since 1965, and in 2004 he claimed the record for the world's longest gum-wrapper chain. He's still adding to it: As of 2015, his total was nearing two million gum wrappers and measured nearly 15 miles.

DRUMMING

Tim Waterston (USA) is one of the world's fastest drummers. In January 2002, he set a speed record, playing 1,407 beats in one minute...with his feet.

NAILING

In October 1999, Chu-Tang-Cuong (Vietnam) drove 116 nails into a wooden board in just 11 minutes. The twist: He did it with his bare hand. (Ouch!)

PROPOSING

In 1976 Keith Redman (USA) asked his girlfriend Beverly to marry him. She said no, the first of 8,801 rejections, a world record. (Happy ending: In 1999 Beverly finally said "Yes" after receiving Redman's proposals at a rate of more than one per day for 23 years.)

COTTAGE CHEESE-EATING

In 1984 Peter Altman (England) shoveled down three pounds of cottage cheese in four minutes. Three years later, Altman set the 30-second record, consuming half a pound of it on a British talk show.

BARF-BAG COLLECTION

Niek Vermeulen (Netherlands) possesses the world's largest collection of airsickness bags He's a frequent flyer, and as of March 2008, owned 5,468 distinct bags from more than 1,065 different airlines, along with 10,000 duplicates. (Note: They are all unused.)

BEAN-EATING

Kerry White (England) holds the world record for eating baked beans, consuming 12,547 beans (in sauce) in a 24-hour period.

Barry Kirk (England) sat in a cold bath of baked beans for 100 hours in September 1986.

What's a Chiasmus?

Glad you asked. A chiasmus is a statement where the second half reverses the first half, resulting in an elegant play on words.

"In America, you can always find a party. In Soviet Russia, the Party always finds you!"
YAKOV SMIRNOFF

"Is man one of God's blunders, or is God one of man's blunders?"
NIETZSCHE

"There is nothing wrong with men possessing riches. The wrong comes when riches possess men."
BILLY GRAHAM

"One should eat to live, not live to eat."
CICERO

"In the case of good books, the point is not how many of them you can get through, but rather how many can get through to you."
MORTIMER J. ADLER

Dumb Crooks
Stoner Edition

Weed been thinking about doing an article like this one for a while.

DUDE, WRONG HOUSE

Andrew Kramer, 22, of Grant County, Washington, who cops said "reeked of pot," was trying to sell baggies of marijuana to passersby. What's so dumb about that? He was doing it in front of the Grant County Courthouse. (He was quickly arrested.)

WRONG WAY TO GET LEGAL ADVICE, DUDE

Robert Michelson, 21, of Farmington, Connecticut, called 911 to ask if he could get arrested for growing just one marijuana plant. The dispatcher said yes, he could. There was a pause. Michelson said, "Thank you," and abruptly hung up. A few minutes later, the police showed up and cited him for growing one pot plant.

SHOULDA LEFT IT AT HOME, DUDE

A 22-year-old Stamford, Connecticut, man was walking to the courthouse to testify in a drug case when he took a quick detour to hide his bag of marijuana under a rock in front of a nearby building. Office workers, seeing the suspicious activity, alerted the police... whose headquarters were across the street from the hiding place. When the man returned, instead of his weed, he found a note that read, "You're under arrest. Look up at the police station." He looked up and saw officers waving at him from the window.

DUDE, WRONG PLANT

A teenager in Daytona Beach, Florida, was arrested for stealing a tomato plant from a neighbor's garden. After he was detained by the homeowner, the boy told the cops he thought it was marijuana...even though it had tomatoes on it.

DUDE, WHY CAN'T WE ALL JUST GET A LAWN?

A 58-year-old Swedish man was busted by police after they witnessed him buying a bag of something from another man. (The other man ran away.) When the officer looked in the bag, he discovered that it wasn't "grass," it was grass—as in lawn clippings. The buyer told the officer that he'd haggled the price down from $62 to $15, and it would have been a great deal had it been actual marijuana. Because it wasn't, the man was not charged.

THERE ARE MORE PET FISH IN AMERICA THAN THERE ARE DOGS AND CATS COMBINED.

261

DUDE, WRONG STASH CONTAINER

A Vero Beach, Florida, man went to the dry cleaners to drop off a bag of what he thought was his dirty laundry. It wasn't. There were three pounds of marijuana inside the bag. Police searched the man's home and found $80,000 worth of illegal drugs.

DUDE, JUST LET IT GO, 'CAUSE IT'S LIKE...GONE

Late one night in 2009, Calvin Hoover, 21, of Salem, Oregon, left the Free Loader Tavern and discovered that someone had broken into his truck and stolen his coat—along with the bag of pot in the pocket. Furious, Hoover called 911 to report that "They stole my weed!" According to the dispatcher, Hoover was difficult to understand "because he kept stopping his truck to vomit." The police found him later that night walking around looking for his weed, and arrested him.

WRONG QUESTION, DUDE

In 2011 Devonte Davon Jeter, 19, was in court on drug possession charges. His public defender told the judge that the marijuana could have belonged to any of the four men who were pulled over that day in Midland, Pennsylvania. Jeter had denied the baggie was his, even though it was found near his feet after he exited the vehicle. Without the officer actually seeing the marijuana on Jeter's person, the judge couldn't convict. But Jeter's case fell apart when the arresting officer testified that after he was released from custody on bail, he asked, "Can I have my weed back?"

BAD DOG, DUDE

San Diego resident Joel Dobrin, 32, was pulled over in 2012 while driving through Oregon. He quickly tried to stuff his stash of hash into a gym sock, but his pit bull had other ideas: He grabbed the sock and started playing tug-of-war. Just as Officer John Terrel approached the truck, the sock flew out of the window and landed at his feet. "I wish everyone traveled with their own personal drug dog," Terrel said. "It sure would make our job easier."

Faces of Death

Who will you encounter after you kick the bucket? The Grim Reaper? Or maybe an entirely different specter? Here are some of Death's strangest personifications.

LEFT: Ymaraj on his loyal water buffalo
RIGHT: Izanagi and Izanami, the not-so-happy couple

Name: Yamaraj
Origin: Hindi culture
Details: Also known as Dharmaraj, or Yama, for short, his name literally means "the Lord of Death." In artistic depictions, he's a portly man with a mustache and, legend says, skin that's "the color of a rain cloud." He rides the plains of existence on a water buffalo, and upon a person's death, ropes the departed soul with a lasso and carries it to Yamalok, the Hindu underworld. His assistant, Chitragupta, keeps track of all the good and bad deeds of every human on the planet, and after checking the records, Yama determines how each soul will be reincarnated. If the person was good, they might return as a tiger. If not: a mosquito.

Name: Giltine
Origin: Eastern Europe, primarily the Baltic states
Details: Before they adopted the more Western depiction of Death as a hooded skeleton with a scythe, people in the Baltic region had Giltine, a grotesque woman with a crooked, blue nose and a sharp, poisonous tongue, whose name means "to sting." According to folklore, she was once a beautiful young woman—until she was trapped in a coffin for seven years and emerged a monster. Then, the legend goes, she collected poison from graveyards and used it to lick the dying to death.

Name: Izanami
Origin: Japan
Details: According to Japanese mythology, a god named Izanagino-Mikoto and his goddess wife, Izanami, helped bridge the gap between Heaven and Earth, creating humanity and the islands of Japan in the process. Izanami died while giving birth to a fire god. Overcome with grief, Izanagi-no-Mikoto went looking for her in Yomi, the land of the dead. He found her, but after discovering that her beauty had been ravaged by death, he fled back to Earth. Enraged by his betrayal,

20,000 LEAGUES EQUALS ABOUT 69,000 MILES. THE DEEPEST SPOT IN ANY OCEAN: ABOUT 6 MILES.

263

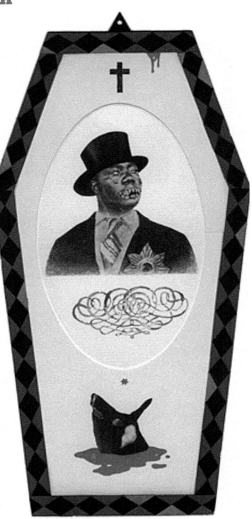

Izanami vowed to take the lives of 1,000 humans per day, becoming the Goddess of Death. Izanagi responded with a vow of his own: to offset her wrath by creating 1,500 people per day.

Name: Santa Muerte
Origin: Mexico
Details: Literally "Saint Death," she is usually portrayed in Mexican folk art as a female skeleton wearing a dress and a large floral hat. The concept emerged from a combination of Meso-American native religions and the Catholicism that dominates the country today. Belief in the skeleton-deity has been condemned over the centuries, with the Catholic Church of Mexico going so far as to dub believers—even if they are also Catholic—a "cult." Nevertheless, millions of Mexicans reportedly worship Santa Muerte, celebrating her during the huge cultural festivities called *Dia de los Muertos* (Day of the Dead) on November 1 of every year and erecting altars to her in their homes. The faithful believe that Santa Muerte not only assists souls in the afterlife but can grant favors to the living, protect them from bodily harm, and make others fall in love with them.

ABOVE: Santa Muerte in her flowing gown
BELOW: Papa Ghede, for whom death seems to be one big party

Name: Papa Ghede
Origin: Haiti
Details: Voodoo practitioners believe that a short, cigar-chomping man in a top hat is waiting for them at the crossroads of Earth and the afterlife. That man is Papa Ghede, who legend says is the living corpse of the first man who ever died. He's aided by four other spirits who handle everything from guarding graveyards to giving voices to the dead during seances. Ghede loves rum and is known for his crass sense of humor and great wisdom, which includes an extensive knowledge of everything that happens in the worlds of the living and the dead. He also reads minds and sometimes even inhabits humans, inspiring them to make love. Ghede is also the patron saint of those who die young. Worshippers offer him rum, cigars, or sacrificed crows to prevent him from taking sick children to the underworld.

Don't Hold the Mayo

Anyone asked to name a favorite condiment might quickly say ketchup or mustard, and sure—those are good. But here's why mayonnaise is the real culinary star.

YOU SAY MAHONNAISE, I SAY AIOLI

Mayonnaise is the bedrock ingredient of numerous condiments and sauces worldwide (rouille, remoulade, tartar sauce, and Thousand Island dressing, for example). Mix a jar of ketchup with mayo and you've got Russian dressing. Mix mustard with mayo, and you've got Helleman's Dijonnaise. The list just goes on and on. There is no definitive source for the origin of the word. Here are a few theories:

● It derives from the Old French word *moyeu* for the yolk of an egg, which is an essential ingredient.

● The French made mayonnaise from a popular Spanish recipe for allioli, an egg-based sauce flavored with lots of garlic.

● A third story says it's from the French verb *manier*, meaning "to mix or blend."

● "Mahonnaise" may be an honorific after the Spanish port of Mahon, where the French Duke de Richelieu defeated the British in a 1756 naval battle. If mayonnaise comes from Mahon, it's more than 250 years old now—and as popular as ever. The first recorded English use of "mayonnaise" appears in an 1841 cookbook.

265

MAYONN-AIZING FACTS

● The world record for eating mayonnaise is held by Russia's Oleg Zhornitskiy; he ate four 32-ounce bowls in eight minutes.

● In Hispanic markets, *Mayonesa con Jugo de Limon* (mayonnaise with lime juice) is so popular that, in 2002, Hellmann's began marketing it as a separate brand. Of the Spanish-speaking countries, Chile is the largest mayonnaise consumer.

● Residents of New Orleans eat 2.4 times as much mayonnaise as citizens of any other U.S. city; people in Omaha, Nebraska, eat the least.

AMERICAN FLAIR

The first commercially manufactured mayo was born in a New York City delicatessen—Richard Hellmann's Columbus Avenue storefront—in 1905. Hellmann sold his wife's homemade salads, which used mayonnaise as a dressing, and soon people were asking to buy it on its own. The condiment became so popular that in 1912 Hellmann built a factory to produce it in large quantities.

Originally, there were two versions of the creamy spread, and to tell them apart, Hellmann tied a blue ribbon around one jar, which was consistently more popular. He called that one Hellmann's Blue Ribbon Mayonnaise.

Meanwhile, across the country, Best Foods introduced Californian consumers to a slightly tangier version of mayonnaise. No one outside the conglomerate knows for sure, but gourmands suspect that the Best Foods formula contains more lemon juice. (Today, Best Foods owns Hellmann's, but maintains both brands and their distinct recipes.) Hellmann's and Best Foods split the costs, but there's one more brand in the American mayo lineup, beloved by Southerners past and present: Duke's. Still made to Mrs. Eugenia Duke's original formula in Greenville, South Carolina, Duke's Mayonnaise ("The Secret of Great Southern Cooks") contains more egg yolks than the other commercial brands and no added sugar.

IT'S ALL IN THE WHISK

True mayonnaise eggheads, however, swear by homemade, even though it's made less often due to the fear of contracting salmonella from raw eggs. Making mayo isn't difficult—just slow and steady.

The essential ingredients are an egg yolk and oil. Additions may include mustard, vinegar, lemon juice, and different oils and seasonings. Mayonnaise making is all in the whisk (or blender or food processor), because the oil has to be added drop by drop to emulsify with the yolk and then is beaten until a thick cream forms.

● The Midwest remains loyal to Miracle Whip, a Depression-era concoction that replaced some of mayonnaise's more expensive fat with starch.

● Mayonnaise can be used in baking to produce moist cakes. It's also touted for many nonfood uses, including lice removal, hair conditioning, and facial masks. It's even said to be effective for bumper sticker and tar removal from cars. And professional florists swear by it to produce clean and shiny leaves.

Govern-mental

Do your civic duty and read these bizarre politics stories from around the globe.

TAX COVEN

In 2011 the cash-strapped Romanian government, in order to generate income, legalized the profession of witchcraft. Now every Romanian witch must pay a 16 percent self-employment tax. Some of the occultists were so incensed that they protested by throwing poisonous mandrake plants into the Danube River. A witch named Alisia complained to reporters, "First they come to us to put spells on their enemies, now they steal from us!" "Queen Witch" Bratara Buzea claimed that she used a dead dog and some cat feces to put a curse on lawmakers. However, at least one witch, Mihaela Minca, was thrilled with the new policy: "It means that our magic gifts are recognized!"

TWO TALL TALES

● In 1989 North Korean Supreme Leader Kim Jong-il released an advertisement for a "wonder drug" that makes people taller. But the whole thing was a ruse. Kim's ulterior motive: to rid the nation of short people. When they showed up to claim their free "cure," they were rounded up and, according to press reports, "sent away to different uninhabited islands in an attempt to end their 'substandard'

A coven of Romanian witches conjuring up a protest

genes from repeating in a new generation." What made this even odder is that Kim himself was only 5'3" tall—he hid it by wearing platform shoes.

● Hajnal Ban, a city councilor in Logan City, Australia, always felt that at 5'0" she wasn't taken seriously, either as a lawyer or as a politician. So in 2001 she went to an orthopedic clinic in Russia and paid $40,000 to have her legs broken in four places. Then, over the course of nine months, surgeons stretched Ban's legs by a millimeter or so every day. After nearly a year of excruciating pain in a foreign hospital, Ban returned to her city council position...three inches taller.

CLOCKWISE, FROM TOP LEFT: Four true patriots—John Wayne, Albert Rivera, Mark Block, and Michele Bachmann

Govern-mental

KOOKY CAMPAIGNERS

● When U.S. Representative Michele Bachmann kicked off her presidential campaign in 2011, she did so from Waterloo, Iowa. "John Wayne was from Waterloo," she boasted in her speech, "That's the kind of spirit that I have, too!" One problem: It was John Wayne Gacy who was from Waterloo—a serial killer who murdered 33 people. John Wayne the movie star was from another town on the other side of Iowa.

● In 2006 a 26-year-old lawyer and swimming champion named Albert Rivera ran for president of Catalonia, an autonomous region of Spain. His campaign strategy: plastering the area's major cities with 10,000 posters of himself naked, with the caption "We don't care where you were born. We don't care which language you speak. We don't care what kind of clothes you wear. We care about you." Rivera, an admitted longshot, said he did it to get young people talking about politics. (He did... and he lost.)

● A weird campaign ad from 2012 featured a mysterious, mustachioed man talking about why the U.S. needs Herman Cain as president. "We can do this," the man says as the camera zooms close in on his face. "We can take this country back!" Then—as the song "I Am America" swells up in the background—the man takes a long drag of a cigarette and then blows the smoke at the camera. End of commercial. Was the ad a joke? Nope. The mustachioed man was Cain's campaign manager, Mark Block, who claimed he was completely serious. Anti-smoking groups were outraged. Block's defense: "I'm not the only one in America who smokes, for God's sake!"

SCIENTISTS SAY: THE HIGHER YOUR IQ, THE MORE YOU DREAM.

EXOPOLITICS

BEAM ME UP, COMRADE

In 2010 Kirsan Ilyumzhinov, the governor of the Russian region of Kalmykia, recounted this story on a Russian TV show: One day in 1997 he was reading a book at his Moscow apartment when a transparent tube appeared on his balcony. "Then I felt that someone was calling me." The next thing he knew, Ilyumzhinov was taking a tour of an alien spaceship.

The aliens spoke to him telepathically, he said, and they passed along a warning: "The day will come when they land on our planet and say: 'You have behaved poorly. Why do you wage wars? Why do you destroy each other?' Then they will pack us all into their spaceships and take us away from this place." Most people just chalked the story up as an amusing antic

by the eccentric millionaire businessman. However, Andrei Lebedev, a member of Russia's parliament, didn't think it was a joke. He immediately requested that Russian president Dmitry Medvedev interrogate the governor to ensure that he didn't give the aliens any state secrets. (Results of the interrogation are unknown.)

VAUDEVILLE

PART II

On page 172, we told you the history of Vaudeville. Here are some highlights.

THE BILL

The formula for a Vaudeville performance was honed and perfected by producers like Keith and Albee to make sure the audience (called "the big black giant," by impresario Oscar Hammerstein) always got its money's worth.

● **Opening Act:** Usually a "silent" act—a juggling troupe or trained dogs, for example—that wouldn't be ruined by the noise of the audience settling in. (Some silent acts, like juggler W. C. Fields and rope trick artist Will Rogers, went on to become headliners when they added comedy to their bits.)

● **Second Act:** A juvenile brother or sister act, like the Gumm Sisters (Frances Gumm became famous later as Judy Garland) or the dancing Nicholas Brothers.

● **Third Act:** A one-act play or comedy sketch featuring "legit" actors, like Sarah Bernhardt, Helen Hayes, or the Barrymores. Famous writers, such as J. M. Barrie (*Peter Pan*) and Jack London (*The Call of the Wild*), often provided material.

● **Fourth Act:** A novelty act, like a magician or mind reader. Escape artist Harry Houdini started in this slot but quickly rose to headliner status.

● **Fifth Act:** Celebrity guest stars held down this spot, which came right before intermission. Sports figures such as boxer John L. Sullivan or baseball's Babe Ruth would come out to answer questions from the crowd. Helen Keller appeared with a translator, who signed questions into the palm of Keller's hand. Carrie Nation, the famous temperance crusader, came on stage wielding the axe she'd used to break up saloons. Convicted murderesses were always a big hit.

● **Sixth Act:** The act right after intermission was always something big and flashy—a lavish production number with lots of dancers and elaborate costumes, or a novelty orchestra. Tiger and lion acts were popular too.

● **Seventh Act:** Called "next to closing," this spot was reserved for the headliners. It was the star spot, and only the top acts earned it. They also made the most money— at a time when a laborer might earn $40 a week, Eddie Cantor was getting $7,700.

● **Closing Act:** Being the closer

ABOVE: **Harry Houdini with chains, in 1906**

was the worst. It meant you were on the way down and out. No one paid attention to you as the crowd put on their coats and headed for the aisles.

Producers often purposely put bad acts in the closing slot to help clear the theater faster, before the next performance. Occasionally the policy backfired with happy results. The Cherry Sisters were possibly the worst act ever to star in Vaudeville. They sang so horribly off-key that they were booed and pelted with rotten fruit.

Then a smart producer realized that the audience actually loved

LEFT: The Marx Brothers in New York, 1928

Variety shows were a staple on early TV, and programs like Sid Caesar's *Your Show of Shows* and *The Ed Sullivan Show* were pure Vaudeville. Where does the ghost of Vaudeville linger today? On *Saturday Night Live* and late-night talk shows, which continue to be a collage of comics, singers, dancers, and even jugglers. As writer Larry Gelbart (*M*A*S*H*) said, "If Vaudeville is dead, TV is the box they put it in."

VAUDEVILLE TERMS WE USE TODAY

● **Hoofers.** A nickname for dancers, who would beat their feet on the stage before their entrance to give the conductor the right tempo. It sounded like a horse stamping its hooves.

● **Corny.** Unsophisticated comedy routines were considered "stuck in the corn," meaning they appealed only to rural audiences. The term became shortened to "corny."

● **Tough act to follow.** When an act got a huge response, the next act had to work twice as hard to win over the audience. So it was a great compliment to a performer to be called "a tough act to follow." For W. C. Fields and Jack Benny, both masters of their craft and never shy about taking on the competition, there was only one act they dreaded following: the Marx Brothers. Benny said after a while he gave up worrying about whether he could top the zany comics: "I just stood in the wings and laughed like hell."

to hate the Cherry Sisters. So he set up a fruit stand in the lobby and sold "ammo" to the audience as they came in. When the sisters went on, they found themselves performing from behind a protective wire screen. As they sang, the crowd howled with laughter and fired away. The Cherry Sisters soon became one of the hottest acts in Vaudeville, commanding top dollar, and remained a big draw for decades.

CURTAIN DOWN

On Friday the 13th in May 1932, the Palace Theatre did the unthinkable. It replaced its two-a-day Vaudeville bill with a movie double feature.

Most historians mark that date as the death of Vaudeville. Several factors were to blame—the growing sophistication of audiences, who now saw Vaudeville as old-fashioned, and the reliance of theaters on ever more lavish and expensive shows. Mostly, though, it was the movies. Films were easier and cheaper for producers to present, and ticket prices were much lower for audiences. Vaudeville limped on until the 1950s, but by 1926, nearly all of the great Vaudeville theaters had been converted to movie houses.

But Vaudeville didn't really die—its influence continued on in the new medium of television.

LIQUID DIET: A LEECH CAN CONSUME 10 TIMES ITS OWN WEIGHT IN BLOOD.

271

Cat Painters

Not people who paint cats, but cats who paint.

FRANK

OSCAR

FIGARO

PINT-SIZED POLLOCKS

Oscar, an orange tabby from Saskatchewan, Canada.
Owner Anna Scott recognized his potential when Oscar started playing with the water in his dish. He swirled it around with his paw before drinking it, and Scott thought he might be trying to express himself. So she mixed food coloring and water, laid down some paper, and let Oscar go to town. The result was a collection of blue, green, and red abstract watercolors that Scott, an artist herself, showed at a local gallery.

Kali and Figaro from Chicago.
These feline friends used nontoxic paint to create swirling red, yellow, and blue patterns.

KALI

Although it looks like a kitty could have made this masterpiece, it's actually a famous Jackson Pollock painting.

Frank, an orphaned feline artist living at an animal shelter in Oregon, used suede for his canvas and crafted a piece called *Three Blind Mice* that made it into a local art show. Patrons sipped wine and called Frank "Pollock with paws," an allusion to what they believed were similarities between the cat and 20th-century abstract painter Jackson Pollock (who would have most likely loathed the comparison). All this attention not only got Frank's paintings into the public eye; it also got him a home. The cat was adopted just before the show's opening night by a family who enjoyed his work.

BUD D. HOLLY

The kitties' paintings don't just adorn refrigerators. They get displayed—and even sold—at art galleries, animal shelters, and regional shows all over the United States. The San Francisco SPCA, for example, sells cat art prints for $15 apiece. The cat artist Bud D. Holly commands up to $250 for an original painting.

273

Pitchers always look so serious on the mound, but off it...

Pitching Zingers

LEFTY GOMEZ, 1934

BILL "SPACEMAN" LEE, 1975

RAY CULP, 1969

"I'm throwing twice as hard as I ever did. It's just not getting there as fast.."
—**Lefty Gomez**

"Baseball's a very simple game. All you have to do is sit on your ass, spit tobacco, and nod at the stupid things your manager says."
—**Bill "Spaceman" Lee**

"Don't tell me I don't know where to play the hitters!"
—**Ray Culp,** after a hit ricocheted off his head and was caught by the centerfielder

ROD BECK, 1993

WHITEY FORD, 1950

GAYLORD PERRY, 1962

"I've never seen anyone on the disabled list with pulled fat."
—**Rod Beck**, on his weight

"The way to make coaches think you're in shape in the spring is to get a tan."
—**Whitey Ford**

"I'd always keep it in at least two places, in case the umpire would ask me to wipe off one. I never wanted to be caught out there without anything. It wouldn't be professional."
—**Gaylord Perry,** on using illegal foreign substances

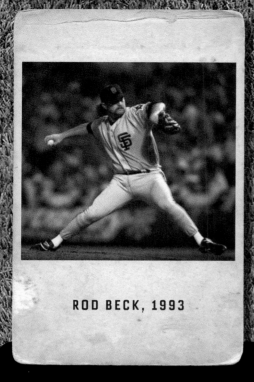

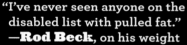

TOMMY JOHN, 1967

BRIAN FUENTES, 2002

BO BELINSKY, 1962

"When they operated on my arm, I told them to put in a Koufax fastball. They did—but it was Mrs. Koufax's."
—**Tommy John**

"Scenario games, like, 'Would you rather open-mouth kiss a bum or get into a sleeping bag with your manager?'"
—**Brian Fuentes,** on reliever, on what goes on in the bullpen

"How can a guy win a game if you don't give him any runs?"
—**Bo Belinsky,** after losing a game 15-0

Jawaharlal Nehru (India's first prime minister) once said, "All my major works have been written in prison. I would recommend prison not only to aspiring writers but to aspiring politicians too." Here are some other notable jailhouse jotters who seem to agree with that advice.

Written in the Pen

NICCOLÒ MACHIAVELLI (1469–1527)
THE PRINCE

Niccolò Machiavelli lived during a time of great plotting and political upheaval in Italy. Initially, he aligned himself with a government that expelled the ruthless and powerful Medici family, which had ruled Florence for 60 years. But when that government fell apart and the Medicis came back with a vengeance, Machiavelli was tossed into prison and tortured. Behind bars, he wrote *The Prince*, a philosophical treatise on politics that said leaders should rule by force instead of by law. In *The Prince*, Machiavelli wrote, "Anyone compelled to choose will find greater security in being feared than in being loved." It was from this book that the term

"Machiavellian" came into use to describe a ruthless, deceitful, and cunning leader. Reportedly, Soviet dictator Joseph Stalin was a fan of *The Prince* and kept a copy next to his bed.

DANIEL DEFOE (1660–1731)
"A HYMN TO THE PILLORY"

Daniel Defoe, most famous for the book *Robinson Crusoe*, wrote perhaps the most immediately useful piece of prison writing while incarcerated. In 1703, he was sentenced to the pillory for three days for satirizing church intolerance. With his head, arms, and legs locked in the wooden frame and then set up in the marketplace, Defoe typically would have been mocked, assaulted, and pelted with garbage by passersby.

ABOVE LEFT: India's first Prime Minister, Jawaharlal Nehru, in the early 1950s

(The goal of the pillory was to shame criminals back to the straight and narrow.) But while in prison awaiting transfer, Defoe quickly wrote "A Hymn to the Pillory," a poem that satirized the punishment he was about to receive. Friends sold copies in front of his pillory, and according to legend, the crowds pelted him with flowers instead of garbage.

OSCAR WILDE (1854–1900)
DE PROFUNDIS

De Profundis is sometimes confused with "The Ballad of Reading Gaol"—the first was written while Irish writer Oscar Wilde was in prison; the second was a poem about his time in prison, but was written after

YELLOW CANARIES THAT ARE FED RED PEPPER WILL TURN BRIGHT ORANGE.

ABOVE, LEFT: Niccolò Machiavelli
ABOVE, CENTER: Oscar Wilde
ABOVE, RIGHT: Martin Luthor King Jr.

FAR LEFT: Daniel Defoe
LEFT: Ezra Pound

he was released. In 1895, Wilde was sentenced to two years of hard labor after being convicted of "gross indecency" (i.e., homosexuality). *De Profundis* ("From the Depths") was a dark and angry 50,000-word letter to his former lover, Lord Alfred Douglas, who had abandoned Wilde when he was convicted.

EZRA POUND (1885–1972)
PISAN CANTOS

At the beginning of World War II, American Ezra Pound lived in Italy and made propaganda radio broadcasts in which he voiced his support of Fascist leader Benito Mussolini and criticized the American government, the British government, and the Jews. After the war, he was charged with treason and imprisoned by the

U.S. Army near the city of Pisa, where wrote 10 of his best cantos for an epic poem. Pound also had a nervous breakdown in prison and spent more than a decade in a series of mental institutions until 1958, when he was labeled incurably insane, but not a danger to others, and released.

MARTIN LUTHER KING JR. (1929–1968)
"LETTER FROM BIRMINGHAM JAIL"

In the spring of 1963, the Southern Christian Leadership Conference, led by Martin Luther King Jr., waged a nonviolent campaign in Birmingham, Alabama, to protest racial discrimination and segregation. The protesters participated in sit-ins at segregated restaurants, marches for voter

registration, and kneel-ins at white churches. These activities were illegal at the time, and King (among others) was arrested and held at the city's jail. While he was there, a group of white clergymen wrote a letter urging African Americans to use the courts instead of protests to further their cause. King drafted "Letter from Birmingham Jail" as a response and argued that civil disobedience was justified when the laws it protested were unjust. The letter—which included famous statements like "injustice anywhere is a threat to justice everywhere"— appeared in national magazines and newspapers and helped bring even more attention to the growing call for civil rights in America.

NASA'S ORIGINAL CALCULATIONS PREDICTED A 5% CHANCE FOR A SUCCESSFUL MOON LANDING.

277

"Saying there appears to be some clotting is like saying there's a traffic jam ahead. Is it a ten-car pileup, or just a really slow bus in the center lane? And if it is a bus, is that bus thrombotic or embolic? I think I pushed the metaphor too far..."

DR GREGORY HOUSE, *HOUSE*

"...Is Like A..."

This page of TV wit is like a glass of orange juice—refreshing and full of pulp.

"The future is like a Japanese game show—you have no idea what's going on."

TRACY, *30 ROCK*

"A conscience is like a boat or a car. If you feel you need one, rent it."

JR EWING, *DALLAS*

"Charlie may be prickly and crusty on the outside, but inside he's all soft and gooey, like a pudding-filled cactus."

ALAN, *TWO AND A HALF MEN*

"Sex is like tennis. When you play an inferior opponent, your game suffers."

EDIE, *DESPERATE HOUSEWIVES*

"Looking at cleavage is like looking at the sun. You don't stare at it. It's too risky. You get a sense of it and then you look away."

JERRY, *SEINFELD*

"Marriage is like a coffin, and each kid is another nail."

HOMER, *THE SIMPSONS*

"What you and I did last night was perfectly natural, like the wind, or not trusting Canadians."

LAURIE, *COUGAR TOWN*

"Now get in there and run that meeting like a shark driving an assault vehicle through a herd of seals wearing chum pants."

VERONICA, *BETTER OFF TED*

Myth-leading

We might assume that the common names we have for things are accurate descriptions of them, but that's not always true.

POISON IVY

It's not a poison, it's an allergen. Poisons are harmful to everybody; allergens only affect some people. Poison ivy can cause severe itching and swelling, but many people aren't even affected by it. It's not ivy, either—it's a member of the sumac family.

BIRTHDAY PARTY

You can only have one birth day—the day you were born. After that, every time you celebrate your birthday you're really throwing an anniversary party.

WILD RICE

It's neither wild, nor rice. Officially known as Zizania aquatica, this once-wild grass seed is now cultivated by farmers worldwide.

RADIATOR

Whether it's in your home or in your car, radiators work by convecting heat—moving it via a liquid or gas, not by radiating. The radiator in your home heats the air currents around it until enough is heated to make the room feel warm. The one in your car transfers heat from the engine to water, which passes it to the atmosphere. The "radiators" radiate a little, but not much.

KILLER WHALE

They're neither killers nor whales. They were once thought to be man-eaters. The 1973 U.S. Navy diving manual even warns that killer whales "will attack human beings at every opportunity." But they were wrong—there are very few documented cases of attacks on human. (Seals and penguins are a different story.) And they're members of the dolphin, not the whale, family.

HEAVY CREAM

When milk producers say "heavy," they actually mean "full of fat," and the fat is the lightest part of the milk. That means that "heavy cream," which contains as much as 30% milk fat, is actually a lot lighter than skim milk, which contains only trace amounts of fat.

RINGWORM

This infection makes "ring-like" marks on skin—but there's no worms involved. It's caused by a fungus.

IN THE YEAR 2000

For a century, people speculated about what life would be like way off in the future—in the year 2000. Now that it's come and gone, we can see just how bizarre some of those predictions were.

HEDGEHOG URINE WAS ONCE BELIEVED TO CURE BALDNESS.

THE DREAM HOUSE OF 2000

"Using wonderful new materials far stronger than steel, but lighter than aluminum...houses will be able to fly....The time may come when whole communities may migrate south in the winter, or move to new lands whenever they feel the need for a change of scenery."

—Arthur C. Clarke, *Vogue*, 1966

"Keeping house will be a breeze by the year 2000. Sonic cleaning devices and air-filtering systems will just about eliminate dusting, scrubbing, and vacuuming. There may be vibrating floor grills by doors to clean shoes, and electrostatic filters will be installed in entrances to remove dust from clothes with ultrasonic waves."

—Staff of the *Wall Street Journal, Here Comes Tomorrow!*, 1966

"When the housewife of 2000 cleans house she simply turns the hose on everything. Why not? Furniture—(upholstery included), rugs, draperies, unscratchable floors—all are made of synthetic fabric or waterproof plastic. After the water has run down a drain in the middle of the floor (later concealed by a rug of synthetic fiber), she turns on a blast of hot air and dries everything."

—Waldemarr Kaempfert, *Popular Mechanics*, 1950

COMMUTING

"Commuters will go to the city, a hundred miles away, in huge aerial buses that hold 200 passengers. Hundreds of thousands more will make such journeys twice a day in their own helicopters."

—Waldemar Kaempfert, *Popular Mechanics*, 1950

"Commuters will rent small four-seater capsules such as we find on a ski lift. These capsules will be linked together into little trains that come into the city. As the train goes out towards the perimeter of the city, the capsule will become an individual unit. One can then drive to wherever he may want to go."

—Ulrich Frantzen, **Prophecy for the Year 2000 (1967)**

"A Seattle executive might board his reserved-seat air-cushion coach at 8:15 A.M. It would lift off the roadbed, whirl around an 'acceleration loop' and plunge into the main tube running from Seattle to San Diego. Little more than half an hour later, the car would peel off onto the 'deceleration loop' in downtown Los Angeles. By 9 a.m. the executive would be at his desk."

—Mitchell Gordon, *Here Comes Tomorrow!*, 1966

THE WORLD OF WORK

"By the year 2000, people will work no more than four days a week and less than eight hours a day. With legal holidays and long vacations, this could result in an annual working period of 147 days on and 218 days off."

—*The New York Times*, October 19, 1967

"By 2000 the machines will be producing so much that everyone in the U.S. will, in effect, be independently wealthy. With government benefits, even nonworking families will have, by one estimate, an annual income of $30,000–$40,000. How to use leisure meaningfully will be a major problem."

—*Time* magazine, February 25, 1966

FIRST ROCK BAND TO PLAY WITH A SYMPHONY ORCHESTRA: DEEP PURPLE (1969).

283

Credits

silvercollection.it ● **p84-85** Jeff Buckley, Dreambrother83, Wikimedia Commons | Tug boat, Shutterstock.com | Chet Baker, Randy Rhoads, Buddy Holly and the Crickets, Ritchie Valens, all Getty Images ● **p86-87** Whistler's Mother, Musée d'Orsay, Wikimedia Commons | Vintage picture frame and vintage wallpaper, Shutterstock.com | Mother Goose's Melody, www.best-books-for-kids.com | Mother Jones, www. lawyersgunsmoneyblog.com ● **p88** Textile mill, Ancoats, Manchester, Wikimedia Commons | Backround corduroy image, Shutterstock.com | Wes Anderson, www.thesartorialist.com | Eddie Veddor, www. sodahead.com ● **p89-91** Express Newspapers/Getty Images | Dana Stone | Tim Page/Corbis | Dennis Hopper, *Apocalypse Now*, Getty Images | www.klinkphoto-info.blogspot.co.uk ● **p92-93** Alcatraz, twins, both Shutterstock.com ● **p94-95** Patrick Duffy, Getty Images | Background image, Shutterstock.com ● **p96-97** *Kimba* images, www.madman.com.au | *The Lion King*, www. imdb.com ● **p98-99** Mark Twain The Humourists lithograph and portrait, both Getty Images | Vintage background, Shutterstock.com ● **p100-101** Baseball park and watching tv illustration, Shutterstock.com ● **p102-103** All illustrations by Sarah Beare, www.sarahbeare.com ● **p104-106** All images, Wikimedia Commons, except vintage background, Shutterstock.com ● **p107** Grand Canyon mules, Sebastian Toncu, Creative Commons Attribution-Share Alike 3.0 Unported, Wikimedia Commons ● **p108-109** Getty Images, except for background, Shutterstock.com ● **p110-111** All images, Shutterstock.com ● **p112-113** Fall leaves, dog, Shutterstock | Quicksand vintage print and Knuckles, Getty Images ● **p114** Russia/USA Bering Straits operational navigation map, Wikimedia Commons ● **p115** x4 portraits, Getty Images ● **p116-117** Night sky background, Science Photo Library | Uranus, Neptune and Pluto, Shutterstock.com ● **p118-119** All images, Shutterstock.com ● **p120-121** Images, www. wired.com ● **p122-123** All pictures Getty Images, except vintage background, Shutterstock.com ● **p124-125** www. sequoitmedia.com | www. engadget.com | www.wadlopen-holwerd.nl | www.slappedham.com | www.snipview.com | Muggle Quidditch and Chess Boxing, Wikimedia Commons ● **p126-127** Lane Jensen, www.whatculture.com | Nut Lady, www.siarchives.si.edu | www.paulies.wordpress.com | Acorn cluster, Shutterstock.com | Alexander Dumas, Google Art Project | Vampires, www.realvampirenews.com ● **p128-129** www.weheartit.com | www.otegony.com | Wikimedia Commons | www.coollinesartwork.com | www.theatlantic. com | www.miragemen.wordpress.com ● **p130-131** www.blueovalforums.com | www.productmobiles.blogspot. co.uk | www.acontinuouslean.com | www.eventxchange.biz | www. prototypesource.com ● **p132-134** WTC, Getty Images | www.newgrounds.com | www.knowyourmeme.com | www.lucasforums.com ● **p135** They Might Be Giants, © Susan Anderson ● **p136-137** www.weburbanist.com | x2 Wikimedia Commons | www. roadsideamerica.com | Lincoln Monument, Pope's Creek, Mira Images, © Andre Jenny/Mira.com ● **p138-139** x4 illustrations, Sarah Beare, sarahbeare.com | Skin background, Shutterstock.com ● **p140-141** Background, Shutterstock.com | x4 dictators, all Getty Images ● **p142-143** x2 illustrations, Sarah Beare, sarahbeare.com ● **p144-145** x2 pictures, both Getty Images ● **p146-147** x2 images, both Shutterstock.com ● **p148-149** Background image, operating theatre, Shutterstock.com ● **p150-151** x4 portraits, Getty Images | Vintage wall background and picture frames, Shutterstock.com ● **p152-153** x2 pictures, Wikimedia Commons | 1958 Chrysler, Getty Images | Desert highway, and vintage soda straws picture, Shutterstock.com ● **p154** Road sign, Shutterstock. com | x3 illustrations, Sarah Beare, sarahbeare.com ● **p155** Vintage ClipArt, Shutterstock.com ● **p156-157** x6 celebrity pictures, Getty Images ● **p158-159** Smelt painting, www.dec.ny.gov | Smelt dipping, Wikimedia Commons | Fresh smelts, www.kitsapsun.com ● **p160-161** Shutterstock.com ● **p162-163** Washington Monument pictures: Vintage engraving by Robert Mills, Getty Images | Two modern views of the monument, Shutterstock.com ● **p164-166** x2 main pictures, Getty Images | Perseid meteors and Background, Shutterstock. com ● **p167** x4 celebrities, Getty Images ● **p168-169** Von Leibig, www.pinterest.com | Hall of Mirrors, Versailles, Shutterstock.com | Keck Observatory, Wikimedia Commons ● **p170-171** Final.fantasy.answers.Wikia.com | www. shaggybevo.com | x2 www.acrosstheboard.blogspot.com | Japanese whaling ship Nisshin Maru,

Shutterstock.com | www.spamarrest.com ● **p172-173** Cat, Shutterstock.com ● **p174-175** Tony Pastor, 14th Street Theater, Fred Allen and Jimmy Durante, Getty Images | Vaudeville Theater, Shutterstock.com ● **p176-177** Gingham tablecloth and all sandwich pictures, Shutterstock.com ● **p178-179** Santa, Shutterstock.com ● **p180-181** Capital Beltway, www.capital-beltway.com | Bible Belt, Borscht Belt, Sun Belt pictures, Shutterstock.com | Kuiper Belt, Sedna, Science Photo Library ● **p182-183** x2 Weird Animal News illustrations, Sarah Beare, sarahbeare.com ● **p184-187** All images, Getty Images ● **p188-189** www.moviemansguide.com | www.jasaseo. com | www.imagefiesta.com | www.digitalspy.co.uk | www.scaredstiffreviews.com | www.news.moviefone.com | www.cinema.theiapolis.com ● **p190-191** x6 celebrities, all Getty Images ● **p192-193** x2 tractors, Wikimedia Commons | U.S. Troops with British Tanks, 1918, Imperial War Museum ● **p194-195** Clouds background, and passenger jet illustration, Shutterstock.com | Pilot illustration, Sarah Beare, sarahbeare.com ● **p196-197** Vintage courtroom background picture, Shutterstock.com ● **p198-199** x6 celebrities, all Getty Images ● **p200-201** Main illustration, Sarah Beare, sarahbeare.com | www.didntyouhear.com | www.tiggerman.com | Paul Winchell and John Fiedler pictures, Getty Images ● **p202-203** Space background and Shuttle pictures, Shutterstock.com ● **p204-205** All images, Shutterstock.com, except Alan Greenspan, Getty Images ● **p206-207** Both illustrations, Sarah Beare, sarahbeare.com | Vintage background, Shutterstock.com ● **p208-209** Color wheel, Shutterstock. com ● **p210-211** Celebrity Haunts montage: John Lennon, Mama Cass, Ben Franklin and Michael Jackson, Getty Images, interiors from Shutterstock.com ● **p212-213** www.blogs.ft.com | Wikimedia Commons | www. pharmafile.com | www.artsbeercans.com ● **p214-215** www. europe1.fr | Helicopter silhouettes, Shutterstock.com ● **p216-217** www.fanpop.com | Wikimedia Commons | www.norse-mythology.org ● **p218-219** All images, Getty Images, except geek, Shutterstock.com ● **p220-221** Lincoln's funeral train, x4 pictures, and Nation's Martyr picture, all Getty Images | Background montage, images from Shutterstock.com ● **p222-223** www. movieposterauthenticating.com/wordpress | Still photograph from *The Sopranos*, © David Chase/HBO ● **p224-225** The *Mona Lisa*, Wikimedia Commons | www.hastac.org | Picasso and Peruggia, Getty Images | Vintage picture frame and background, Shutterstock.com ● **p226-228** Billie Holiday, Sinead O'Connor, Elvis Costello, all Getty Images ● **p229-231** All images, Shutterstock.com, except The Great John Toilet brochure, www.buzzfeed.com ● **p232-233** www.kansascity.com ● **p234-235** www.amazon.com | Wikimedia Commons | www.bbc.com ● **p236-237** All pictures, Getty Images, except background, Shutterstock.com ● **p238-239** www. feedergoldfish.typepad.com | All other images, Shutterstock.com ● **p240-241** www.newenglandhistoricalsociety. com | www.drsphinx.wordpress.com | www.suehubbard.com | www.theguardian.com | www.melissabititci.com | www.rcplondon.ac.uk ● **p242-243** www.theapricity.com | www.domsweirdnews.blogspot.co.uk | Associated Press | Silhouette graphics, Shutterstock.com ● **p244-245** Illustrations by Sarah Beare, sarahbeare.com | Vintage background, Shutterstock.com ● **p246-247** Lucky Lorhke and American G.I. photos, all Getty Images | background, Shutterstock.com ● **p248** All components, Shutterstock.com ● **p249-250** All components, Shutterstock.com ● **p251-252** Both pictures from Getty Images ● **p253-254** Chicken photo and hypnotic backgrounds, Shutterstock.com | Chicken illustrations by Sarah Beare, sarahbeare.com ● **p255-257** Frontier Women photos by Getty Images, background by Shutterstock.com ● **p258-259** Illustrations by Sarah Beare, sarahbeare.com | all other images from Shutterstock.com ● **p260** All images from Getty Images ● **p261-262** All images from Shutterstock.com ● **p263-264** Papa Guede art by Stefan Danielsson at Loyal Gallery, www. loyalgallery.com/gl012_stefan_danielsson.html | Izanagi and Izanami, Getty Images | Sanata Muerte, Wikimedia Commons ● **p265-266** www.southbyse.com | www.sterlingbrands.com | Miracle Whip, Shutterstock.com ● **p267-269** Associated Press | www.nydailynews.com | www. lamentable.org | Wikimedia Commons | Alien abduction, Shutterstock.com ● **p270-271** Harry Houdini, the Marx Brothers, Getty Images ● **p272-273** All components, Shutterstock.com ● **p274-275** Baseball player portraits, Getty Images | Old photo cards, pitcher graphic, and grass background, Shutterstock.com ● **p276-277** x6 writers, all Getty Images | Background, Shutterstock.com ● **p278-279** www.wallpaperscraft.com | www.youtube.com | Wikimedia Commons | www.fanpop.com | © Christopher Lane/Guardian | www. simpsons.wikia.com ● **p280-281** All images, Shutterstock.com ● **p282-283** Shutterstock.com ● **p287** Shutterstock.com ● **p288** Shutterstock.com

March of the Sioux, 1905

The Last Page

Fellow Trivia Hounds:

The fight for good bathroom reading should never be taken loosely—we must do our duty and sit firmly for what we believe in, even while the rest of the world is taking potshots at us.

We'll be brief. Now that we've proven we're not simply a flush-in-the-pan, we invite you to take the plunge: Sit Down and Be Counted! Log on to *www.bathroomreader.com* and earn a permanent spot on the BRI honor roll!

If you like reading our books...visit the BRI's website!

- Receive our irregular newsletters via e-mail
- Order additional Bathroom Readers
- Like us on Facebook
- Tweet us on Twitter
- Blog us on our blog

Go with the Flow...

Well, we're out of space, and when you've gotta go, you've gotta go.
Thanks for all your support.
Hope to hear from you soon. Meanwhile, remember...

Keep on flushin'!